The Tales of
Edgar Allan Poe

A Kaplan SAT Score-Raising Classic

The Tales of
Edgar Allan Poe

A Kaplan SAT Score-Raising Classic

Simon & Schuster

New York ✦ London ✦ Sydney ✦ Toronto

Kaplan Publishing
Published by Simon & Schuster, Inc.
1230 Avenue of the Americas
New York, NY 10020

For bulk sales to schools, colleges, and universities, please contact: Order Department, Simon & Schuster, Inc. 100 Front Street, Riverside, NJ 08075. Phone: 1-800-223-2336. Fax: 1-800-943-9831.

For information regarding special discounts for other bulk purchases, please contact Simon & Schuster Special Sales at 1-800-456-6798 or business@simonandschuster.com

Cover Design: Cheung Tai
Cover Illustration: Greg Copeland
Interior Page Design and Production: Lori DeGeorge
Editor: Helena Santini

Manufactured in the United States of America

January 2005

10 9 8 7 6.

Library of Congress Cataloging-in-Publication Data is available.

ISBN: 0-7432-6468-1

How To Use This Book

———◆———

Edgar Allan Poe's stories are not only filled with mystery and intrigue—they're also filled with SAT words! Now Kaplan makes it as easy as 1-2-3 for you to learn these vocabulary words as you read the stories.

On the right-hand pages you'll find selected stories from Edgar Allan Poe with words **bolded** throughout. These bolded words are frequently found on the SAT. On the left-hand pages, Kaplan defines these SAT words, as well as gives you the part of speech, pronunciation, and synonyms for each word—everything you need to know to improve your vocabulary and to acc the SAT.

Some of the most challenging vocabulary words found in *The Tales of Edgar Allan Poe* aren't likely to appear on the SAT, but we thought you might want to learn those, too. That's why we've <u>underlined</u> them throughout the text and added their definitions to a glossary at the end of the book. After all—you never know where they might pop up next!

There's also an endnotes section that clarifies the occasional mythological character or French phrase that Edgar Allan Poe liked to throw in from time to time. The words explained in this section are numbered throughout the text.

So what are you waiting for? Start reading!

TABLE OF CONTENTS

ACUTE (uh <u>kyoot</u>) *adj.*
  1. sensitive, heightened; sharp, pointed; severe
     Synonyms: perceptive; piercing; intense, fierce
  2. clever, shrewd
     Synonyms: ingenious, keen

The Tell-Tale Heart

True! Nervous—very, very dreadfully nervous I had been and am; but why *will* you say that I am mad? The disease had sharpened my senses, not destroyed, not dulled them. Above all was the sense of hearing **acute**. I heard all things in the heaven and in the earth. I heard many things in hell. How, then, am I mad? <u>Hearken</u> and observe how healthily, how calmly I can tell you the whole story.

It is impossible to say how first the idea entered my brain; but once conceived, it haunted me day and night. Object there was none. Passion there was none. I loved the old man. He had never wronged me. He had never given me insult. For his gold I had no desire. I think it was his eye! Yes, it was this! One of his eyes resembled that of a vulture—a pale blue eye, with a film over it. Whenever it fell upon me, my blood ran cold; and so by degrees, very gradually, I made up my mind to take the life of the old man, and thus rid myself of the eye forever.

Now this is the point. You fancy me mad. Madmen know nothing. But you should have seen me. You should have seen how wisely I proceeded—with what caution, with what foresight, with what <u>dissimulation</u> I went to work! I was never kinder to the old man than during the whole week before I killed him. And every night, about midnight, I turned the latch of his door and opened it—oh, so gently! And then, when I had made an opening sufficient for my head, I put in a dark lantern, all closed, closed, so that no light shone out, and then I thrust in my head. Oh, you would have laughed to see how cunningly I thrust it in! I moved it slowly—very, very slowly, so that I might not disturb the old man's sleep. It took me an hour to place my whole head within the opening so far that I

VEX (vehks) *v.* **-ing,-ed.**
  to irritate, annoy; confuse, puzzle
    Synonyms: bother, plague, afflict, irk; perplex, perturb

PROFOUND (pruh <u>fownd</u>) (proh <u>fownd</u>) *adj.*
  intelligent; difficult to understand; deep, infinite
    Synonyms: smart; thorough, weighty; bottomless,
    unending

SAGACITY (suh <u>gaa</u> sih tee) *n.*
  shrewdness, intelligence
    Synonyms: astuteness, perspicacity, wisdom

could see him as he lay upon his bed. Ha! Would a madman have been so wise as this? And then, when my head was well in the room, I undid the lantern cautiously—oh, so cautiously (for the hinges creaked) I undid it just so much that a single thin ray fell upon the vulture eye. And this I did for seven long nights—every night just at midnight—but I found the eye always closed; and so it was impossible to do the work; for it was not the old man who **vexed** me, but his Evil Eye. And every morning, when the day broke, I went boldly into the chamber, and spoke courageously to him, calling him by name in a hearty tone, and inquiring how he had passed the night. So you see, he would have been a very **profound** old man indeed to suspect that every night, just at twelve, I looked in upon him while he slept.

Upon the eighth night I was more than usually cautious in opening the door. A watch's minute hand moves more quickly than did mine. Never before that night had I *felt* the extent of my own powers—of my **sagacity**. I could scarcely contain my feelings of triumph. To think that there I was, opening the door, little by little, and he not even to dream of my secret deeds or thoughts. I fairly chuckled at the idea, and perhaps he heard me, for he moved on the bed suddenly, as if startled. Now you may think that I drew back, but no. His room was as black as pitch with the thick darkness (for the shutters were close fastened, through fear of robbers), and so I knew that he could not see the opening of the door, and I kept pushing it on steadily, steadily.

I had my head in, and was about to open the lantern, when my thumb slipped upon the tin fastening, and the old man sprang up in the bed, crying out, "Who's there?"

I kept quite still and said nothing. For a whole hour I did not move a muscle, and in the meantime I did not hear him lie down. He was still sitting up in the bed listening, just as I have done, night after night, hearkening to the death watches in the wall.

STIFLED (<u>stie</u> fuhld) *adj.*
    suppressed or held back; smothered or suffocated
        Synonyms: muted, muffled, restrained; deadened

STALK (stahk) *v.* **-ing,-ed.**
    to hunt, pursue
        Synonyms: track, shadow, trail, dog, hound

RESOLVE (rih <u>sahlv</u>) *v.* **-ing,-ed.**
    to determine or to make a firm decision about
        Synonyms: solve, decide

STEALTHILY (<u>stehl</u> thuh lee) *adv.*
    quietly and cautiously
        Synonyms: furtively, secretly, surreptitiously,
        covertly

ACUTENESS (uh <u>kyoot</u> nehs) *n.*
    sharpness, severity
        Synonym: intensity

Presently I heard a slight groan, and I knew it was the groan of mortal terror. It was not a groan of pain or of grief—oh, no! It was the low stifled sound that arises from the bottom of the soul when overcharged with awe. I knew the sound well. Many a night, just at midnight, when all the world slept, it has welled up from my own bosom, deepening with its dreadful echo, the terrors that distracted me. I say I knew it well. I knew what the old man felt, and pitied him, although I chuckled at heart. I knew that he had been lying awake ever since the first slight noise when he had turned in the bed. His fears had been ever since growing upon him. He had been trying to fancy them causeless, but could not. He had been saying to himself, "It is nothing but the wind in the chimney; it is only a mouse crossing the floor," or "it is merely a cricket which has made a single chirp." Yes, he has been trying to comfort himself with these suppositions, but he had found all in vain. *All in vain*, because Death, in approaching him, had stalked with his black shadow before him, and enveloped the victim. And it was the mournful influence of the unperceived shadow that caused him to feel—although he neither saw nor heard—to *feel* the presence of my head within the room.

When I had waited a long time, very patiently, without hearing him lie down, I resolved to open a little—a very, very little crevice in the lantern. So I opened it—you cannot imagine how stealthily, stealthily—until, at length, a single dim ray, like the thread of a spider, shot out from the crevice and full upon the vulture eye.

It was open—wide, wide open—and I grew furious as I gazed upon it. I saw it with perfect distinctness—all a dull blue, with a hideous veil over it that chilled the very marrow in my bones. But I could see nothing else of the old man's face or person, for I had directed the ray as if by instinct, precisely upon the damned spot.

And now have I not told you that what you mistake for madness is but over-acuteness of the senses? Now, I say,

VEX (vehks) *v.* **-ing,-ed.**
  to irritate, annoy; confuse, puzzle
    Synonyms: bother, plague, afflict, irk; perplex, perturb

WANE (wayn) *v.* **-ing,-ed.**
  to decrease gradually
    Synonyms: dwindle, flag, fade, shrink, diminish

there came to my ears a low, dull, quick sound, such as a watch makes when enveloped in cotton. I knew *that* sound well too. It was the beating of the old man's heart. It increased my fury, as the beating of a drum stimulates the soldier into courage.

But even yet I refrained and kept still. I scarcely breathed. I held the lantern motionless. I tried how steadily I could to maintain the ray upon the eye. In the meantime the hellish tattoo of the heart increased. It grew quicker and quicker, and louder and louder every instant. The old man's terror *must* have been extreme! It grew louder, I say, louder every moment! Do you mark me well? I have told you that I am nervous, so I am. And now at the dead hour of the night, amid the dreadful silence of that old house, so strange a noise as this excited me to uncontrollable terror. Yet, for some minutes longer I refrained and stood still. But the beating grew louder, louder! I thought the heart must burst. And now a new anxiety seized me—the sound would be heard by a neighbor! The old man's hour had come! With a loud yell, I threw open the lantern and leaped into the room. He shrieked once—once only. In an instant I dragged him to the floor and pulled the heavy bed over him. I then smiled gaily, to find the deed so far done. But, for many minutes, the heart beat on with a muffled sound. This, however, did not vex me; it would not be heard through the wall. At length it ceased. The old man was dead. I removed the bed and examined the corpse. Yes, he was stone, stone dead. I placed my hand upon the heart and held it there many minutes. There was no pulsation. He was stone dead. His eye would trouble me no more.

If still you think me mad, you will think so no longer when I describe the wise precautions I took for the concealment of the body. The night waned, and I worked hastily, but in silence. First of all I dismembered the corpse. I cut off the head and the arms and the legs.

WARY (<u>way</u> ree) *adj.*
    careful, cautious
        Synonyms: watchful, vigilant, alert, guarded,
        suspicious

SUAVITY (<u>swahv</u> ih tee) *n.*
    smooth grace or politeness, courtesy
        Synonyms: urbanity, diplomacy, pleasantness

AUDACITY (aw <u>daa</u> sih tee) *n.*
    boldness, daring
        Synonyms: courage, bravery, recklessness
REPOSE (rih <u>pohz</u>) *v.* **-ing,-ed.**
    to lie dead; to relax or rest
        Synonyms: pass on; sleep, slumber

I then took up three planks from the flooring of the chamber and deposited all between the scantlings. I then replaced the boards so cleverly, so cunningly, that no human eye—not even *his*—could have detected any thing wrong. There was nothing to wash out, no stain of any kind, no blood-spot whatsoever. I had been too **wary** for that. A tub had caught all. Ha! Ha!

When I had made an end of these labors, it was four o'clock and still dark as midnight. As the bell sounded the hour, there came a knocking at the street door. I went down to open it with a light heart, for what had I *now* to fear? There entered three men, who introduced themselves, with perfect **suavity**, as officers of the police. A shriek had been heard by a neighbor during the night; suspicion of foul play had been aroused; information had been lodged at the police office, and they (the officers) had been deputed to search the premises.

I smiled, for *what* had I to fear? I bade the gentlemen welcome. The shriek, I said, was my own in a dream. The old man, I mentioned, was absent in the country. I took my visitors all over the house. I bade them search—search *well*. I led them, at length, to *his* chamber. I showed them his treasures, secure, undisturbed. In the enthusiasm of my confidence, I brought chairs into the room, and desired them *here* to rest from their fatigues, while I myself, in the wild **audacity** of my perfect triumph, placed my own seat upon the very spot beneath which **reposed** the corpse of the victim.

The officers were satisfied. My manner had convinced them. I was singularly at ease. They sat, and while I answered cheerily, they chatted about familiar things. But, ere long, I felt myself getting pale and wished them gone. My head ached, and I fancied a ringing in my ears; but still they sat and chatted. The ringing became more distinct—it continued and became more distinct. I talked more freely to get rid of the feeling, but it continued and

VEHEMENTLY (<u>vee</u> huh muhnt lee) *adv.*
strongly, urgently
Synonyms: intensely, passionately, ardently

TRIFLE (<u>trie</u> fuhl) *n.*
something of slight worth or little importance
Synonyms: triviality, novelty, trinket

GESTICULATION (jeh stih kyuh <u>lay</u> shuhn) *n.*
the act of making gestures; a particularly expressive gesture
Synonyms: motion, indication; signal, expression

DERISION (dih <u>rih</u> zhuhn) *n.*
mockery, ridicule
Synonyms: taunting, jeering, insult, teasing

HYPOCRITICAL (hih puh <u>krih</u> tih kuhl) *adj.*
expressing feelings or virtues that one doesn't really have
Synonyms: fraudulent, deceitful, insincere, phony

gained definitiveness until, at length, I found that the noise was *not* within my ears.

No doubt I now grew *very* pale, but I talked more fluently, and with a heightened voice. Yet the sound increased—and what could I do? It was a *low, dull, quick sound—much such a sound as a watch makes when enveloped in cotton*. I gasped for breath, and yet the officers heard it not. I talked more quickly, more **vehemently**; but the noise steadily increased. I arose and argued about **trifles** in a high key and with violent **gesticulations**, but the noise steadily increased. Why *would* they not be gone? I paced the floor to and fro with heavy strides as if excited to fury by the observation of the men, but the noise steadily increased. Oh God! What *could* I do? I foamed—I raved—I swore! I swung the chair upon which I had been sitting, and grated it upon the boards, but the noise arose over all and continually increased. It grew louder—louder—*louder!* And still the men chatted pleasantly and smiled. Was it possible they heard not? Almighty God! No, no, they heard—they suspected— they *knew!* They were making a mockery of my horror! This I thought, and this I think. But any thing was better than this agony! Any thing was more tolerable than this **derision!** I could bear those **hypocritical** smiles no longer! I felt that I must scream or die! And now again, hark! Louder! Louder! Louder! *Louder!*—

"Villains," I shrieked, "dissemble no more! I admit the deed! Tear up the planks! Here, here! It is the beating of his hideous heart!"

KEENLY (<u>keen</u> lee) *adv.*
  intensely, sharply
    Synonyms: acutely, quickly, perceptively

CORPULENT (<u>kohr</u> pyuh luhnt) *adj.*
  obese, bulky
    Synonyms: stout, rotund, portly, plump

INIMITABLE (ih <u>nihm</u> it uh buhl) *adj.*
  unable to be copied or imitated
    Synonyms: matchless, exceptional, unrivaled

PREDISPOSE (pree dih <u>spohz</u>) *v.* **-ing,-ed.**
  to incline or give a tendency to beforehand; to put in
  place, to settle in advance
    Synonyms: determine, motivate; organize, position

RETAIN (rih <u>tayn</u>) *v.* **-ing,-ed.**
  to hold, keep possession of
    Synonyms: withhold, reserve, maintain, remember

MOTLEY (<u>maht</u> lee) *n.*
  1. the colorful attire of a jester
    Synonym: clown suit
  2. an assortment, mixture
    Synonyms: miscellany, variety

HOP-FROG

I never knew anyone so **keenly** alive to a joke as the king was. He seemed to live only for joking. To tell a good story of the joke kind, and to tell it well, was the surest road to his favor. Thus it happened that his seven ministers were all noted for their accomplishments as jokers. They all took after the king, too, in being large, **corpulent**, oily men, as well as **inimitable** jokers. Whether people grow fat by joking or whether there is something in fat itself which **predisposes** to a joke, I have never been quite able to determine; but certain it is that a lean joker is a *rara avis in terris*.[1]

About the refinements, or as he called them, the "ghosts" of wit, the king troubled himself very little. He had a special admiration for *breadth* in a jest, and would often put up with *length* for the sake of it. Overniceties wearied him. He would have preferred Rabelais' "Gargantua" to the "Zadig" of Voltaire, and upon the whole, practical jokes suited his taste far better than verbal ones.

At the date of my narrative, professing jesters had not altogether gone out of fashion at court. Several of the great continental "powers" still **retained** their "fools," who wore **motley**, with caps and bells, and who were expected to be always ready with sharp <u>witticisms</u> at a moment's notice, in consideration of the crumbs that fell from the royal table.

Our king, as a matter of course, **retained** his "fool." The fact is, he *required* something in the way of folly—if only to counterbalance the heavy wisdom of the seven wise men who were his ministers, not to mention himself.

GAIT (gayt) *n.*
the way one moves on foot, a manner of walking
Synonyms: tread, walk, march, pace
ILLIMITABLE (ih lih miht uh buhl) *adj.*
not having a limit or boundary, endless
Synonyms: infinite, vast, immeasurable
CONSOLATION (kahn suh lay shuhn) *n.*
something providing comfort or solace for a loss or
hardship
Synonym: condolence
CONSTITUTIONAL (kahn stih too shuh nuhl) *adj.*
having to do with the physical structure or health of
something or someone
Synonyms: natural, inherent, innate
PRODIGIOUS (pruh dih juhs) *adj.*
vast, enormous, extraordinary
Synonyms: huge, gigantic, impressive, marvelous
BESTOW (bih stoh) *v.* **-ing,-ed.**
to give as a gift; to apply or devote time or effort
Synonyms: endow, confer, present; allocate, dedicate
COMPENSATION (kahm pehn say shuhn) *n.*
something that makes up for the faults of something
else; repayment, reimbursement
Synonyms: balance, counteraction; indemnity,
retribution
DEXTERITY (dehk stayr ih tee) *n.*
physical or mental skill, ability
Synonyms: aptitude, adroitness, proficiency
BARBAROUS (baar buh ruhs) *adj.*
lacking culture or refinement; mercilessly cruel
Synonyms: crude; savage, vulgar, inhumane

His fool, or professional jester, was not only a fool, however. His value was <u>trebled</u> in the eyes of the king, by the fact of his being also a dwarf and a cripple. Dwarfs were as common at court in those days as fools, and many monarchs would have found it difficult to get through their days (days are rather longer at court than elsewhere) without both a jester to laugh *with*, and a dwarf to laugh *at*. But as I have already observed, your jesters, in ninety-nine cases out of a hundred, are fat, round, and unwieldy—so that it was no small source of <u>self-gratulation</u> with our king that, in Hop-Frog (this was the fool's name), he possessed a triplicate treasure in one person.

I believe the name "Hop-Frog" was *not* that given to the dwarf by his sponsors at baptism, but it was conferred upon him, by general consent of the seven ministers, on account of his inability to walk as other men do. In fact, Hop-Frog could only get along by a sort of <u>interjectional gait</u>—something between a leap and a wriggle—a movement that afforded **illimitable** amusement, and of course **consolation**, to the king, for (notwithstanding the <u>protuberance</u> of his stomach and a **constitutional** swelling of the head) the king, by his whole court, was accounted as a capital figure.

But although Hop-Frog, through the distortion of his legs, could move only with great pain and difficulty along a road or floor, the **prodigious** muscular power which nature seemed to have **bestowed** upon his arms, by way of **compensation** for deficiency in the lower limbs, enabled him to perform many feats of wonderful **dexterity**, where trees or ropes were in question, or anything else to climb. At such exercises he certainly much more resembled a squirrel, or a small monkey, than a frog.

I am not able to say with precision, from what country Hop-Frog originally came. It was from some **barbarous** region, however, that no person ever heard of—a vast distance from the court of our king. Hop-Frog, and a young girl very little less dwarfish than himself (although of

MASQUERADE (maas kuh <u>rayd</u>) *n.*
    a costume ball; disguise, action that conceals the truth
    Synonyms: carnival, party; charade, façade

exquisite proportions, and a marvellous dancer), had been forcibly carried off from their respective homes in adjoining provinces, and sent as presents to the king by one of his ever-victorious generals.

Under these circumstances, it is not to be wondered that a close intimacy arose between the two little captives. Indeed, they soon became sworn friends. Hop-Frog, who although he made a great deal of sport was by no means popular, had it not in his power to render Trippetta many services; but *she*, on account of her grace and exquisite beauty (although a dwarf), was universally admired and petted; so she possessed much influence and never failed to use it whenever she could, for the benefit of Hop-Frog.

On some grand state occasion—I forget what—the king determined to have a **masquerade**, and whenever a **masquerade**, or any thing of that kind, occurred at our court, then the talents both of Hop-Frog and Trippetta were sure to be called into play. Hop-Frog especially was so inventive in the way of getting up pageants, suggesting novel characters, and arranging costume for masked balls, that nothing could be done, it seems, without his assistance.

The night appointed for the *fête* had arrived. A gorgeous hall had been fitted up under Trippetta's eye, with every kind of device which could possibly give *éclat* to a **masquerade**. The whole court was in a fever of expectation. As for costumes and characters, it might well be supposed that everybody had come to a decision on such points. Many had made up their minds (as to what roles they should assume) a week, or even a month, in advance. In fact, there was not a particle of indecision anywhere except in the case of the king and his seven ministers. Why *they* hesitated I never could tell, unless they did it by way of a joke. More probably, they found it difficult, on account of being so fat, to make up their minds. At all events, time flew, and as a last resort, they sent for Trippetta and Hop-Frog.

NOVEL (<u>nah</u> vuhl) *adj.*
  new, original
    Synonyms: fresh, newfangled, innovative, unusual,
    different

When the two little friends obeyed the summons of the king, they found him sitting at his wine with the seven members of his cabinet council; but the monarch appeared to be in a very ill humor. He knew that Hop-Frog was not fond of wine; for it excited the poor cripple almost to madness, and madness is no comfortable feeling. But the king loved his practical jokes, and took pleasure in forcing Hop-Frog to drink and (as the king called it) "to be merry."

"Come here, Hop-Frog," said he, as the jester and his friend entered the room. "Swallow this bumper to the health of your absent friends [here Hop-Frog sighed] and then let us have the benefit of your invention. We want characters—*characters*, man,—something **novel**, out of the way. We are wearied with this everlasting sameness. Come, drink! The wine will brighten your wits."

Hop-Frog endeavored, as usual, to get up a jest in reply to these advances from the king, but the effort was too much. It happened to be the poor dwarf's birthday, and the command to drink to his "absent friends" forced tears to his eyes. Many large, bitter drops fell into the goblet as he took it humbly from the hand of the tyrant.

"Ah! Ha, ha, ha!" roared the latter, as the dwarf reluctantly drained the beaker. "See what a glass of good wine can do! Why, your eyes are shining already!"

Poor fellow! His large eyes *gleamed* rather than shone, for the effect of wine on his excitable brain was not more powerful than instantaneous. He placed the goblet nervously on the table, and looked round upon the company with a half-insane stare. They all seemed highly amused at the success of the king's "joke."

"And now to business," said the prime minister, a *very* fat man.

"Yes," said the king. "Come, Hop-Frog, lend us your assistance. Characters, my fine fellow, we stand in need of characters—all of us—ha, ha, ha!" and as this was seriously meant for a joke, his laugh was chorused by the seven.

21

NOVEL (<u>nah</u> vuhl) *adj.*
new, original
Synonyms: fresh, newfangled, innovative, unusual, different

IMPLORE (ihm <u>plohr</u>) *v.* **-ing,-ed.**
to call upon in supplication, beg
Synonyms: plead, entreat, solicit

AUDACITY (aw <u>daa</u> sih tee) *n.*
boldness, daring
Synonyms: courage, bravery, recklessness

INDIGNATION (ihn dihg <u>nay</u> shun) *n.*
anger caused by something mean or unjust
Synonyms: fury, ire, wrath

PROTRACTED (proh <u>traak</u> tihd) *adj.*
prolonged, drawn out, extended
Synonyms: lengthy, elongated, stretched

EJACULATE (ih <u>jaak</u> yuh layt) *v.* **-ing,-ed.**
to exclaim suddenly
Synonyms: blurt, shout, declare

Hop-Frog also laughed, although feebly and somewhat vacantly.

"Come, come," said the king, impatiently. "Have you nothing to suggest?"

"I am endeavoring to think of something *novel*," replied the dwarf abstractedly, for he was quite bewildered by the wine.

"Endeavoring!" cried the tyrant, fiercely. "What do you mean by *that?* Ah, I perceive. You are sulky and want more wine. Here, drink this!" He poured out another goblet full and offered it to the cripple, who merely gazed at it, gasping for breath.

"Drink, I say!" shouted the monster, "or by the fiends—"

The dwarf hesitated. The king grew purple with rage. The courtiers smirked. Trippetta, pale as a corpse, advanced to the monarch's seat, and, falling on her knees before him, implored him to spare her friend.

The tyrant regarded her for some moments, in evident wonder at her audacity. He seemed quite at a loss what to do or say—how most becomingly to express his indignation. At last, without uttering a syllable, he pushed her violently from him and threw the contents of the brimming goblet in her face.

The poor girl got up as best she could, and not daring even to sigh, resumed her position at the foot of the table.

There was a dead silence for about half a minute, during which the falling of a leaf, or of a feather, might have been heard. It was interrupted by a low but harsh and protracted grating sound which seemed to come at once from every corner of the room.

"What—what—*what* are you making that noise for?" demanded the king, turning furiously to the dwarf.

The latter seemed to have recovered, in great measure, from his intoxication, and looking fixedly but quietly into the tyrant's face, merely ejaculated:

"I—I? How could it have been me?"

WHET (weht) *v.* **-ting,-ted.**
to sharpen, stimulate
Synonyms: hone, edge, strop, grind
VAGABOND (<u>vaa</u> guh bahnd) *n.*
one who moves from place to place with no fixed home
Synonyms: wanderer, floater, vagrant, nomad
REPULSIVE (rih <u>puhl</u> sihv) *adj.*
sickening, disgusting; repellant
Synonyms: nauseating; offensive
PACIFY (<u>paa</u> suh fie) *v.* **-ing,-ied.**
to restore calm, bring peace
Synonyms: mollify, conciliate, appease, placate
MASQUERADE (maas kuh <u>rayd</u>) *n.*
a costume ball; disguise, action that conceals the truth
Synonyms: carnival, party; charade, façade

ACUTE (uh <u>kyoot</u>) *adj.*
1. clever, shrewd
Synonyms: ingenious, keen
2. sensitive, heightened; sharp, pointed; severe
Synonyms: perceptive; piercing; intense, fierce
DIVERSION (dih <u>vuhr</u> zhuhn) (die <u>vuhr</u> zhuhn) *n.*
an amusing or relaxing activity; a distraction
Synonyms: entertainment, recreation; deviation
DRAW *v.* **-ing, drew, drawn**
to pull, drag; to lead, to bring about on purpose;
to attract or be attracted to
Synonyms: haul, tow, yank; provoke, elicit; lure,
entice

"The sound appeared to come from without," observed one of the courtiers. "I fancy it was the parrot at the window, whetting his bill upon his cage-wires."

"True," replied the monarch, as if much relieved by the suggestion, "but, on the honor of a knight, I could have sworn that it was the gritting of this vagabond's teeth."

Hereupon the dwarf laughed (the king was too confirmed a joker to object to anyone's laughing) and displayed a set of large, powerful, and very repulsive teeth. Moreover, he avowed his perfect willingness to swallow as much wine as desired. The monarch was pacified; and having drained another bumper with no very perceptible ill effect, Hop-Frog entered at once, and with spirit, into the plans for the masquerade.

"I cannot tell what was the association of ideas," observed he, very tranquilly and as if he had never tasted wine in his life, "but *just after* your majesty had struck the girl and thrown the wine in her face—*just after* your majesty had done this, and while the parrot was making that odd noise outside the window, there came into my mind a capital diversion—one of my own country frolics—often enacted among us at our masquerades. But here it will be new altogether. Unfortunately, however, it requires a company of eight persons, and—"

"Here we are!" cried the king, laughing at his acute discovery of the coincidence. "Eight to a fraction—I and my seven ministers. Come! What is the diversion?"

"We call it," replied the cripple, "the Eight Chained Ourang-Outangs, and it really is excellent sport if well enacted."

"*We* will enact it," remarked the king, drawing himself up and lowering his eyelids.

"The beauty of the game," continued Hop-Frog, "lies in the fright it occasions among the women."

"Capital!" roared in chorus the monarch and his ministry.

"I will equip you as Ourang-Outangs," proceeded the dwarf. "Leave all that to me. The resemblance shall be so

MASQUERADER (maas kuh <u>ray</u> duhr) *n.*
　one who attends a costume ball; a person in disguise
　　Synonyms: partygoer; pretender, fooler, impostor

MASQUERADE (maas kuh <u>rayd</u>) *n.*
　a costume ball; disguise, action that conceals the truth
　　Synonyms: carnival, party; charade, façade

INIMITABLE (ih <u>nihm</u> it uh buhl) *adj.*
　unable to be copied or imitated
　　Synonyms: matchless, exceptional, unrivaled

EXECUTION (ehk sih <u>kyoo</u> shuhn) *n.*
　1. the act of performing or carrying out a task
　　Synonyms: operation, enactment, accomplishment,
　　achievement
　2. the act of putting to death
　　Synonyms: killing, suicide, murder

CIVILIZED (<u>sih</u> vuhl iezd) *adj.*
　relating to human lifestyle as opposed to the wild,
　humane; politely sophisticated, cultured
　　Synonyms: refined, cultivated; courteous, pleasant,
　　affable

PROCURE (proh <u>kyoor</u>) *v.* **-ing,-ed.**
　to obtain
　　Synonyms: acquire, secure, get, gain

striking that the company of **masqueraders** will take you for real beasts, and of course, they will be as much terrified as astonished."

"Oh, this is exquisite!" exclaimed the king. "Hop-Frog! I will make a man of you."

"The chains are for the purpose of increasing the confusion by their jangling. You are supposed to have escaped, *en masse*, from your keepers. Your majesty cannot conceive the effect produced, at a **masquerade**, by eight chained Ourang-Outangs, imagined to be real ones by most of the company, and rushing in with savage cries, among the crowd of delicately and gorgeously <u>habited</u> men and women. The contrast is **inimitable**."

"It *must* be," said the king, and the council arose hurriedly (as it was growing late), to put in **execution** the scheme of Hop-Frog.

His mode of equipping the party as Ourang-Outangs was very simple, but effective enough for his purposes. The animals in question had, at the <u>epoch</u> of my story, very rarely been seen in any part of the **civilized** world; and as the imitations made by the dwarf were sufficiently beast-like and more than sufficiently hideous, their truthfulness to nature was thus thought to be secured.

The king and his ministers were first encased in tight-fitting stockinet shirts and drawers. They were then saturated with tar. At this stage of the process, some one of the party suggested feathers; but the suggestion was at once overruled by the dwarf, who soon convinced the eight, by <u>ocular</u> demonstration, that the hair of such a brute as the Ourang-Outang was much more efficiently represented by *flax*. A thick coating of the latter was accordingly plastered upon the coating of tar. A long chain was now **procured**. First, it was passed about the waist of the king and tied; then about another of the party, and also tied; then about all successively, in the same manner. When this chaining arrangement was complete, and the party stood as far apart from each other as

RESIDUE (<u>reh</u> suh doo) *n.*
  remainder, remnant
    Synonyms: rest, balance, surplus, excess, overflow

MASQUERADE (maas kuh <u>rayd</u>) *n.*
  a costume ball; disguise, action that conceals the truth
    Synonyms: carnival, party; charade, façade

DETRIMENTAL (deht ruh <u>mehn</u> tuhl) *adj.*
  causing harm or injury
    Synonyms: adverse, deleterious, inimical,
    destructive, hurtful

MASQUERADER (maas kuh <u>ray</u> duhr) *n.*
  one who attends a costume ball; a person in disguise
    Synonyms: partygoer; pretender, fooler, impostor
IMPEDIMENT (ihm <u>pehd</u> uh muhnt) *n.*
  barrier, obstacle; speech disorder
    Synonyms: obstruction, hindrance, hurdle; lisp
PRODIGIOUS (pruh <u>dih</u> juhs) *adj.*
  vast, enormous, extraordinary
    Synonyms: huge, gigantic, impressive, marvelous

possible, they formed a circle; and to make all things appear natural, Hop-Frog passed the **residue** of the chain, in two diameters, at right angles, across the circle, after the fashion adopted at the present day by those who capture chimpanzees, or other large apes, in Borneo.

The grand saloon in which the **masquerade** was to take place was a circular room, very lofty, and receiving the light of the sun only through a single window at top. At night (the season for which the apartment was especially designed) it was illuminated principally by a large chandelier, <u>depending</u> by a chain from the centre of the sky-light and lowered, or elevated, by means of a counter-balance as usual; but (in order not to look unsightly) this latter passed outside the <u>cupola</u> and over the roof.

The arrangements of the room had been left to Trippetta's superintendence; but in some particulars, it seems she had been guided by the calmer judgment of her friend the dwarf. At his suggestion it was that on this occasion the chandelier was removed. Its waxen drippings (which, in weather so warm, it was quite impossible to prevent) would have been seriously **detrimental** to the rich dresses of the guests who, on account of the crowded state of the saloon, could not *all* be expected to keep from out its centre—that is to say, from under the chandelier. Additional sconces were set in various parts of the hall, out of the way; and a flambeau, emitting sweet odor, was placed in the right hand of each of the <u>Caryatides</u> that stood against the wall—some fifty or sixty all together.

The eight Ourang-Outangs, taking Hop-Frog's advice, waited patiently until midnight (when the room was thoroughly filled with **masqueraders**) before making their appearance. No sooner had the clock ceased striking, however, when they rushed, or rather rolled in, all together—for the **impediments** of their chains caused most of the party to fall, and all to stumble as they entered.

The excitement among the **masqueraders** was **prodigious**, and filled the heart of the king with glee. As had been

EXPIATE (<u>ehk</u> spee ayt) *v.* **-ing,-ed.**
  to atone for, make amends for
    Synonyms: answer, compensate, pay

TUMULT (<u>tuh</u> muhlt) *n.*
  state of confusion; agitation
    Synonyms: disturbance, turmoil, din, commotion,
    chaos

MASQUERADER (maas kuh <u>ray</u> duhr) *n.*
  one who attends a costume ball; a person in disguise
    Synonyms: partygoer; pretender, fooler, impostor

DRAW *v.* **-ing, drew, drawn**
  to pull, drag; to lead, to bring about on purpose;
  to attract or be attracted to
    Synonyms: haul, tow, yank; provoke, elicit; lure,
    entice

DESCEND (dih <u>sehnd</u>) (dee <u>sehnd</u>) *v.* **-ing,-ed.**
  to pass from a higher place to a lower place
    Synonyms: fall, dismount, gravitate

INCITE (ihn <u>siet</u>) *v.* **-ing,-ed.**
  to move to action, to activate, to urge on
    Synonyms: encourage, actuate, motivate, stimulate

INEVITABLE (ihn <u>ehv</u> ih tuh buhl) *adj.*
  certain, unavoidable
    Synonyms: inescapable, sure, predictable

CONTRIVED (kuhn <u>trievd</u>) *adj.*
  devised, planned, or managed; formed in an artistic
  manner
    Synonyms: concocted, created, schemed; designed

DIN (dihn) *n.*
  blaring noise
    Synonyms: loudness, clamor, cacophony, commotion

anticipated, there were not a few of the guests who supposed the ferocious-looking creatures to be beasts of *some* kind in reality, if not precisely Ourang-Outangs. Many of the women swooned with affright; and had not the king taken the precaution to exclude all weapons from the saloon, his party might soon have **expiated** their frolic in their blood. As it was, a general rush was made for the doors; but the king had ordered them to be locked immediately upon his entrance, and, at the dwarf's suggestion, the keys had been deposited with *him*.

While the **tumult** was at its height, and each **masquerader** attentive only to his own safety (for, in fact, there was much *real* danger from the pressure of the excited crowd), the chain by which the chandelier ordinarily hung and which had been **drawn** up on its removal, might have been seen very gradually to **descend**, until its hooked extremity came within three feet of the floor.

Soon after this, the king and his seven friends having reeled about the hall in all directions, found themselves, at length, in its centre, and, of course, in immediate contact with the chain. While they were thus situated, the dwarf, who had followed noiselessly at their heels, **inciting** them to keep up the commotion, took hold of their own chain at the intersection of the two portions which crossed the circle <u>diametrically</u> and at right angles. Here, with the rapidity of thought, he inserted the hook from which the chandelier had been wont to <u>depend</u> and in an instant, by some unseen agency, the chandelier-chain was **drawn** so far upward as to take the hook out of reach, and, as an **inevitable** consequence, to drag the Ourang-Outangs together in close connection, and face to face.

The **masqueraders**, by this time, had recovered in some measure from their alarm; and, beginning to regard the whole matter as a well-**contrived** pleasantry, set up a loud shout of laughter at the predicament of the apes.

"Leave them to *me!*" now screamed Hop-Frog, his shrill voice making itself easily heard through all the **din**.

AGILITY (uh <u>jihl</u> ih tee) *n.*
   great coordination, nimbleness
      Synonyms: spryness, dexterity, litheness

SUSPEND (suh <u>spehnd</u>) *v.* **-ing,-ed.**
   to hang; to delay, interrupt
   Synonyms: dangle, depend; defer, cease, disrupt,
      halt, discontinue

ASCENT (uh <u>sehnt</u>) *n.*
   movement upward; an upward slope; a climb or rising
   to another level
      Synonyms: scaling, escalation; incline, upgrade;
      mounting

COUNTENANCE (<u>kown</u> tuh nuhns) *n.*
   appearance, facial expression
      Synonyms: face, features, visage
SCRUTINIZE (<u>skroot</u> niez) *v.* **-ing,-ed.**
   to observe carefully
      Synonyms: examine, study, survey

"Leave them to me. I fancy I know them. If I can only get a good look at them, *I* can soon tell who they are."

Here, scrambling over the heads of the crowd, he managed to get to the wall. When, seizing a flambeau from one of the <u>Caryatides</u>, he returned, as he went, to the centre of the room and leaped, with the **agility** of a monkey, upon the king's head and thence clambered a few feet up the chain, holding down the torch to examine the group of Ourang-Outangs, and still screaming: "*I* shall soon find out who they are!"

And now, while the whole assembly (the apes included) were convulsed with laughter, the jester suddenly uttered a shrill whistle. The chain flew violently up for about thirty feet, dragging with it the dismayed and struggling Ourang-Outangs, and leaving them **suspended** in mid-air between the sky-light and the floor. Hop-Frog, clinging to the chain as it rose, still maintained his relative position in respect to the eight maskers, and still (as if nothing were the matter) continued to thrust his torch down toward them, as though endeavoring to discover who they were.

So thoroughly astonished was the whole company at this **ascent**, that a dead silence of about a minute's duration <u>ensued</u>. It was broken by just such a low, harsh, grating sound, as had before attracted the attention of the king and his councilors when the former threw the wine in the face of Trippetta. But, on the present occasion, there could be no question as to *whence* the sound issued. It came from the fang-like teeth of the dwarf, who ground them and gnashed them as he foamed at the mouth, and glared, with an expression of maniacal rage, into the upturned **countenances** of the king and his seven companions.

"Ah, ha!" said at length the infuriated jester. "Ah, ha! I begin to see who these people are, now!" Here, pretending to **scrutinize** the king more closely, he held the flambeau to the flaxen coat which enveloped him, and which instantly burst into a sheet of vivid flame. In less than half a minute the whole eight Ourang-Outangs were blazing

MULTITUDE (<u>muhl</u> tuh tood) *n.*
  a crowd, the state of being many, a great number
    Synonyms: mass, myriad, slew

VIRULENCE (<u>veer</u> uh luhnts) *n.*
  extreme harmfulness; malignancy
    Synonyms: harshness, destructiveness; infection,
    toxicity, pestilence

SCRUPLE (<u>skroo</u> puhl) *v.* **-ing,-ed.**
  to hesitate because of one's moral conscience; to make
  a wise ethical or moral decision
    Synonyms: balk, waver, question; reconsider, restrain

ABET (uh <u>beht</u>) *v.* **-ting,-ted.**
  to act as an accomplice, to help
    Synonyms: assist, collaborate

ADHERE (aad <u>heer</u>) *v.* **-ing,-ed.**
  to cling to; to follow without deviation
    Synonyms: stick, affix, fasten; cleave, abide

VENGEANCE (<u>vehn</u> juhns) *n.*
  punishment inflicted in retaliation; vehemence
    Synonyms: revenge, repayment; wrath

FETID (<u>feh</u> tihd) *adj.*
  foul-smelling, putrid
    Synonyms: stinky, funky, malodorous, rank

fiercely, amid the shrieks of the **multitude** who gazed at them from below, horror-stricken, and without the power to render them the slightest assistance.

At length the flames, suddenly increasing in **virulence**, forced the jester to climb higher up the chain to be out of their reach; and, as he made this movement, the crowd again sank, for a brief instant, into silence. The dwarf seized his opportunity, and once more spoke.

"I now see *distinctly*," he said, "what manner of people these maskers are. They are a great king and his seven privy-councilors—a king who does not **scruple** to strike a defenceless girl, and his seven councillors who **abet** him in the outrage. As for myself, I am simply Hop-Frog, the jester—and *this is my last jest*."

Owing to the high combustibility of both the flax and the tar to which it **adhered**, the dwarf had scarcely made an end of his brief speech before the work of **vengeance** was complete. The eight corpses swung in their chains, a **fetid**, blackened, hideous, and indistinguishable mass. The cripple hurled his torch at them, clambered leisurely to the ceiling, and disappeared through the sky-light.

It is supposed that Trippetta, stationed on the roof of the saloon, had been the accomplice of her friend in his fiery revenge, and that together, they effected their escape to their own country; for neither was seen again.

SOLICIT (suh <u>lih</u> siht) *v.* **-ing,-ed.**
   to petition persistently, to seek out
      Synonyms: entice, tempt, request, entreat

SUCCINCTLY (suh <u>sihnkt</u> lee) *adv.*
   tersely, briefly, concisely
      Synonyms: bluntly, curtly
EXPOUND (ihk <u>spownd</u>) *v.* **-ing,-ed.**
   to explain or describe in detail
      Synonyms: elucidate, elaborate, explicate

DOCILITY (dah <u>sih</u> lih tee) *n.*
   tameness, a willingness to be taught, good behavior
      Synonyms: mildness, obedience
DISPOSITION (dihs puh <u>zih</u> shuhn) *n.*
   mood or temperament
      Synonyms: behavior, tendency, inclination, nature
INDULGE (ihn <u>duhlj</u>) *v.* **-ing,-ed.**
   to spoil; to give in, as to a craving or desire
      Synonyms: pamper; humor, gratify, allow
DERIVE (dih <u>riev</u>) *v.* **-ing,-ed.**
   to receive from a source, to originate
      Synonyms: infer, descend, deduce, come (from)
SAGACIOUS (suh <u>gay</u> shuhs) *adj.*
   intelligent, shrewd, clever
      Synonyms: astute, perspicacious, wise, judicious
DERIVABLE (dih <u>riev</u> uh buhl) *adj.*
   able to be received from a source, obtainable
      Synonyms: inferable, deducible, resultant

THE BLACK CAT

For the most wild yet most homely narrative which I am about to pen, I neither expect nor **solicit** belief. Mad indeed would I be to expect it, in a case where my very senses reject their own evidence. Yet, mad am I not—and very surely do I not dream. But tomorrow I die, and today I would unburden my soul. My immediate purpose is to place before the world, plainly, **succinctly**, and without comment, a series of mere household events. In their consequences, these events have terrified, have tortured, have destroyed me. Yet I will not attempt to **expound** them. To me, they have presented little but horror—to many they will seem less terrible than *baroques*.[2] Hereafter, perhaps, some intellect may be found which will reduce my phantasm to the commonplace—some intellect more calm, more logical, and far less excitable than my own, which will perceive, in the circumstances I detail with awe, nothing more than an ordinary succession of very natural causes and effects.

From my infancy I was noted for the **docility** and humanity of my **disposition**. My tenderness of heart was even so <u>conspicuous</u> as to make me the jest of my companions. I was especially fond of animals, and was **indulged** by my parents with a great variety of pets. With these I spent most of my time, and never was so happy as when feeding and caressing them. This peculiarity of character grew with my growth, and, in my manhood, I **derived** from it one of my principal sources of pleasure. To those who have cherished an affection for a faithful and **sagacious** dog, I need hardly be at the trouble of explaining the nature or the intensity of the gratification thus **derivable**. There is something in the unselfish and

PALTRY (<u>pahl</u> tree) *adj.*
pitifully small or worthless
Synonyms: trivial, trifling, petty, picayune, meager

FIDELITY (fih <u>dehl</u> ih tee) (fie <u>dehl</u> ih tee) *n.*
loyalty
Synonyms: allegiance, fealty, faithfulness

DISPOSITION (dihs puh <u>zih</u> shuhn) *n.*
mood or temperament
Synonyms: behavior, tendency, inclination, nature

UNCONGENIAL (uhn kuhn <u>jee</u> nee uhl) *adj.*
dissimilar in tastes and habits; having an unpleasant manner
Synonyms: discordant, conflicting; discourteous, rude

PARTIALITY (pahr shee <u>aal</u> ih tee) *n.*
a special liking for something; favoritism or favorable bias
Synonyms: fondness, fancy; preference, inclination

PROCURE (proh <u>kyoor</u>) *v.* **-ing,-ed.** *(See page 26.)*

SAGACIOUS (suh <u>gay</u> shuhs) *adj.* *(See page 36.)*

ALLUSION (uh <u>loo</u> zhuhn) *n.*
indirect reference
Synonyms: intimation, suggestion

TEMPERAMENT (<u>tehm</u> puhr uh mehnt) *n.*
an attitude, a manner of behaving
Synonyms: disposition, mood, mentality

INTEMPERANCE (ihn <u>tehm</u> puhr uhnts) *n.*
lack of restraint or self-control (for example, with alcohol)
Synonyms: carelessness, wildness, spontaneity

INTEMPERATE (ihn <u>tehm</u> puhr iht) *adj.*
excessive with regards to one's behavior, immoderate
Synonyms: careless, wild, spontaneous

RETAIN (rih <u>tayn</u>) *v.* **-ing,-ed.** *(See page 14.)*

RESTRAIN (rih <u>strayn</u>) *v.* **-ing,-ed.**
to control, repress, restrict, hold back
Synonyms: hamper, bridle, curb, check

SCRUPLE (<u>skroo</u> puhl) *n.*
an ethical and moral belief that prevents action; a hesitation caused by moral conscience
Synonyms: principle; restraint, qualm, misgiving

self-sacrificing love of a brute, which goes directly to the heart of him who has had frequent occasion to test the **paltry** friendship and gossamer **fidelity** of mere *Man*.

I married early, and was happy to find in my wife a **disposition** not **uncongenial** with my own. Observing my **partiality** for domestic pets, she lost no opportunity of **procuring** those of the most agreeable kind. We had birds, gold-fish, a fine dog, rabbits, a small monkey, and a cat.

This latter was a remarkably large and beautiful animal, entirely black, and **sagacious** to an astonishing degree. In speaking of his intelligence, my wife, who at heart was not a little <u>tinctured</u> with superstition, made frequent **allusion** to the ancient popular notion, which regarded all black cats as witches in disguise. Not that she was ever *serious* upon this point—and I mention the matter at all for no better reason than that it happens, just now, to be remembered.

Pluto—this was the cat's name—was my favorite pet and playmate. I alone fed him, and he attended me wherever I went about the house. It was even with difficulty that I could prevent him from following me through the streets.

Our friendship lasted in this manner for several years, during which my general **temperament** and character—through the instrumentality of the Fiend **Intemperance**—had (I blush to confess it) experienced a radical alteration for the worse. I grew day by day more moody, more irritable, more regardless of the feelings of others. I suffered myself to use **intemperate** language to my wife. At length, I even offered her personal violence. My pets, of course, were made to feel the change in my disposition. I not only neglected, but ill-used them. For Pluto, however, I still **retained** sufficient regard to **restrain** me from maltreating him, as I made no **scruple** of maltreating the rabbits, the monkey, or even the dog, when, by accident, or through affection, they came in my way. But my disease grew upon me—for what disease is like Alcohol!—

MALEVOLENCE (muh <u>lehv</u> uh luhnts) *n.*
ill-will, desire to cause evil or harm to others; hatred
Synonyms: spite, unkindness; animosity, malice
ATROCITY (uh <u>trah</u> sih tee) *n.*
revolting wickedness, cruelty
Synonyms: horror, barbarity, abomination, outrage
DEBAUCH (dih <u>bahch</u>) *n.*
excessive eating or drinking, overindulgence;
corruption, seduction from virtue or duty
Synonyms: intemperance; riot, debasement
SENTIMENT (<u>sehn</u> tuh muhnt) *n.*
an attitude, thought, or judgment prompted by
feeling; a romantic or nostalgic feeling
Synonyms: idea; emotion
REMORSE (rih <u>mohrs</u>) *n.*
a gnawing distress arising from a sense of guilt
Synonyms: anguish, ruefulness, shame, penitence
EQUIVOCAL (ih <u>kwihv</u> uh kuhl) *adj.*
ambiguous, open to more than one interpretation;
equal in name, but not in reality
Synonyms: doubtful, uncertain; misleading
IRREVOCABLE (ih <u>rehv</u> uh kuh buhl) *adj.*
conclusive, irreversible
Synonyms: permanent, indelible, irreparable
PERVERSENESS (puhr <u>vuhrs</u> nehs) *n.*
deliberate disobedience or misbehavior; contrariness
Synonyms: unruliness; immorality, irrationality
IMPULSE (<u>ihm</u> puhls) *n.*
sudden tendency, inclination
Synonyms: urge, whim
FACULTY (<u>faa</u> kuhl tee) *n.*
the ability to act or do
Synonyms: aptitude, capability, sense, skill

and at length even Pluto, who was now becoming old, and consequently somewhat <u>peevish</u>—even Pluto began to experience the effects of my ill temper.

One night, returning home much intoxicated from one of my haunts about town, I fancied that the cat avoided my presence. I seized him. In his fright at my violence, he inflicted a slight wound upon my hand with his teeth. The fury of a demon instantly possessed me. I knew myself no longer. My original soul seemed, at once, to take its flight from my body; and a more than fiendish **malevolence**, gin-nurtured, thrilled every fibre of my frame. I took from my waistcoat-pocket a penknife, opened it, grasped the poor beast by the throat, and deliberately cut one of its eyes from the socket! I blush, I burn, I shudder, while I pen the damnable **atrocity**.

When reason returned with the morning—when I had slept off the fumes of the night's **debauch**—I experienced a **sentiment** half of horror, half of **remorse**, for the crime of which I had been guilty; but it was, at best, a feeble and **equivocal** feeling, and the soul remained untouched. I again plunged into excess, and soon drowned in wine all memory of the deed.

In the meantime, the cat slowly recovered. The socket of the lost eye presented, it is true, a frightful appearance, but he no longer appeared to suffer any pain. He went about the house as usual, but, as might be expected, fled in extreme terror at my approach. I had so much of my old heart left, as to be at first grieved by this evident dislike on the part of a creature which had once so loved me. But this feeling soon gave place to irritation. And then came, as if to my final and **irrevocable** overthrow, the spirit of PERVERSENESS. Of this spirit philosophy takes no account. Yet I am not more sure that my soul lives, than I am that **perverseness** is one of the primitive **impulses** of the human heart—one of the indivisible primary **faculties**, or **sentiments**, which give direction to the character of Man. Who has not, a hundred times, found

PERPETUAL (puhr <u>peht</u> chyoo uhl) *adj.*
  endless, lasting
    Synonyms: continuous, constant, ceaseless, eternal,
    perennial

INCLINATION (ihn cluh <u>nay</u> shuhn) *n.*
  tendency toward
    Synonyms: leaning, trend, preference, disposition,
    propensity

PERVERSENESS (puhr <u>vuhrs</u> nehs) *n.*
  deliberate disobedience or misbehavior; contrariness
    Synonyms: unruliness; immorality, irrationality

UNFATHOMABLE (uhn <u>faath</u> uhm uh buhl) *adj.*
  very difficult to understand; incapable of being
  measured
    Synonyms: incomprehensible; infinite, unending

VEX (vehks) *v.* **-ing,-ed.**
  to irritate, annoy; confuse, puzzle
    Synonyms: bother, plague, afflict, irk; perplex, perturb

CONSUMMATE (<u>kahn</u> suh mayt) *v.* **-ing,-ed.**
  to accomplish, to complete
    Synonyms: conclude, fulfill, perfect

REMORSE (rih <u>mohrs</u>) *n.*
  a gnawing distress arising from a sense of guilt
    Synonyms: anguish, ruefulness, shame, penitence

CONFLAGRATION (kahn fluh <u>gray</u> shuhn) *n.*
  a big, destructive fire; an intense scene
    Synonyms: blaze, holocaust, inferno; spectacle

ATROCITY (uh <u>trah</u> sih tee) *n.*
  revolting wickedness, cruelty
    Synonyms: horror, barbarity, abomination, outrage

himself committing a vile or a stupid action, for no other reason than because he knows he should *not*? Have we not a **perpetual inclination**, in the teeth of our best judgment, to violate that which is law, merely because we understand it to be such? This spirit of **perverseness**, I say, came to my final overthrow. It was this **unfathomable** longing of the soul to **vex** itself—to offer violence to its own nature—to do wrong for the wrong's sake only—that urged me to continue and finally to **consummate** the injury I had inflicted upon the unoffending brute. One morning, in cold blood, I slipped a noose about its neck and hung it to the limb of a tree, hung it with the tears streaming from my eyes, and with the bitterest **remorse** at my heart, hung it *because* I knew that it had loved me, and *because* I felt it had given me no reason of offence, hung it because I knew that in so doing I was committing a sin, a deadly sin that would so jeopardize my immortal soul as to place it—if such a thing were possible—even beyond the reach of the infinite mercy of the Most Merciful and Most Terrible God.

On the night of the day on which this most cruel deed was done, I was aroused from sleep by the cry of fire. The curtains of my bed were in flames. The whole house was blazing. It was with great difficulty that my wife, a servant, and myself, made our escape from the **conflagration**. The destruction was complete. My entire worldly wealth was swallowed up, and I resigned myself thenceforward to despair.

I am above the weakness of seeking to establish a sequence of cause and effect, between the disaster and the **atrocity**. But I am detailing a chain of facts, and wish not to leave even a possible link imperfect. On the day succeeding the fire, I visited the ruins. The walls, with one exception, had fallen in. This exception was found in a compartment wall, not very thick, which stood about the middle of the house, and against which had rested the head of my bed. The plastering had here, in great

APPARITION (aa puh <u>rih</u> shuhn) *n.*
    an unexpected or unusual sight or appearance; a
    ghostly figure
        Synonyms: illusion; spirit, specter
ADJACENT (uh <u>jay</u> suhnt) *adj.*
    next to, close, bordering
        Synonyms: neighboring, adjoining, abutting

SENTIMENT (<u>sehn</u> tuh muhnt) *n.*
    an attitude, thought, or judgment prompted by
    feeling; a romantic or nostalgic feeling
        Synonyms: idea; emotion
REMORSE (rih <u>mohrs</u>) *n.*
    a gnawing distress arising from a sense of guilt
        Synonyms: anguish, ruefulness, shame, penitence
STUPEFIED (<u>stoo</u> puh fied) *adj.*
    having dull senses; stunned, astonished
        Synonyms: dazed, bemused, benumbed; amazed
INFAMY (<u>ihn</u> fuh mee) *n.*
    reputation for bad deeds
        Synonyms: disgrace, dishonor, shame, ignominy
DRAW *v.* **-ing, drew, drawn**
    to attract or be attracted to; to pull, drag; to lead, to
    bring about on purpose
        Synonyms: lure, entice; haul, tow, yank; provoke, elicit

measure, resisted the action of the fire—a fact which I attributed to its having been recently spread. About this wall a dense crowd were collected, and many persons seemed to be examining a particular portion of it with very minute and eager attention. The words "strange!" "singular!" and other similar expressions, excited my curiosity. I approached and saw, as if <u>graven</u> in *bas-relief*[3] upon the white surface, the figure of a gigantic cat. The impression was given with an accuracy truly marvellous. There was a rope about the animal's neck.

When I first beheld this **apparition**—for I could scarcely regard it as less—my wonder and my terror were extreme. But at length reflection came to my aid. The cat, I remembered, had been hung in the garden **adjacent** to the house. Upon the alarm of fire, this garden had been immediately filled by the crowd—by someone of whom the animal must have been cut from the tree and thrown, through an open window, into my chamber. This had probably been done with the view of arousing me from sleep. The falling of other walls had compressed the victim of my cruelty into the substance of the freshly-spread plaster; the lime of which, with the flames, and the *ammonia* from the carcass, had then accomplished the portraiture as I saw it.

Although I thus readily accounted to my reason, if not altogether to my conscience for the startling fact just detailed, it did not the less fail to make a deep impression upon my fancy. For months I could not rid myself of the phantasm of the cat; and, during this period, there came back into my spirit a half-**sentiment** that seemed, but was not, **remorse**. I went so far as to regret the loss of the animal, and to look about me, among the vile haunts which I now habitually frequented, for another pet of the same species and of somewhat similar appearance, with which to supply its place.

One night as I sat, half **stupefied**, in a den of more than **infamy**, my attention was suddenly **drawn** to some black

REPOSE (rih <u>pohz</u>) *v.* **-ing,-ed.**
    to relax or rest; to lie dead
        Synonyms: sleep, slumber; pass on
CONSTITUTE (kahn stih <u>toot</u>) *v.* **-ing,-ed.**
    to be the parts or components of something,
    to compose; to equal
        Synonyms: comprise, form, make up; amount to

EVINCE (ih <u>vihns</u>) *v.* **-ing,-ed.**
    to show clearly or display
        Synonyms: express, exhibit, demonstrate, manifest
DISPOSITION (dihs puh <u>zih</u> shuhn) *n.*
    mood or temperament
        Synonyms: behavior, tendency, inclination, nature

LOATHING (<u>lohth</u> ing) *adj.*
    hatred or dislike
        Synonyms: detestation, abhorrence
ODIOUS (<u>oh</u> dee uhs) *adj.*
    hateful, contemptible
        Synonyms: detestable, obnoxious, offensive,
        repellent, loathsome
PESTILENCE (<u>peh</u> stihl ehnts) *n.*
    epidemic, plague, illness
        Synonyms: contagion, scourge, sickness, disease

object, **reposing** upon the head of one of the immense hogsheads of gin, or of rum, which **constituted** the chief furniture of the apartment. I had been looking steadily at the top of this hogshead for some minutes, and what now caused me surprise was the fact that I had not sooner perceived the object thereupon. I approached it and touched it with my hand. It was a black cat—a very large one—fully as large as Pluto, and closely resembling him in every respect but one. Pluto had not a white hair upon any portion of his body, but this cat had a large, although indefinite splotch of white, covering nearly the whole region of the breast.

Upon my touching him, he immediately arose, purred loudly, rubbed against my hand, and appeared delighted with my notice. This, then, was the very creature of which I was in search. I at once offered to purchase it from the landlord, but this person made no claim to it, knew nothing of it, had never seen it before.

I continued my caresses, and when I prepared to go home, the animal **evinced** a **disposition** to accompany me. I permitted it to do so, occasionally stooping and patting it as I proceeded. When it reached the house it domesticated itself at once, and became immediately a great favorite with my wife.

For my own part, I soon found a dislike to it arising within me. This was just the reverse of what I had anticipated but—I know not how or why it was—its evident fondess for myself rather disgusted and annoyed me. By slow degrees these feelings of disgust and annoyance rose into the bitterness of hatred. I avoided the creature, a certain sense of shame, and the remembrance of my former deed of cruelty, preventing me from physically abusing it. I did not for some weeks strike or otherwise violently ill use it, but gradually—very gradually—I came to look upon it with unutterable **loathing**, and to flee silently from its **odious** presence, as from the breath of a **pestilence**.

AVERSION (uh <u>vuhr</u> zhuhn) *n.*
  intense dislike
    Synonyms: antagonism, antipathy, abhorrence,
    repulsion, repugnance
PARTIALITY (pahr shee <u>aal</u> ih tee) *n.*
  a special liking for something; favoritism or favorable
  bias
    Synonyms: fondness, fancy; preference, inclination
PERTINACITY (puhr tih <u>naa</u> sih tee) *n.*
  stubborn persistence
    Synonyms: obstinacy, diligence
LOATHSOME (<u>lohth</u> suhm) *adj.*
  abhorrent, hateful
    Synonyms: offensive, disgusting

CHIMERA (kie <u>meer</u> uh) (kih <u>meer</u> uh) *n.*
  a fantasy or dream
    Synonyms: illusion, vision, impossibility
CONSTITUTE (kahn stih <u>toot</u>) *v.* **-ing,-ed.**
  to be the parts or components of something,
  to compose; to equal
    Synonyms: comprise, form, make up; amount to

LOATHE (lohth) *v.* **-ing,-ed.**
  to abhor, despise, hate
    Synonyms: abominate, execrate, detest, condemn

What added, no doubt, to my hatred of the beast, was the discovery, on the morning after I brought it home, that, like Pluto, it also had been deprived of one of its eyes. This circumstance, however, only endeared it to my wife, who, as I have already said, possessed in a high degree that humanity of feeling which had once been my distinguishing trait, and the source of many of my simplest and purest pleasures.

With my **aversion** to this cat, however, its **partiality** for myself seemed to increase. It followed my footsteps with a **pertinacity** which it would be difficult to make the reader comprehend. Whenever I sat, it would crouch beneath my chair or spring upon my knees, covering me with its **loathsome** caresses. If I arose to walk, it would get between my feet and thus nearly throw me down or, fastening its long and sharp claws in my dress, clamber, in this manner, to my breast. At such times, although I longed to destroy it with a blow, I was yet withheld from so doing, partly by a memory of my former crime, but chiefly—let me confess it at once—by absolute *dread* of the beast.

This dread was not exactly a dread of physical evil and yet I should be at a loss how otherwise to define it. I am almost ashamed to own—yes, even in this felon's cell, I am almost ashamed to own—that the terror and horror with which the animal inspired me, had been heightened by one of the merest **chimeras** it would be possible to conceive. My wife had called my attention more than once to the character of the mark of white hair, of which I have spoken, and which **constituted** the sole visible difference between the strange beast and the one I had destroyed. The reader will remember that this mark, although large, had been originally very indefinite. But by slow degrees—degrees nearly imperceptible, and which for a long time my reason struggled to reject as fanciful—it had, at length, assumed a rigorous distinctness of outline. It was now the representation of an object that I shudder to name, and for this, above all, I **loathed** and dreaded, and

CONTEMPTUOUSLY (kuhn <u>tehmp</u> choo uhs lee) *adv.*
scornfully
    Synonyms: derisively, disdainfully, superciliously

INCARNATE (ihn <u>kahr</u> niht) *adj.*
having human or bodily form; personified
    Synonyms: embodied, corporal, physical; typefied
INCUMBENT (ihn <u>kuhm</u> buhnt) *adj.*
leaning or pressing upon something else
    Synonyms: lying, resting

COMPEL (kuhm <u>pehl</u>) *v.* **-ling,-led.**
to urge or force
    Synonyms: coerce, oblige, constrain
EXASPERATE (ihg <u>zaas</u> puhr ayt) *v.* **-ing,-ed.**
to irritate
    Synonyms: frustrate, annoy, vex, pique
WRATH (raath) *n.*
anger, rage
    Synonyms: fury, ire, resentment, indignation
DESCEND (dih <u>sehnd</u>) (dee <u>sehnd</u>) *v.* **-ing,-ed.**
to pass from a higher place to a lower place
    Synonyms: fall, dismount, gravitate
GOAD (gohd) *v.* **-ing,-ed.**
to prod or urge
    Synonyms: impel, incite, stimulate, provoke, rouse

would have rid myself of the monster *had I dared.* It was now, I say, the image of a hideous—of a ghastly thing— of the <u>GALLOWS</u>! Oh, mournful and terrible engine of Horror and of Crime, of Agony and of Death!

And now was I indeed wretched beyond the wretchedness of mere Humanity. A brute beast—whose fellow I had **contemptuously** destroyed—a brute beast to work out for *me*—for me, a man fashioned in the image of the High God—so much of insufferable woe! Alas, neither by day nor by night knew I the blessing of rest anymore! During the former the creature left me no moment alone, and in the latter I started hourly from dreams of unutterable fear to find the hot breath of *the thing* upon my face, and its vast weight—an **incarnate** nightmare that I had no power to shake off—**incumbent** eternally upon my *heart!*

Beneath the pressure of torments such as these the feeble remnant of the good within me <u>succumbed</u>. Evil thoughts became my sole intimates—the darkest and most evil of thoughts. The moodiness of my usual temper increased to hatred of all things and of all mankind; while from the sudden, frequent, and ungovernable outbursts of a fury to which I now blindly abandoned myself, my uncomplaining wife, alas, was the most usual and the most patient of sufferers.

One day she accompanied me, upon some household errand, into the cellar of the old building which our poverty **compelled** us to inhabit. The cat followed me down the steep stairs, and, nearly throwing me headlong, **exasperated** me to madness. Uplifting an axe and forgetting in my **wrath** the childish dread which had hitherto stayed my hand, I aimed a blow at the animal, which, of course, would have proved instantly fatal had it **descended** as I wished. But this blow was arrested by the hand of my wife. **Goaded** by the interference into a rage more than demoniacal, I withdrew my arm from her grasp and buried the axe in her brain. She fell dead upon the spot without a groan.

RESOLVE (rih <u>sahlv</u>) *v.* **-ing,-ed.**
    to determine or to make a firm decision about
        Synonyms: solve, decide

EXPEDIENT (ihk <u>spee</u> dee uhnt) *n.*
    something that speeds up a process or meets an
    urgent need; a method; a resource
        Synonyms: contrivance; use, way; device,
        instrument
ADAPTED (uh <u>daap</u> tihd) *adj.*
    accustomed, equipped
        Synonyms: prepared, fit, accomodating

PROCURE (proh <u>kyoor</u>) *v.* **-ing,-ed.**
    to obtain
        Synonyms: acquire, secure, get, gain

MINUTE (mie <u>noot</u>) (mih <u>noot</u>) *adj.*
    precise, detailed; very small
        Synonyms: attentive, critical; tiny, diminutive,
        infinitesimal

This hideous murder accomplished, I set myself forthwith, and with entire deliberation, to the task of concealing the body. I knew that I could not remove it from the house, either by day or by night, without the risk of being observed by the neighbors. Many projects entered my mind. At one period I thought of cutting the corpse into minute fragments and destroying them by fire. At another, I resolved to dig a grave for it in the floor of the cellar. Again, I deliberated about casting it in the well in the yard, about packing it in a box, as if merchandise, with the usual arrangements, and so getting a porter to take it from the house. Finally I hit upon what I considered a far better expedient than either of these. I determined to wall it up in the cellar, as the monks of the Middle Ages are recorded to have walled up their victims.

For a purpose such as this the cellar was well adapted. Its walls were loosely constructed, and had lately been plastered throughout with a rough plaster, which the dampness of the atmosphere had prevented from hardening. Moreover, in one of the walls was a projection, caused by a false chimney, or fireplace, that had been filled up and made to resemble the rest of the cellar. I made no doubt that I could readily displace the bricks at this point, insert the corpse, and wall the whole up as before, so that no eye could detect anything suspicious.

And in this calculation I was not deceived. By means of a crowbar I easily dislodged the bricks and, having carefully deposited the body against the inner wall, I propped it in that position, while with little trouble I relaid the whole structure as it originally stood. Having procured mortar, sand, and hair, with every possible precaution, I prepared a plaster which could not be distinguished from the old, and with this I very carefully went over the new brick-work. When I had finished, I felt satisfied that all was right. The wall did not present the slightest appearance of having been disturbed. The rubbish on the floor was picked up with the minutest care. I

RESOLVE (rih <u>sahlv</u>) *v.* **-ing,-ed.**
    to determine or to make a firm decision about
        Synonyms: solve, decide
FORBEAR (fohr <u>bayr</u>) *v.* **-ing,-bore.**
    to refrain or resist; to tolerate or put up with
        Synonym: avoid, withhold, inhibit; endure, suffer
DETESTED (dee <u>tehst</u> ihd) *adj.*
    intensely hated
        Synonyms: disgusting, despicable, loathsome

INSCRUTABILITY (ihn skroo tuh <u>bihl</u> ih tee) *n.*
    the inability to be fully seen or understood
        Synonyms: mystery, seclusion, concealment, enigma

DESCEND (dih <u>sehnd</u>) (dee <u>sehnd</u>) *v.* **-ing,-ed.**
    to pass from a higher place to a lower place
        Synonyms: fall, dismount, gravitate

looked around triumphantly and said to myself: "Here at least, then, my labor has not been in vain."

My next step was to look for the beast which had been the cause of so much wretchedness, for I had, at length, firmly resolved to put it to death. Had I been able to meet with it at the moment, there could have been no doubt of its fate; but it appeared that the crafty animal had been alarmed at the violence of my previous anger and forbore to present itself in my present mood. It is impossible to describe or to imagine the deep, the blissful sense of relief which the absence of the detested creature occasioned in my bosom. It did not make its appearance during the night; and thus for one night, at least, since its introduction into the house, I soundly and tranquilly slept aye, *slept* even with the burden of murder upon my soul.

The second and the third day passed, and still my tormentor came not. Once again I breathed as a freeman. The monster, in terror, had fled the premises forever! I should behold it no more! My happiness was supreme! The guilt of my dark deed disturbed me but little. Some few inquiries had been made, but these had been readily answered. Even a search had been instituted—but of course nothing was to be discovered. I looked upon my future felicity as secured.

Upon the fourth day of the assassination, a party of the police came, very unexpectedly, into the house and proceeded again to make rigorous investigation of the premises. Secure, however, in the inscrutability of my place of concealment, I felt no embarrassment whatsoever. The officers bade me to accompany them in their search. They left no nook or corner unexplored. At length, for the third or fourth time, they descended into the cellar. I quivered not in a muscle. My heart beat calmly as that of one who slumbers in innocence. I walked the cellar from end to end. I folded my arms upon my bosom and roamed easily to and fro. The police were thoroughly satisfied and prepared to depart. The glee at

RESTRAIN (rih <u>strayn</u>) *v.* **-ing,-ed.**
   to control, repress, restrict, hold back
      Synonyms: hamper, bridle, curb, check
ASCEND (uh <u>sehnd</u>) *v.* **-ing,-ed.**
   to rise to another level or climb; to move upward
      Synonyms: elevate, escalate, mount; hoist, lift
ALLAY (uh <u>lay</u>) *v.* **-ing,-ed.**
   to lessen, ease, or soothe
      Synonyms: alleviate, assuage, quell, mitigate,
      palliate

ARCH (ahrch) *adj.*
   having the highest rank, most important;
   mischievous, roguish
      Synonyms: chief, top; impish, saucy, ironic

ANOMALOUS (uh <u>nah</u> moh luhs) *adj.*
   irregular or deviating from the norm
      Synonyms: odd, strange, peculiar, abnormal
EXULT (ihg <u>suhlt</u>) *v.* **-ing,-ed.**
   to be extremely joyful, to rejoice
      Synonyms: celebrate, delight, jubilate

my heart was too strong to be **restrained**. I burned to say if but one word, by way of triumph, and to render doubly sure their assurance of my guiltlessness.

"Gentlemen," I said at last, as the party **ascended** the steps, "I delight to have **allayed** your suspicions. I wish you all health and a little more courtesy. By the bye, gentlemen, this, this is a very well-constructed house." (In the rabid desire to say something easily, I scarcely knew what I uttered at all.) "I may say an *excellently* well-constructed house. These walls—are you going, gentlemen? These walls are solidly put together." And here, through the mere frenzy of bravado, I rapped heavily with a cane which I held in my hand, upon that very portion of the brickwork behind which stood the corpse of the wife of my bosom.

But may God shield and deliver me from the fangs of the **Arch**-Fiend! No sooner had the reverberation of my blows sunk into silence, than I was answered by a voice from within the tomb! By a cry, at first muffled and broken, like the sobbing of a child, and then quickly swelling into one long, loud, and continuous scream, utterly **anomalous** and inhuman—a howl—a wailing shriek, half of horror and half of triumph, such as might have arisen only out of hell, conjointly from the throats of the damned in their agony and of the demons that **exult** in the damnation.

Of my own thoughts it is folly to speak. Swooning, I staggered to the opposite wall. For one instant the party on the stairs remained motionless, through extremity of terror and awe. In the next a dozen stout arms were toiling at the wall. It fell bodily. The corpse, already greatly decayed and clotted with gore, stood erect before the eyes of the spectators. Upon its head, with red extended mouth and solitary eye of fire, sat the hideous beast whose craft had seduced me into murder and whose informing voice had <u>consigned</u> me to the hangman. I had walled the monster up within the tomb.

PERVADE (puhr <u>vayd</u>) *v.* **-ing,-ed.**
 to become diffused throughout every part of
  Synonyms: permeate, spread, fill, transfuse
SINGULAR (<u>sihn</u> gyuh luhr) *adj.*
 uncommon, peculiar
  Synonyms: unusual, odd, rare, unique, individual
PLACID (<u>plaa</u> sihd) *adj.*
 calm
  Synonyms: tranquil, serene, peaceful, complacent
ENTHRALLING (ehn <u>thrah</u> lihng) *adj.*
 captivating, enchanting, enslaving
  Synonyms: bewitching, fascinating, enrapturing,
  transfixing, mesmerizing
ELOQUENCE (<u>eh</u> luh kwuhns) *n.*
 persuasive and effective speech
  Synonyms: expressiveness, fluency
STEALTHILY (<u>stehl</u> thuh lee) *adv.*
 quietly and cautiously
  Synonyms: furtively, secretly, surreptitiously,
  covertly
ADAPT (uh <u>daapt</u>) *v.* **-ing,-ed.**
 to accommodate; to adjust
  Synonyms: conform, fit, reconcile
PATERNAL (puh <u>tuhr</u> nuhl) *adj.*
 inherited from the father; fatherly, related to the
 characteristics of fatherhood
  Synonyms: hereditary; parental

LIGEIA

And the will therein lieth, which dieth not. Who knoweth the mysteries of the will, with its vigor? For God is but a great will pervading all things by nature of its intentness. Man doth not yield himself to the angels, nor onto death utterly, save only through the weakness of his feeble will.—*Joseph Glanvill*

I cannot, for my soul, remember how, when, or even precisely where, I first became acquainted with the lady Ligeia. Long years have since elapsed, and my memory is feeble through much suffering. Or, perhaps, I cannot *now* bring these points to mind, because, in truth, the character of my beloved, her rare learning, her **singular** yet **placid** cast of beauty, and the thrilling and **enthralling eloquence** of her low musical language, made their way into my heart by paces so steadily and **stealthily** progessive, that they have been unnoticed and unknown. Yet I believe that I met her first and most frequently in some large, old, decaying city near the Rhine. Of her family I have surely heard her speak. That it is of a remotely ancient date cannot be doubted. Ligeia! Ligeia! Buried in studies of a nature more than all else **adapted** to deaden impressions of the outward world, it is by that sweet word alone—by Ligeia—that I bring before mine eyes in fancy the image of her who is no more. And now, while I write, a recollection flashes upon me that I have *never known* the **paternal** name of her who was my friend and my betrothed, and who became the partner of my studies, and finally the wife of my bosom. Was it a playful charge on the part of my Ligeia? Or was it a test of my strength of affection, that I should institute no inquiries upon this

CAPRICE (kuh <u>prees</u>) *n.*
   an impulsive change of mind, fickleness
      Synonym: whim

WAN (wahn) *adj.*
   sickly pale
      Synonyms: ashen, pallid, blanched, pasty

EMACIATED (ih <u>may</u> shee ay tihd) *adj.*
   very thin due to hunger or disease; feeble
      Synonyms: bony, gaunt, haggard, skeletal

DEMEANOR (dih <u>meen</u> uhr) *n.*
   one's behavior or conduct
      Synonyms: attitude, disposition, manner, presence

HEATHEN (<u>hee</u> thuhn) *n.*
   pagan, an uncivilized and irreligious person
      Synonyms: idolater, polytheist

PERVADE (puhr <u>vayd</u>) *v.* **-ing,-ed.**
   to become diffused throughout every part of
      Synonyms: permeate, spread, fill, transfuse

REPOSE (rih <u>pohz</u>) *n.*
   a state of peace or tranquility; relaxation, leisure
      Synonyms: calmness, serenity; rest, ease, idleness

point? Or was it rather a **caprice** of my own—a wildly romantic offering on the shrine of the most passionate devotion? I but indistinctly recall the fact itself—what wonder that I have utterly forgotten the circumstances which originated or attended it? And indeed, if ever that spirit which is entitled *Romance*—if ever she, the **wan** and the misty-winged *Ashtophet*[4] of idolatrous Egypt, presided, as they tell, over marriages ill-omened, then most surely she presided over mine.

There is one dear topic, however, on which my memory fails me not. It is the *person* of Ligeia. In stature she was tall, somewhat slender, and, in her latter days, even **emaciated**. I would in vain attempt to portray the majesty, the quiet ease of her **demeanor**, or the incomprehensible lightness and elasticity of her footfall. She came and departed as a shadow. I was never made aware of her entrance into my closed study, save by the dear music of her low, sweet voice, as she placed her marble hand upon my shoulder. In beauty of face no maiden ever equalled her. It was the radiance of an opium dream—an airy and spirit-lifting vision more wildly divine than the phantasies that hovered about the slumbering souls of the daughters of Delos. Yet her features were not of that regular mould which we have been falsely taught to worship in the classical labors of the **heathen**. "There is no exquisite beauty," says Bacon, Lord Verulam, speaking truly of all the forms and <u>genera</u> of beauty, "without some *strangeness* in the proportion." Yet, although I saw that the features of Ligeia were not of a classic regularity—although I perceived that her loveliness was indeed "exquisite," and felt that there was much of "strangeness" **pervading** it, yet I have tried in vain to detect the irregularity and to trace home my own perception of "the strange." I examined the contour of the lofty and pale forehead—it was faultless— how cold indeed that word when applied to a majesty so divine! The skin rivalling the purest ivory, the commanding extent and **repose**, the gentle prominence of the

LUXURIANT (luhg <u>zhoor</u> ee uhnt) *adj.*
  extravagantly abundant; elegant, lavish
    Synonyms: profuse, plentiful; opulent, rich
EPITHET (<u>eh</u> puh theht) *n.*
  a descriptive term or phrase substituted for a real
  name; an abusive word or phrase
    Synonyms: nickname, motto, catchphrase
LUXURIOUS (luhg <u>zhoor</u> ee uhs) *adj.*
  sensual, pleasurably indulgent
    Synonyms: elaborate, fancy, impressive, posh

SERENE (suh <u>reen</u>) *adj.*
  calm, peaceful
    Synonyms: tranquil, composed, content, placid
PLACID (<u>plaa</u> sihd) *adj.*
  calm
    Synonyms: tranquil, serene, peaceful, complacent
EXULTINGLY (ihg <u>suhl</u> tihng lee) *adv.*
  joyfully, rejoicingly
    Synonyms: gleefully, delightfully, jubilantly
SCRUTINIZE (<u>skroot</u> niez) *v.* **-ing,-ed.**
  to observe carefully
    Synonyms: examine, study, survey
ALLUDE (uh <u>lood</u>) *v.* **-ing,-ed.**
  to make an indirect reference
    Synonyms: intimate, suggest, hint

regions above the temples, and then the raven-black, the glossy, the **luxuriant** and naturally-curling tresses, setting forth the full force of the Homeric **epithet**, "hyacinthine!"[5] I looked at the delicate outlines of the nose—and nowhere but in the graceful medallions of the Hebrews had I beheld a similar perfection. There were the same **luxurious** smoothness of surface, the same scarcely perceptible tendency to the <u>aquiline</u>, the same harmoniously curved nostrils speaking the free spirit. I regarded the sweet mouth. Here was indeed the triumph of all things heavenly—the magnificent turn of the short upper lip, the soft, voluptuous slumber of the under, the dimples which sported, and the color which spoke, the teeth glancing back, with a brilliancy almost startling, every ray of the holy light which fell upon them in her **serene** and **placid** yet most **exultingly** radiant of all smiles. I **scrutinized** the formation of the chin—and, here too, I found the gentleness of breadth, the softness and the majesty, the fullness and the spirituality, of the Greek— the contour which the god Apollo revealed but in a dream, to Cleomenes, the son of the Athenian. And then I peered into the large eyes of Ligeia.

For eyes we have no models in the remotely antique. It might have been, too, that in these eyes of my beloved lay the secret to which Lord Verulam **alludes**. They were, I must believe, far larger than the ordinary eyes of our own race. They were even fuller than the fullest of the gazelle eyes of the tribe of the valley of Nourjahad. Yet it was only at intervals—in moments of intense excitement— that this peculiarity became more than slightly noticeable in Ligeia. And at such moments was her beauty—in my heated fancy thus it appeared perhaps—the beauty of beings either above or apart from the earth, the beauty of the fabulous Houri of the Turk. The hue of the <u>orbs</u> was the most brilliant of black, and far over them hung jetty lashes of great length. The brows, slightly irregular in outline, had the same tint. The "strangeness," however,

PONDER (<u>pahn</u> duhr) *v.* **-ing,-ed.**
to consider or think about something in depth
Synonyms: contemplate, reflect, ruminate

FATHOM (<u>faath</u> uhm) *v.* **-ing,-ed.**
to understand fully, to gauge; to measure the depth of
Synonyms: comprehend; sound

PROFOUND (pruh <u>fownd</u>) (proh <u>fownd</u>) *adj.*
deep, infinite; intelligent; difficult to understand
Synonyms: bottomless, unending; smart; thorough,
weighty

DEVOUT (dih <u>vowt</u>) *adj.*
devoted, as to religion
Synonyms: pious, observant, sincere, earnest, reverent

ANOMALY (uh <u>nah</u> moh lee) *n.*
an irregularity or deviation from the norm
Synonyms: oddity, aberration, deviance, peculiarity,
abnormality

SCRUTINY (<u>skroot</u> nee) *n.*
careful observation
Synonyms: examination, study, surveillance

ANALOGY (uh <u>naal</u> uh jee) *n.*
a relation or likeness, parallelism
Synonyms: correlation, comparison, similarity

SUBSEQUENTLY (<u>suhb</u> suh kwehnt lee) *adv.*
in time or order, in succession, behind
Synonyms: next, afterward

DERIVE (dih <u>riev</u>) *v.* **-ing,-ed.**
to receive from a source, to originate
Synonyms: infer, descend, deduce, come (from)

SENTIMENT (<u>sehn</u> tuh muhnt) *n.*
an attitude, thought, or judgment prompted by
feeling, a romantic or nostalgic feeling
Synonyms: idea, emotion

LUMINOUS (<u>loo</u> muhn uhs) *adj.*
bright, brilliant, glowing
Synonyms: radiant, incandescent, effulgent

which I found in the eyes was of a nature distinct from the formation, or the color, or the brilliancy of the features, and must, after all, be referred to as the *expression*. Ah, word of no meaning! Behind whose vast latitude of mere sound we intrench our ignorance of so much of the spiritual. The expression of the eyes of Ligeia! How for long hours have I **pondered** upon it! How have I, through the whole of a midsummer night, struggled to **fathom** it! What was it—that something more **profound** than the well of Democritus[55]—which lay far within the pupils of my beloved? What was it? I was possessed with a passion to discover. Those eyes! Those large, those shining, those divine orbs! They became to me twin stars of Leda, and I to them **devoutest** of astrologers.

There is no point, among the many incomprehensible **anomalies** of the science of mind, more thrillingly exciting than the fact—never, I believe, noticed in the schools— that in our endeavors to recall to memory something long forgotten, we often find ourselves upon the very verge of remembrance, without being able, in the end, to remember. And thus how frequently in my intense **scrutiny** of Ligeia's eyes, have I felt approaching the full knowledge of their expression—felt it approaching—yet not quite be mine—and so at length entirely depart! And (strange, oh, strangest mystery of all!) I found, in the commonest objects of the universe, a circle of **analogies** to that expression. I mean to say that, **subsequently** to the period when Ligeia's beauty passed into my spirit, there dwelling as in a shrine, I **derived** from many existences in the material world a **sentiment** such as I felt always around, within me, by her large and **luminous** orbs. Yet not the more could I define that **sentiment**, or analyze, or even steadily view it. I recognized it, let me repeat, sometimes in the survey of a rapidly growing vine—in the contemplation of a moth, a butterfly, a chrysalis, a stream of running water. I have felt it in the ocean, in the falling of a meteor. I have felt it in the glances of unusually aged people. And

SCRUTINY (<u>skroot</u> nee) *n.*
careful observation
Synonyms: examination, study, surveillance
INNUMERABLE (ih <u>noo</u> muhr uh buhl)
(ih <u>nyoo</u> muhr uh buhl) *adj.*
too many to be counted, inestimable
Synonyms: incalculable, immeasurable, infinite
SENTIMENT (<u>sehn</u> tuh muhnt) *n. (See page 64.)*
PERVADE (puhr <u>vayd</u>) *v.* **-ing,-ed.**
to become diffused throughout every part of
Synonyms: permeate, spread, fill, transfuse
SUBSEQUENT (<u>suhb</u> suh kwehnt) *adj.*
following in time or order
Synonyms: succeeding, next, afterward
VOLITION (vuh <u>lih</u> shuhn) *n.*
free choice, free will
Synonyms: decision, autonomy
PLACID (<u>plaa</u> sihd) *adj.*
calm
Synonyms: tranquil, serene, peaceful, complacent
TUMULTUOUS (tuh <u>muhl</u> choo uhs) *adj.*
confusing or disorderly, agitated
Synonyms: disturbed, turbulent, chaotic, hectic
APPALL (uh <u>pahl</u>) *v.* **-ing,-ed.**
to overcome with shock or dismay
Synonyms: horrify, astound, petrify
MODULATION (mah juh <u>lay</u> shuhn) *n.*
the act of tuning to a key or pitch; the act of passing
from one musical key to another
Synonyms: adjustment, transition, inflection
PROFICIENT (proh <u>fihsh</u> ehnt) *adj.*
expert, skilled in a certain subject
Synonyms: adept, skillful, deft, experienced,
accomplished
DIALECT (<u>die</u> uh lehkt) *n.*
regional style of speaking
Synonyms: idiom, patois, jargon, vernacular

there are one or two stars in heaven (one especially, a star of the sixth magnitude, double and changeable, to be found near the large star in Lyra) in a telescopic **scrutiny** of which I have been made aware of the feeling. I have been filled with it by certain sounds from stringed instruments, and not unfrequently by passages from books. Among **innumerable** other instances, I well remember something in a volume of Joseph Glanvill, which (perhaps merely from its quaintness—who shall say?) never failed to inspire me with the **sentiment**, "And the will therein lieth, which dieth not. Who knoweth the mysteries of the will, with its vigor? For God is but a great will **pervading** all things by nature of its intentness. Man doth not yield him to the angels, nor unto death utterly, save only through the weakness of his feeble will."

Length of years and **subsequent** reflection have enabled me to trace, indeed, some remote connection between this passage in the English moralist and a portion of the character of Ligeia. An intensity in thought, action, or speech was possibly, in her, a result, or at least an index, of that gigantic **volition** which, during our long intercourse, failed to give other and more immediate evidence of its existence. Of all the women whom I have ever known, she, the outwardly calm, the ever-**placid** Ligeia, was the most violently a prey to the **tumultuous** vultures of stern passion. And of such passion I could form no estimate, save by the miraculous expansion of those eyes which at once so delighted and **appalled** me—by the almost magical melody, **modulation**, distinctness, and **placidity** of her very low voice, and by the fierce energy (rendered doubly effective by contrast with her manner of utterance) of the wild words which she habitually uttered.

I have spoken of the learning of Ligeia; it was immense, such as I have never known in woman. In the classical tongues was she deeply **proficient**, and as far as my own acquaintance extended in regard to the modern **dialects** of Europe, I have never known her at fault.

ERUDITION (ehr yuh <u>dih</u> shuhn) (ehr uh <u>dih</u> shuhn) *n.*
  serious, scholarly learning
    Synonyms: knowledge, education
TRAVERSE (truh <u>vuhrs</u>) (<u>traa</u> vuhrs) *v.* **-ing,-ed.**
  to travel or move across; to turn or move laterally
    Synonyms: cross, intersect, pass through; swivel,
    zigzag

CHAOTIC (kay <u>ah</u> ti**hk**) *adj.*
  extremely disorder**ed**
    Synonyms: incoherent, random, disorganized
ETHEREAL (ih <u>theer</u> ee uhl) *adj.*
  not earthly, spiritual, delicate
    Synonyms: intangible, diaphanous, airy, gossamer,
    sheer

POIGNANT (<u>poy</u> nyaant) *adj.*
  emotionally moving
    Synonyms: stirring, touching, pathetic, piquant
LUMINOUS (<u>loo</u> muhn uhs) *adj.*
  bright, brilliant, glowing
    Synonyms: radiant, incandescent, effulgent
IMMERSE (ih <u>muhrs</u>) *v.* **-ing,-ed.**
  to engross, preoccupy; to bathe, dip
    Synonyms: engage, absorb; douse, dunk, submerge
PORE (pohr) *v.* **-ing,-ed.**
  to study closely or meditatively
    Synonyms: peruse, gaze, ponder
IMPETUOUSLY (ihm <u>peh</u> choo uhs lee) *adv.*
  rapidly, forcefully; in a quick manner without
  thinking
    Synonyms: fiercely; impulsively, passionately

Indeed upon any theme of the most admired, simply the most <u>abstruse</u> of the boasted **erudition** of the Academy, have I *ever* found Ligeia at fault? How singularly—how thrillingly, this one point in the nature of my wife has forced itself, at this late period only, upon my attention! I said her knowledge was such as I have never known in woman—but where breathes the man who has **traversed**, and successfully, *all* the wide areas of moral, physical, and mathematical science? I saw not then what I now clearly perceive, that the acquisitions of Ligeia were gigantic, were astounding; yet I was sufficiently aware of her infinite supremacy to resign myself, with a child-like confidence, to her guidance through the **chaotic** world of <u>metaphysical</u> investigation at which I was most busily occupied during the earlier years of our marriage. With how vast a triumph—with how vivid a delight—with how much of all that is **ethereal** in hope did I *feel*, as she bent over me in studies but little sought—but less known— that delicious vista by slow degrees expanding before me, down whose long, gorgeous, and all untrodden path, I might at length pass onward to the goal of a wisdom too divinely precious not to be forbidden!

How **poignant**, then, must have been the grief with which, after some years, I beheld my well-grounded expectations take wings to themselves and fly away! Without Ligeia I was but as a child groping <u>benighted</u>. Her presence, her readings alone, rendered vividly **luminous** the many mysteries of the <u>transcendentalism</u> in which we were **immersed**, wanting the radiant lustre of her eyes, letters, <u>lambent</u> and golden, grew duller than Saturnian[6] lead. And now those eyes shone less and less frequently upon the pages over which I **pored**. Ligeia grew ill. The wild eyes blazed with a too, too glorious <u>effulgence</u>; the pale fingers became of the transparent waxen hue of the grave; and the blue veins upon the lofty forehead swelled and sank **impetuously** with the tides of the most gentle emotion. I saw that she must die, and I

SOLACE (<u>sah</u> lihs) *n.*
  comfort in distress, consolation
    Synonyms: succor, balm, cheer, condolence
PLACIDITY (plaa <u>sih</u> dih tee) *n.*
  calmness
    Synonyms: tranquility, serenity, complacency
DEMEANOR (dih <u>meen</u> uhr) *n.*
  one's behavior or conduct
    Synonyms: attitude, disposition, manner, presence
ASPIRATION (aa spuhr <u>ay</u> shuhn) *n.*
  a great hope or goal
    Synonyms: intention, purpose, expectation
DETAIN (dih <u>tayn</u>) (dee <u>tayn</u>) *v.* **-ing,-ed.**
  to hold as if in custody; to restrain from continuing on
    Synonyms: keep, apprehend; delay, inhibit
DILATE (<u>die</u> layt) (die <u>layt</u>) *v.* **-ing,-ed.**
  to explain or expand on; to enlarge, swell, extend
    Synonyms: expound, discuss; spread, distend
ABANDONMENT (uh <u>baan</u> duhn mehnt) *n.*
  total lack of inhibition
    Synonyms: exuberance, enthusiasm
UNMERITED (uhn <u>mehr</u> iht ihd) *adj.*
  undeserved
    Synonyms: unworthy, unearned, unwarranted
BESTOW (bih <u>stoh</u>) *v.* **-ing,-ed.**
  to give as a gift; to apply or devote time or effort
    Synonyms: endow, confer, present; allocate, dedicate
VEHEMENCE (<u>vee</u> huh muhnts) *n.*
  strength, urgency
    Synonyms: fervor, intensity, ferocity, passion, ardor

struggled desperately in spirit with the grim Azrael.[7] And the struggles of the passionate wife were, to my astonishment, even more energetic than my own. There had been much in her stern nature to impress me with the belief that, to her, death would have come without its terrors, but not so. Words are <u>impotent</u> to convey any just idea of the fierceness of resistance with which she wrestled with the Shadow. I groaned in anguish at the pitiable spectacle. I would have soothed—I would have reasoned; but in the intensity of her wild desire for life—for life—*but* for life— **solace** and reason were alike the uttermost of folly. Yet not until the last instance, amid the most convulsive writhings of her fierce spirit, was shaken the external **placidity** of her **demeanor.** Her voice grew more gentle— grew more low—yet I would not wish to dwell upon the wild meaning of the quietly uttered words. My brain reeled as I <u>hearkened</u>, entranced, to a melody more than mortal, to assumptions and **aspirations** which mortality had never before known.

That she loved me I should not have doubted; and I might have been easily aware that, in a bosom such as hers, love would have reigned no ordinary passion. But in death only was I fully impressed with the strength of her affection. For long hours, **detaining** my hand, would she pour out before me the overflowing of a heart whose more than passionate devotion amounted to <u>idolatry</u>. How had I deserved to be so blessed by such confessions? How had I deserved to be so cursed with the removal of my beloved in the hour of my making them? But upon this subject I cannot bear to **dilate.** Let me say only, that in Ligeia's more than womanly **abandonment** to a love, alas—all **unmerited,** all unworthily **bestowed,** I at length recognized the principle of her longing, with so wildly earnest a desire, for the life which was now fleeing so rapidly away. It is this wild longing—it is this eager **vehemence** of desire for life—*but* for life—that I have no power to portray—no utterance capable of expressing.

PEREMPTORILY (puhr <u>ehm</u> tohr uh lee) *adv.*
   absolutely, in a commanding manner; immediately
   putting an end to
      Synonyms: urgently, imperatively; decisively, finally

MOTLEY (<u>maht</u> lee) *adj.*
   composed of diverse parts; many colored
      Synonyms: miscellaneous, heterogeneous, mixed,
      varied, assorted; showy, splashy, hued

MIMIC (<u>mih</u> mihk) *n.*
   an imitator, one who copies
      Synonyms: ape, simulator, impersonator

At high noon of the night in which she departed, beckoning me **peremptorily** to her side, she bade me repeat certain verses composed by herself not many days before. I obeyed her. They were these:

Lo! 'tis a gala night
Within the lonesome latter years!
An angel <u>throng</u>, bewinged, bedight
In veils, and drowned in tears,
Sit in a theatre, to see
A play of hopes and fears,
While the orchestra breathes fitfully
The music of the spheres.

Mimes, in the form of God on high,
Mutter and mumble low,
And hither and thither fly;
Mere puppets they, who come and go
At bidding of vast formless things
That shift the scenery to and fro,
Flapping from out their condor wings
Invisible Woe!

That **motley** drama!—oh, be sure
It shall not be forgot!
With its Phantom chased for evermore,
By a crowd that seize it not,
Through a circle that ever returneth in
To the self-same spot;
And much of Madness, and more of Sin
And Horror, the soul of the plot!

But see, amid the **mimic** rout
A crawling shape intrude!
A blood-red thing that writhes from out
The scenic solitude!
It writhes!—it writhes!—with mortal pangs

SERAPH (<u>seh</u> ruhf) *n.*
angel, guardian
Synonyms: heavenly being, cherub, spirit
IMBUE (ihm <u>byoo</u>) *v.* **-ing,-ed.**
to infuse; to dye, wet
Synonyms: charge, freight, permeate; moisten

PALLID (<u>paa</u> lihd) *adj.*
lacking color or liveliness
Synonyms: pale, wan, ashen, blanched, ghostly
WAN (wahn) *adj.*
sickly pale
Synonyms: ashen, pallid, blanched, pasty
AFFIRM (uh <u>fihrm</u>) *v.* **-ing,-ed.**
to state positively, to assert as valid or confirmed
Synonyms: declare, avow, maintain
UNDEVIATINGLY (uhn dee vee <u>ay</u> tihng lee) *adv.*
absolutely, in a straightforward manner
Synonyms: consistently, regularly, unvaryingly

SOLEMNLY (<u>sah</u> luhm lee) *adv.*
seriously or somberly
Synonyms: quietly, earnestly, ceremonially

DESOLATION (deh suh <u>lay</u> shuhn) *n.*
sadness, loneliness; barren wasteland
Synonyms: despair; bleakness, devastation, ruin

The mimes become its food,
And the **seraphs** sob at vermin fangs
In human gore **imbued**.

Out—out are the lights—out all!
And over each quivering form,
The curtain, a funeral pall,
Comes down with the rush of a storm—
And the angels, all **pallid** and **wan**,
Uprising, unveiling, **affirm**
That the play is the tragedy, "Man,"
And its hero, the conqueror Worm.

"O God!" half shrieked Ligeia, leaping to her feet and extending her arms aloft with a spasmodic movement, as I made an end of these lines. "O God! O Divine Father! Shall these things be **undeviatingly** so? Shall this conqueror be not once conquered? Are we not part and parcel in Thee? Who—who knoweth the mysteries of the will with its vigor? Man doth not yield him to the angels, nor unto death utterly, save only through the weakness of his feeble will."

And now, as if exhausted with emotion, she suffered her white arms to fall, and returned **solemnly** to her bed of death. And as she breathed her last sighs, there came mingled with them a low murmur from her lips. I bent to them my ear, and distinquished, again, the concluding words of the passage in Glanvill. "*Man doth not yield him to the angels, nor unto death utterly, save only through the weakness of his feeble will.*"

She died, and I, crushed into the very dust with sorrow, could no longer endure the lonely **desolation** of my dwelling in the dim and decaying city by the Rhine. I had no lack of what the world calls wealth. Ligeia had brought me far more, very far more, than ordinarily falls to the lot of mortals. After a few months, therefore, of weary and aimless wandering, I purchased and put in

MELANCHOLY (mehl uhn <u>kahl</u> ee) *adj.*
  sad, depressing
    Synonyms: dejected, despondent, woeful, sorrowful
VERDANT (<u>vuhr</u> dnt) *adj.*
  green with vegetation; inexperienced
    Synonyms: grassy, leafy, wooded; immature
PERVERSITY (puhr <u>vuhr</u> sih tee) *n.*
  deliberate misbehavior
    Synonyms: disobedience, defiance, opposition
ALLEVIATE (uh <u>lee</u> vee ayt) *v.* **-ing,-ed.**
  to relieve, improve partially
    Synonyms: allay, assuage, palliate, mitigate, quell
INCIPIENT (ihn <u>sihp</u> ee uhnt) *adj.*
  beginning to exist or appear, in an initial stage
    Synonyms: dawning, nascent, inchoate
SOLEMN (<u>sah</u> luhm) *adj.*
  somberly impressive; quiet, deeply serious
    Synonyms: dignified, ceremonial; earnest, brooding

ALIENATION (ay lee uhn <u>ay</u> shuhn)
(ayl yuhn <u>ay</u> shuhn) *n.*
  derangement of the mind; separation or isolation
    Synonyms: madness, insanity; estrangement,
    disaffectation
HAUGHTY (<u>haw</u> tee) (<u>hah</u> tee) *adj.*
  arrogant and condescending
    Synonyms: proud, disdainful, supercilious, scornful
MINUTELY (mie <u>noot</u> lee) (mih <u>noot</u> lee) *adv.*
  precisely, in a detailed manner
    Synonyms: attentively, critically

some repair an <u>abbey</u>, which I shall not name, in one of the wildest and least frequented portions of fair England. The gloomy and dreary grandeur of the building, the almost savage aspect of the domain, the many **melancholy** and time-honored memories connected with both, had much in unison with the feelings of utter abandonment which had driven me into that remote and unsocial region of the country. Yet although the external abbey, with its **verdant** decay hanging about it, suffered but little alteration, I gave way, with a child-like **perversity**, and perchance with a faint hope of **alleviating** my sorrows, to a display of more than regal magnificence within. For such follies, even in childhood, I had <u>imbibed</u> a taste, and now they came back to me as if in the <u>dotage</u> of grief. Alas, I feel how much even of **incipient** madness might have been discovered in the gorgeous and fantastic draperies, in the **solemn** carvings of Egypt, in the wild cornices and furniture, in the Bedlam patterns of the carpets of tufted gold! I had become a bound slave in the <u>trammels</u> of opium, and my labors and my orders had taken a coloring from my dreams. But these absurdities I must not pause to detail. Let me speak only of that one chamber, ever accursed, whither, in a moment of mental **alienation**, I led from the altar as my bride—as the successor of the unforgotten Ligeia—the fair-haired and blue-eyed Lady Rowena Trevanion, of Tremaine.

There is no individual portion of the architecture and decoration of that bridal chamber which is not now visibly before me. Where were the souls of the **haughty** family of the bride when, through thirst of gold, they permitted to pass the threshold of an apartment so bedecked a maiden and a daughter so beloved? I have said that I **minutely** remember the details of the chamber, yet I am sadly forgetful of topics of deep moment; and here there was no system, no keeping, in the fantastic display, to take hold upon the memory. The room lay in a high turret of the <u>castellated</u> abbey, was pentagonal in shape, and of

LIGEIA

CAPACIOUS (kuh <u>pay</u> shuhs) *adj.*
  large, roomy, extensive
    Synonyms: ample, commodious

MELANCHOLY (mehl uhn <u>kahl</u> ee) *adj.*
  sad, depressing
    Synonyms: dejected, despondent, woeful, sorrowful
CONTRIVED (kuhn <u>trievd</u>) *adj.*
  formed in an artistic manner; devised, planned, or
  managed
    Synonyms: designed; concocted, created, schemed

capacious size. Occupying the whole southern face of the pentagon was the sole window—an immense sheet of unbroken glass from Venice—a single pane, and tinted of a leaden hue, so that the rays of either the sun or moon passing through it, fell with a ghastly lustre on the objects within. Over the upper portion of this huge window, extended the trellis-work of an aged vine, which clambered up the massy walls of the turret. The ceiling of gloomy-looking oak was excessively lofty, vaulted, and elaborately <u>fretted</u> with the wildest and most grotesque specimens of a semi-Gothic, semi-Druidical[8] device. From out the most central recess of this **melancholy** vaulting, <u>depended</u>, by a single chain of gold with long links, a huge <u>censer</u> of the same metal, Saracenic[9] in pattern, and with many perforations so **contrived** that there writhed in and out of them, as if <u>endued</u> with a serpent vitality, a continual succession of parti-colored fires.

Some few ottomans and golden candelabra, of Eastern figure, were in various stations about; and there was the couch, too—the bridal couch—of an Indian model, low and sculptured of solid ebony, with a pall-like canopy above. In each of the angles of the chamber stood on end a gigantic <u>sarcophagus</u> of black granite, from the tombs of the kings over against Luxor, with their aged lids full of immemorial sculpture. But in the draping of the apartment lay, alas, the chief phantasy of all. The lofty walls, gigantic in height—even unproportionably so—were hung from summit to foot, in vast folds, with a heavy and massive-looking tapestry—tapestry of a material which was found alike as a carpet on the floor, as a covering for the ottomans and the ebony bed, as a canopy for the bed and as the gorgeous <u>volutes</u> of the curtains which partially shaded the window. The material was the richest cloth of gold. It was spotted all over, at irregular intervals, with <u>arabesque</u> figures, about a foot in diameter, and wrought upon the cloth in patterns of the most jetty black. But these figures partook of the true character of

CONTRIVANCE (kuhn <u>triev</u> ehnts) *n.*
 the act of creating art or an artistic creation; a plan
  Synonyms: design, project; concoction, scheme
ANTIQUITY (aan <u>tih</u> kwih tee) *n.*
 ancient times; the quality of being very old
  Synonyms: history; hoariness
ANIMATION (aa nih <u>may</u> shuhn) *n.*
 the quality or condition of being alive, spirited,
 active or vigorous
  Synonyms: life, vitality, invigoration, liveliness
UNHALLOWED (un <u>haa</u> lohd) *adj.*
 unholy, immoral
  Synonyms: irreligious, desecrated
DISQUIETUDE (dihs <u>kwie</u> eh tood) *n.*
 anxiety; lack of peace or tranquility
  Synonyms: edginess; uneasiness
LOATHE (lohth) *v.* **-ing,-ed.**
 to abhor, despise, hate
  Synonyms: abominate, execrate, detest, condemn
AUGUST (aw <u>guhst</u>) *adj.*
 dignified, grandiose
  Synonyms: grand, majestic, admirable, awesome
REVEL (<u>reh</u> vuhl) *v.* **-ling,-led.**
 to take pleasure in
  Synonyms: merrymake, delight
ETHEREAL (ih <u>theer</u> ee uhl) *adj.*
 not earthly, spiritual, delicate
  Synonyms: intangible, diaphanous, airy, gossamer,
 sheer
FETTER (<u>feh</u> tuhr) *v.* **-ing,-ed.**
 to bind, chain, confine
  Synonyms: manacle, handcuff, curb, tether
SOLEMN (<u>sah</u> luhm) *adj.*
 quiet, deeply serious; somberly impressive
  Synonyms: earnest, brooding; dignified, ceremonial
ARDOR (<u>ahr</u> duhr) *n.*
 passion, enthusiasm
  Synonyms: intensity, vehemence

the arabesque only when regarded from a single point of view. By a **contrivance** now common, and indeed traceable to a very remote period of **antiquity**, they were made changeable in aspect. To one entering the room, they bore the appearance of simple monstrosities; but upon a farther advance, this appearance gradually departed, and step by step as the visitor moved his station in the chamber, he saw himself surrounded by an endless succession of the ghastly forms which belong to the superstition of the Norman, or arise in the guilty slumbers of the monk. The phantasmagoric effect was vastly heightened by the artificial introduction of a strong continual current of wind behind the draperies, giving a hideous and uneasy **animation** to the whole.

In halls such as these—in a bridal chamber such as this—I passed, with the Lady of Tremaine, the **unhallowed** hours of the first month of our marriage, passed them with but little **disquietude**. That my wife dreaded the fierce moodiness of my temper—that she shunned me, and loved me but little—I could not help perceiving; but it gave me rather pleasure than otherwise. I **loathed** her with a hatred belonging more to demon than to man. My memory flew back (oh, with what intensity of regret!) to Ligeia, the beloved, the **august**, the beautiful, the entombed. I **revelled** in recollections of her purity, of her wisdom, of her lofty, her **ethereal** nature, of her passionate, her idolatrous love. Now, then, did my spirit fully and freely burn with more than all the fires of her own. In the excitement of my opium dreams (for I was habitually **fettered** in the shackles of the drug), I would call aloud upon her name, during the silence of the night or among the sheltered recesses of the glens by day, as if through the wild eagerness, the **solemn** passion, the consuming **ardor** of my longing for the departed, I could restore her to the pathways she had abandoned—ah, *could* it be for ever?—upon the earth.

PERTURBED (puhr <u>tuhrbd</u>) *adj.*
disturbed
>Synonyms: bothered, annoyed, distressed, confused, upset

CONVALESCENT (kahn vuhl <u>ehs</u> uhnt) *adj.*
partially recovered from an illness
>Synonyms: healed, recuperated, healthy

CONSTITUTION (kahn stih <u>too</u> shuhn) *n.*
the physical structure or health of something or someone; the sum of components, composition
>Synonyms: disposition, nature, stature; formation, design, architecture, make-up

ERADICATE (ih <u>raad</u> ih kayt) *v.* **-ing,-ed.**
to erase or wipe out
>Synonyms: abolish, eliminate, annihilate

TEMPERAMENT (<u>tehm</u> puhr uh mehnt) *n.*
an attitude, a manner of behaving
>Synonyms: disposition, mood, mentality

PERTINACIOUSLY (puhr tihn <u>ay</u> shuhs lee) *adv.*
stubbornly, persistently
>Synonyms: obstinately, tenaciously, steadily, doggedly

ALLUDE (uh <u>lood</u>) *v.* **-ing,-ed.**
to make an indirect reference
>Synonyms: intimate, suggest, hint

EMACIATED (ih <u>may</u> shee ay tihd) *adj.*
very thin due to hunger or disease; feeble
>Synonyms: bony, gaunt, haggard, skeletal

COUNTENANCE (<u>kown</u> tuh nuhns) *n.*
appearance, facial expression
>Synonyms: face, features, visage

INARTICULATE (ihn ahr <u>tihk</u> yuh liht) *adj.*
unable to speak clearly
>Synonyms: incomprehensible, unintelligible

About the commencement of the second month of the marriage, the Lady Rowena was attacked with sudden illness, from which her recovery was slow. The fever which consumed her rendered her nights uneasy; and in her **perturbed** state of half-slumber, she spoke of sounds, and of motions, in and about the chamber of the turret, which I concluded had no origin except in the distemper of her fancy, or perhaps in the <u>phantasmagoric</u> influences of the chamber itself. She became at length **convalescent**—finally, well. Yet but a brief period elapsed, ere a second more violent disorder again threw her upon a bed of suffering; and from this attack her frame, at all times feeble, never altogether recovered. Her illnesses were, after this <u>epoch</u>, of alarming character, and of more alarming recurrence, defying alike the knowledge and the great exertions of her physicians. With the increase of the chronic disease, which had thus apparently taken too sure hold upon her **constitution** to be **eradicated** by human means, I could not fail to observe a similar increase in the nervous irritation of her **temperament** and in her excitability by trivial causes of fear. She spoke again, and now more frequently and **pertinaciously**, of the sounds—of the slight sounds—and of the unusual motions among the tapestries, to which she had formerly **alluded**.

One night, near the closing in of September, she pressed this distressing subject with more than usual emphasis upon my attention. She had just awakened from an unquiet slumber, and I had been watching with feelings half of anxiety, half of vague terror, the workings of her **emaciated countenance**. I sat by the side of her ebony bed, upon one of the ottomans of India. She partly arose and spoke, in an earnest low whisper, of sounds which she *then* heard, but which I could not hear—of motions which she *then* saw, but which I could not perceive. The wind was rushing hurriedly behind the tapestries, and I wished to show her (what, let me confess it, I could not *all* believe) that those almost **inarticulate** breathings and

PROCURE (proh <u>kyoor</u>) *v.* **-ing,-ed.**
 to obtain
   Synonyms: acquire, secure, get, gain
PALPABLE (<u>paalp</u> uh buhl) *adj.*
 obvious, real, tangible
   Synonyms: perceptible, appreciable, discernable,
   concrete, material

IMMODERATE (ih <u>mah</u> duhr iht) *adj.*
 extreme, unreasonable
   Synonyms: extravagant, exorbitant

FORBEAR (fohr <u>bayr</u>) *v.* **-ing,-bore.**
 to refrain or resist; to tolerate or put up with
   Synonym: avoid, withhold, inhibit; endure, suffer
MORBIDLY (<u>mohr</u> bihd lee) *adv.*
 gruesomely, gloomily
   Synonyms: darkly, horridly, psychotically
SUBSEQUENT (<u>suhb</u> suh kwehnt) *adj.*
 following in time or order
   Synonyms: succeeding, next, afterward

those very gentle variations of the figures upon the wall were but the natural effects of that customary rushing of the wind. But a deadly <u>pallor</u>, overspreading her face, had proved to me that my exertions to reassure her would be fruitless. She appeared to be fainting, and no attendants were within call. I remembered where was deposited a <u>decanter</u> of light wine which had been ordered by her physicians and hastened across the chamber to **procure** it. But as I stepped beneath the light of the <u>censer</u>, two circumstances of a startling nature attracted my attention. I had felt that some **palpable** although invisible object had passed lightly by my person and I saw that there lay upon the golden carpet, in the very middle of the rich lustre thrown from the <u>censer</u>, a shadow—a faint, indefinite shadow of angelic aspect—such as might be fancied for the shadow of a shade. But I was wild with the excitement of an **immoderate** dose of opium, and heeded these things but little, nor spoke of them to Rowena. Having found the wine, I re-crossed the chamber, and poured out a gobletful, which I held to the lips of the fainting lady. She had now partially recovered, however, and took the vessel herself, while I sank upon an ottoman near me, with my eyes fastened upon her person. It was then that I became distinctly aware of a gentle footfall upon the carpet, and near the couch; and in a second thereafter, as Rowena was in the act of raising the wine to her lips, I saw, or may have dreamed that I saw, fall within the goblet, as if from some invisible spring in the atmosphere of the room, three or four large drops of a brilliant and ruby colored fluid. If this I saw—not so Rowena. She swallowed the wine unhesitatingly, and I **forbore** to speak to her of a circumstance which must, after all, I considered, have been but the suggestion of a vivid imagination, rendered **morbidly** active by the terror of the lady, by the opium, and by the hour.

Yet I cannot conceal it from my own perception that, immediately **subsequent** to the fall of the ruby-drops, a

SUBSEQUENT (<u>suhb</u> suh kwehnt) *adj.*
following in time or order
Synonyms: succeeding, next, afterward
SHROUD or ENSHROUD (shrowd) *v.* **-ing,-ed.**
to wrap up, hide from sight
Synonyms: blanket, obscure, conceal, cloak,
envelop
ENGENDERED (ehn <u>gehn</u> duhrd) *adj.*
produced, caused
Synonyms: propagated, originated, generated

PALLID (<u>paa</u> lihd) *adj.*
lacking color or liveliness
Synonyms: pale, wan, ashen, blanched, ghostly
TURBULENT (<u>tuhr</u> byoo luhnt) *adj.*
chaotic, disordered
Synonyms: disturbed, agitated, riotous, tumultuous
WANE (wayn) *v.* **-ing,-ed.**
to decrease gradually
Synonyms: dwindle, flag, fade, shrink, diminish
REVERY or REVERIE (<u>rehv</u> uh rcc) *n.*
a daydream
Synonyms: dream, absorption, muse, meditation

RESOLUTELY (reh suh <u>loot</u> lee) *adv.*
with determination; with a clear purpose
Synonyms: firmly, unwaveringly; intently
PERSEVERINGLY (pehr suh <u>veer</u> ihng lee) *adv.*
with unwavering determination
Synonyms: persistently, enduringly, ploddingly
TINGE (tihnj) *n.*
a slight shade of color, stain, odor, or taste
Synonyms: h<u>int</u>, hue, tincture, tone, wash

rapid change for the worse took place in the disorder of my wife, so that, on the third **subsequent** night, the hands of her <u>menials</u> prepared her for the tomb, and on the fourth, I sat alone with her **shrouded** body, in that fantastic chamber which had received her as my bride. Wild visions, opium-**engendered**, flitted, shadow-like before me. I gazed with unquiet eye upon the <u>sarcophagi</u> in the angles of the room, upon the varying figures of the drapery, and upon the writhing of the parti-colored fires in the <u>censer</u> overhead. My eyes then fell, as I called to mind the circumstances of a former night, to the spot beneath the glare of the <u>censer</u> where I had seen the faint traces of the shadow. It was there, however, no longer; and breathing with greater freedom, I turned my glances to the **pallid** and rigid figure upon the bed. Then rushed upon me a thousand memories of Ligeia, and then came back upon my heart, with the **turbulent** violence of a flood, the whole of that unutterable woe with which I had regarded *her* thus **enshrouded**. The night **waned** and still, with a bosom full of bitter thoughts of the one only and supremely beloved, I remained gazing upon the body of Rowena.

It might have been midnight, or perhaps earlier or later, for I had taken no note of time, when a sob, low, gentle, but very distinct, startled me from my **revery**. I *felt* that it came from the bed of ebony—the bed of death. I listened in an agony of superstitious terror—but there was no repetition of the sound. I strained my vision to detect any motion in the corpse, but there was not the slightest perceptible. Yet I could not have been deceived. I *had* heard the noise, however faint, and my soul was awakened within me. I **resolutely** and **perseveringly** kept my attention riveted upon the body. Many minutes elapsed before any circumstance occurred tending to throw light upon the mystery. At length it became evident that a slight, a very feeble, and barely noticeable **tinge** of color had flushed up within the cheeks and along the sunken small veins of the eyelids. Through a species of

PRECIPITATE (preh <u>sih</u> puh tiht) *adj*.
  hasty and presumptuous; abrupt
    Synonyms: impetuous, headlong, reckless; sudden, rash

WANNESS (<u>wahn</u> nehs) *n*.
  sickly paleness
    Synonyms: pallor, lividity
REPULSIVE (rih <u>puhl</u> sihv) *adj*.
  sickening, disgusting; repellant
    Synonyms: nauseating; offensive

DISCLOSE (dihs <u>klohs</u>) *v*. **-ing,-ed.**
  to expose, divulge
    Synonyms: confess, reveal, impart
PROFOUND (pruh <u>fownd</u>) (proh <u>fownd</u>) *adj*.
  difficult to understand; deep, infinite; intelligent
    Synonyms: thorough, weighty; bottomless, unending; smart
PERVADE (puhr <u>vayd</u>) *v*. **-ing,-ed.**
  to become diffused throughout every part of
    Synonyms: permeate, spread, fill, transfuse

unutterable horror and awe, for which the language of mortality has no sufficiently energetic expression, I felt my heart cease to beat, my limbs grow rigid where I sat. Yet a sense of duty finally operated to restore my self-possession. I could no longer doubt that we had been **precipitate** in our preparations—that Rowena still lived. It was necessary that some immediate exertion be made; yet the turret was altogether apart from the portion of the abbey tenanted by the servants—there were none within call—I had no means of summoning them to my aid without leaving the room for many minutes, and this I could not venture to do. I therefore struggled alone in my endeavors to call back the spirit still hovering. In a short period it was certain, however, that a relapse had taken place; the color disappeared from both eyelid and cheek, leaving a **wanness** even more than that of marble; the lips became doubly shrivelled and pinched up in the ghastly expression of death; a **repulsive** clamminess and coldness overspread rapidly the surface of the body; and all the usual rigorous stiffness immediately <u>supervened</u>. I fell back with a shudder upon the couch from which I had been so startlingly aroused and again gave myself up to passionate waking visions of Ligeia.

An hour thus elapsed, when (could it be possible?) I was a second time aware of some vague sound issuing from the region of the bed. I listened in extremity of horror. The sound came again—it was a sigh. Rushing to the corpse, I saw—distinctly saw—a tremor upon the lips. In a minute afterward they relaxed, **disclosing** a bright line of the pearly teeth. Amazement now struggled in my bosom with the **profound** awe which had hitherto reigned there alone. I felt that my vision grew dim, that my reason wandered, and it was only by a violent effort that I at length succeeded in nerving myself to the task which duty thus once more had pointed out. There was now a partial glow upon the forehead and upon the cheek and throat. A perceptible warmth **pervaded** the whole frame; there was even

ARDOR (<u>ahr</u> duhr) *n.*
  passion, enthusiasm
    Synonyms: intensity, vehemence

LIVID (<u>lih</u> vihd) *adj.*
  pale; discolored from a bruise; reddened with anger
    Synonyms: ashen, pallid; black-and-blue; furious
LOATHSOME (<u>lohth</u> suhm) *adj.*
  abhorrent, hateful
    Synonyms: offensive, disgusting

MINUTELY (mie <u>noot</u> lee) (mih <u>noot</u> lee) *adv.*
  precisely, in a detailed manner
    Synonyms: attentively, critically

APPALLING (uh <u>pahl</u> lihng) *adj.*
  shocking, dismaying
    Synonyms: horrifying, dreadful, ghastly, awful
COUNTENANCE (<u>kown</u> tuh nuhns) *n.*
  appearance, facial expression
    Synonyms: face, features, visage
IMPART (ihm <u>pahrt</u>) *v.* **-ing,-ed.**
  to give or share, to pass on
    Synonyms: bestow, contribute, reveal, convey

a slight pulsation at the heart. The lady *lived*, and with redoubled **ardor** I betook myself to the task of restoration. I chafed and bathed the temples and the hands, and used every exertion which experience, and no little medical reading, could suggest. But in vain. Suddenly, the color fled, the pulsation ceased, the lips resumed the expression of the dead, and, in an instant afterward, the whole body took upon itself the icy chilliness, the **livid** hue, the intense rigidity, the sunken outline, and all the **loathsome** peculiarities of that which has been, for many days, a tenant of the tomb.

And again I sunk into visions of Ligeia and again (what marvel that I shudder while I write?), *again* there reached my ears a low sob from the region of the ebony bed. But why shall I **minutely** detail the unspeakable horrors of that night? Why shall I pause to relate how, time after time, until near the period of the gray dawn, this hideous drama of <u>revivification</u> was repeated; how each terrific relapse was only into a sterner and apparently more irredeemable death; how each agony wore the aspect of a struggle with some invisible foe; and how each struggle was succeeded by I know not what of wild change in the personal appearance of the corpse? Let me hurry to a conclusion.

The greater part of the fearful night had worn away, and she who had been dead once again stirred—and now more vigorously than hitherto, although arousing from a <u>dissolution</u> more **appalling** in its utter hopelessness than any. I had long ceased to struggle or to move and remained sitting rigidly upon the ottoman, a helpless prey to a whirl of violent emotions, of which extreme awe was perhaps the least terrible, the least consuming. The corpse, I repeat, stirred, and now more vigorously than before. The hues of life flushed up with <u>unwonted</u> energy into the **countenance**—the limbs relaxed—and, save that the eyelids were yet pressed heavily together, and that the bandages and draperies of the grave still **imparted** their

FETTERS (<u>feh</u> tuhrs) *n.*
item that confines or binds, chains
Synonyms: shackles, manacles, handcuffs, tethers

TOTTERING (<u>tah</u> tuhr ihng) *adj.*
barely standing
Synonyms: unsteady, wobbly, swaying, reeling, staggering

ENSHROUD or SHROUD (ehn <u>shrowd</u>) *v.* **-ing,-ed.**
to wrap up, hide from sight
Synonyms: blanket, obscure, conceal, cloak, envelop

PALPABLY (<u>paalp</u> uh blee) *adv.*
apparently, tangibly
Synonyms: perceptibly, substantially, clearly

DEMEANOR (dih <u>meen</u> uhr) *n.*
one's behavior or conduct
Synonyms: attitude, disposition, manner, presence

APPARITION (aa puh <u>rih</u> shuhn) *n.*
a ghostly figure; an unexpected or unusual sight or appearance
Synonyms: spirit, specter; illusion

TUMULT (<u>tuh</u> muhlt) *n.*
state of confusion, agitation
Synonyms: disturbance, turmoil, din, commotion

UNAPPEASABLE (uhn uh <u>pees</u> uh buhl) *adj.*
unable to be calmed; unable to be satisfied
Synonyms: relentless, inexorable; insatiable

MALADY (<u>maal</u> uh dee) *n.*
illness
Synonyms: disease, disorder, ailment, affliction, infirmity

DISHEVELLED (dih <u>shehv</u> uhld) *adj.*
untidy, disarranged, unkempt
Synonyms: disordered, messy, rumpled

charnel character to the figure, I might have dreamed that Rowena had indeed shaken off, utterly, the **fetters** of Death. But if this idea was not, even then, altogether adopted, I could at least doubt no longer when, arising from the bed, **tottering**, with feeble steps, with closed eyes, and with the manner of one bewildered in a dream, the thing that was **enshrouded** advanced boldly and **palpably** into the middle of the apartment.

I trembled not—I stirred not—for a crowd of unutterable fancies connected with the air, the stature, the **demeanor** of the figure, rushing hurriedly through my brain, had paralyzed—had chilled me into stone. I stirred not, but gazed upon the **apparition**. There was a mad disorder in my thoughts—a **tumult unappeasable**. Could it, indeed, be the *living* Rowena who confronted me? Could it, indeed, be Rowena *at all*—the fair-haired, the blue-eyed Lady Rowena Trevanion of Tremaine? Why, why should I doubt it? The bandage lay heavily about the mouth—but then might it not be the mouth of the breathing Lady of Tremaine? And the cheeks—there were the roses as in her noon of life—yes, these might indeed be the fair cheeks of the living Lady of Tremaine. And the chin, with its dimples, as in health, might it not be hers? But *had she then grown taller since her malady?* What inexpressible madness seized me with that thought? One bound and I had reached her feet! Shrinking from my touch, she let fall from her head, unloosened, the ghastly cerements which had confined it, and there streamed forth into the rushing atmosphere of the chamber huge masses of long and **dishevelled** hair; *it was blacker than the raven wings of midnight!* And now slowly opened the eyes of the figure which stood before me. "Here then, at least," I shrieked aloud, "can I never—can I never be mistaken—these are the full, and the black, and the wild eyes—of my lost love—of the Lady—of the LADY LIGEIA."

SQUANDER (<u>skwan</u> duhr) *v.* **-ing,-ed.**
   to waste
      Synonyms: dissipate, fritter, misspend

MULTITUDE (<u>muhl</u> tuh tood) *n.*
   a crowd, the state of being many, a great number
      Synonyms: mass, myriad, slew

SOPHIST (<u>soh</u> fihst) *n.*
   one who specializes in elaborate philosophy and
   argumentation
      Synonyms: scholar, thinker

DENOUNCE (dih <u>nowns</u>) *v.* **-ing,-ed.**
   to condemn; to accuse, blame
      Synonyms: censure; criticize, vilify, brand

STALK (stahk) *v.* **-ing,-ed.**
   to hunt, pursue
      Synonyms: track, shadow, trail, dog, hound

THE ASSIGNATION

Stay for me there! I will not fail
To meet thee in that hollow vale.

[*Exequy on the death of his wife,
by Henry King, Bishop of Chichester*]

Ill-fated and mysterious man, bewildered in the brilliancy of thine own imagination, and fallen in the flames of thine own youth! Again in fancy I behold thee! Once more thy form hath risen before me! Not, oh, not as thou art in the cold valley and shadow but as thou *shouldst* be—**squandering** away a life of magnificent meditation in that city of dim visions, thine own Venice—which is a star-beloved Elysium[10] of the sea, and the wide windows of whose Palladian[11] palaces look down with a deep and bitter meaning upon the secrets of her silent waters. Yes! I repeat it—as thou *shouldst* be. There are surely other worlds than this—other thoughts than the thoughts of the **multitude**—other speculations than the speculations of the **sophist**. Who then shall call thy conduct into question? Who shall blame thee for thy visionary hours, or **denounce** those occupations as a wasting away of life, which were but the overflowings of thine everlasting energies?

It was at Venice beneath the covered archway there called the *Ponte di Sospiri* that I met, for the third or fourth time, the person of whom I speak. It is with a confused recollection that I bring to mind the circumstances of that meeting. Yet I remember—ah, how should I forget?—the deep midnight, the Bridge of Sighs, the beauty of woman, and the Genius of Romance that **stalked** up and down the narrow canal.

LIVID (<u>lih</u> vihd) *adj.*
  eerily luminous; pale; discolored from a bruise;
  reddened with anger
    Synonyms: deathlike; ashen, pallid; black-and-blue;
    furious
PRETERNATURAL (pree tuhr <u>naach</u> uh ruhl) *adj.*
  extraordinary or unnatural
    Synonyms: abnormal, mysterious, odd, unearthly
PLACIDLY (<u>plaa</u> sihd lee) *adv.*
  calmly
    Synonyms: tranquilly, serenely, peacefully,
    complacently

It was a night of unusual gloom. The great clock of the Piazza had sounded the fifth hour of the Italian evening. The square of the Campanile lay silent and deserted, and the lights in the old Ducal Palace were dying fast away. I was returning home from the Piazzetta by way of the Grand Canal. But as my gondola arrived opposite the mouth of the canal San Marco, a female voice from its recesses broke suddenly upon the night, in one wild, hysterical, and long-continued shriek. Startled at the sound, I sprang upon my feet; while the gondolier, letting slip his single oar, lost it in the pitchy darkness beyond a chance of recovery, and we were consequently left to the guidance of the current which here sets from the greater into the smaller channel. Like some huge and sable-feathered condor, we were slowly drifting down toward the Bridge of Sighs, when a thousand flambeaux flashing from the windows and down the staircases of the Ducal Palace, turned all at once that deep gloom into a livid and preternatural day.

A child, slipping from the arms of its own mother, had fallen from an upper window of the lofty structure into the deep and dim canal. The quiet waters had closed placidly over their victim; and, although my own gondola was the only one in sight, many a stout swimmer, already in the stream, was seeking in vain upon the surface, the treasure which was to be found, alas, only within the abyss. Upon the broad black marble flagstones at the entrance of the palace, and a few steps above the water, stood a figure which none who then saw can have ever since forgotten. It was the Marchesa Aphrodite—the adoration of all Venice—the gayest of the gay—the most lovely where all were beautiful—but still the young wife of the old and intriguing Mentoni, and the mother of that fair child, her first and only one, who now, deep beneath the murky water, was thinking in bitterness of heart upon her sweet caresses, and exhausting its little life in struggles to call upon her name.

SULLEN (<u>suh</u> luhn) *adj.*
   brooding, gloomy
      Synonyms: morose, sulky, somber, glum
STIFLING (<u>stie</u> flihng) *adj.*
   smothering, suffocating
      Synonyms: strangling, gasping
NICHE (nihch) *n.*
   recess in a wall; best position for something
      Synonyms: alcove, cranny, crevice; place, station
SOLEMN (<u>sah</u> luhm) *adj.*
   somberly impressive; quiet, deeply serious
      Synonyms: dignified, ceremonial; earnest, brooding
INNUMERABLE (ih <u>noo</u> muhr uh buhl)
(ih <u>nyoo</u> muhr uh buhl) *adj.*
   too many to be counted, inestimable
      Synonyms: incalculable, immeasurable, infinite
ENNUYÉ or **ENNUI** (ahn <u>wee</u>) (ahn wee) *adj.*
   bored, lacking interest or energy
      Synonyms: tedious, listless, world-weary
STUPEFIED (<u>stoo</u> puh fied) *adj.*
   stunned, astonished; having dull senses
      Synonyms: amazed; dazed, bemused, benumbed
AGITATED (<u>aa</u> gih tay tihd) *adj.*
   upset or uneasy
      Synonyms: disturbed, flustered, bothered
OMINOUS (<u>ah</u> mihn uhs) *adj.*
   menacing, threatening, indicating misfortune
      Synonyms: inauspicious, unpropitious, sinister, dire,
      baleful
COUNTENANCE (<u>kown</u> tuh nuhns) *n.*
   appearance, facial expression
      Synonyms: face, features, visage

She stood alone. Her small, bare, and silvery feet gleamed in the black mirror of marble beneath her. Her hair, not as yet more than half loosened for the night from its ball-room array, clustered, amid a shower of diamonds, round and round her classical head in curls like those of the young hyacinth. A snowy-white and gauze-like drapery seemed to be nearly the sole covering to her delicate form; but the mid-summer and midnight air was hot, **sullen**, and still, and no motion in the statue-like form itself, stirred even the folds of that raiment of very vapor which hung around it as the heavy marble hangs around the Niobe. Yet—strange to say!—her large lustrous eyes were not turned downward upon that grave wherein her brightest hope lay buried, but riveted in a widely different direction! The prison of the Old Republic is, I think, the stateliest building in all of Venice—but how could that lady gaze so fixedly upon it, when beneath her lay **stifling** her own child? Yon dark, gloomy **niche**, too, yawns right opposite her chamber window—what, then, *could* there be in its shadows—in its architecture—in its ivy-wreathed and **solemn** cornices—that the Marchesa di Mentoni had not wondered at a thousand times before? Nonsense! Who docs not remember that, at such a time as this, the eye, like a shattered mirror, multiplies the images of its sorrow, and sees in **innumerable** far-off places, the woe which is close at hand?

Many steps above the Marchesa and within the arch of the water-gate stood, in full dress, the Satyr-like figure of Mentoni himself. He was occasionally occupied in thrumming a guitar, and seemed **ennuyé** to the very death, as at intervals he gave directions for the recovery of his child. **Stupefied** and aghast, I had myself no power to move from the upright position I had assumed upon first hearing the shriek and must have presented to the eyes of the **agitated** group a spectral and **ominous** appearance, as with pale **countenance** and rigid limbs, I floated down among them in that funereal gondola.

NICHE (nihch) *n.*
  recess in a wall; best position for something
    Synonyms: alcove, cranny, crevice; place, station

DESCENT (dih <u>sehnt</u>) (dee <u>sehnt</u>) *n.*
  1. a decline; the passing from a higher place to a
     lower place
     Synonyms: slope; lowering, dismount, gravitation
  2. one's ancestry
     Synonyms: here**dity, lineage**

COUNTENANCE (<u>kown</u> tuh nuhns) *n.*
  appearance, facial expression
    Synonyms: face, features, visage

All efforts proved in vain. Many of the most energetic in the search were relaxing their exertions and yielding to a gloomy sorrow. There seemed but little hope for the child; (how much less than for the mother!) but now, from the interior of that dark **niche** which has been already mentioned as forming a part of the Old Republican prison, and as fronting the <u>lattice</u> of the Marchesa, a figure muffled in a cloak, stepped out within reach of the light, and, pausing a moment upon the verge of the giddy **descent**, plunged headlong into the canal. As, in an instant afterward, he stood with the still living and breathing child within his grasp, upon the marble flagstones by the side of the Marchesa, his cloak, heavy with the drenching water, became unfastened, and, falling in folds about his feet, discovered to the wonder-stricken spectators the graceful person of a very young man, with the sound of whose name the greater part of Europe was then ringing.

No word spoke the deliverer. But the Marchesa! She will now receive her child—she will press it to her heart— she will cling to its little form, and smother it with her caresses. Alas! *Another's* arms have taken it from the stranger—*another's* arms have taken it away, and borne it afar off, unnoticed, into the palace! And the Marchesa! Her lip—her beautiful lip trembles; tears are gathering in her eyes—those eyes which, like Pliny's acanthus,[12] are "soft and almost liquid." Yes! Tears are gathering in those eyes—and see! The entire woman thrills throughout the soul, and the statue has started into life! The <u>pallor</u> of the marble **countenance**, the swelling of the marble bosom, the very purity of the marble feet, we behold suddenly flushed over with a tide of ungovernable crimson; and a slight shudder quivers about her delicate frame, as a gentle air at Napoli about the rich silver lilies in the grass.

Why *should* that lady blush! To this demand there is no answer—except that, having left, in the eager haste and terror of a mother's heart, the privacy of her own *boudoir*,

TUMULT (<u>tuh</u> muhlt) *n.*
    state of confusion; agitation
        Synonyms: disturbance, turmoil, din, commotion,
        chaos

AGITATION (aa gih <u>tay</u> shuhn) *n.*
    uneasiness; commotion, excitement
        Synonyms: restlessness, anxiety; disturbance
CIVILITY (sih <u>vihl</u> ih tee) *n.*
    a courteous behavior or politeness
        Synonyms: compliment, pleasantry

MINUTE (mie <u>noot</u>) (mih <u>noot</u>) *adj.*
    precise, detailed; very small
        Synonyms: attentive, critical; tiny, diminutive,
        infinitesimal

BELIE (bih <u>lie</u>) *v.* **belying,-ied.**
    to misrepresent, expose as false
        Synonyms: distort, refute
EVINCE (ih <u>vihns</u>) *v.* **-ing,-ed.**
    to show clearly or display
        Synonyms: express, exhibit, demonstrate, manifest

she has neglected to <u>enthral</u> her tiny feet in their slippers, and utterly forgotten to throw over her Venetian shoulders that drapery which is their due. What other possible reason could there have been for her so blushing, for the glance of those wild appealing eyes? For the unusual **tumult** of that throbbing bosom? For the convulsive pressure of that trembling hand? That hand which fell, as Mentoni turned into the palace, accidentally, upon the hand of the stranger. What reason could there have been for the low—the singularly low tone of those unmeaning words which the lady uttered hurriedly in bidding him adieu? "Thou hast conquered," she said, or the murmurs of the water deceived me. "Thou hast conquered, one hour after sunrise. We shall meet—so let it be!"

———◆———

The **tumult** had subsided, the lights had died away within the palace, and the stranger, whom I now recognised, stood alone upon the flags. He shook with inconceivable **agitation** and his eye glanced around in search of a gondola. I could not do less than offer him the service of my own, and he accepted the **civility**. Having obtained an oar at the water-gate, we proceeded together to his residence, while he rapidly recovered his self-possession and spoke of our former slight acquaintance in terms of great apparent cordiality.

There are some subjects upon which I take pleasure in being **minute**. The person of the stranger—let me call him by this title, who to all the world was still a stranger—the person of the stranger is one of these subjects. In height he might have been below rather than above medium size, although there were moments of intense passion when his frame actually *expanded* and **belied** the assertion. The light, almost slender symmetry of his figure promised more of that ready activity which he **evinced** at the Bridge of Sighs than of that Herculean strength which he has been known to wield without an effort upon occasions of

PROFUSION (pruh <u>fyoo</u> zhuhn) *n.*
  abundance, outpouring
    Synonyms: plenty, extravagance

COUNTENANCE (<u>kown</u> tuh nuhns) *n.*
  appearance, facial expression
    Synonyms: face, features, visage

RETAIN (rih <u>tayn</u>) *v.* **-ing,-ed.**
  to hold, keep possession of
    Synonyms: withhold, reserve, maintain, remember
VESTIGE (<u>veh</u> stihj) *n.*
  trace, remnant
    Synonyms: relic, remains, token, sign, spoor
SOLICIT (suh <u>lih</u> siht) *v.* **-ing,-ed.**
  to petition persistently, to seek out
    Synonyms: entice, tempt, request, entreat

LUXURIOUSNESS (luhg <u>zhoor</u> ee uhs nehs) *adj.*
  grandeur, opulence, pleasurable indulgence
    Synonyms: magnificence, splendor, richness

more dangerous emergency. With the mouth and chin of a deity—singular, wild, full, liquid eyes, whose shadows varied from pure hazel to intense and brilliant jet—and a **profusion** of curling, black hair, from which a forehead of unusual breadth gleamed forth at intervals all light and ivory—his were features than which I have seen none more classically regular, except, perhaps, the marble ones of the Emperor Commodus. Yet his **countenance** was, nevertheless, one of those which all men have seen at some period of their lives, and have never afterward seen again. It had no peculiar, it had no settled predominant expression to be fastened upon the memory, a **countenance** seen and instantly forgotten, but forgotten with a vague and neverceasing desire of recalling it to mind. Not that the spirit of each rapid passion failed at any time to throw its own distinct image upon the mirror of that face—but that the mirror, mirror-like, **retained** no **vestige** of the passion, when the passion had departed.

Upon leaving him on the night of our adventure, he **solicited** me in what I thought an urgent manner, to call upon him *very* early the next morning. Shortly after sunrise, I found myself accordingly at his palazzo, one of those huge structures of gloomy yet fantastic pomp, which tower above the waters of the Grand Canal in the vicinity of the Rialto. I was shown up a broad winding staircase of mosaics, into an apartment whose unparalleled splendor burst through the opening door with an actual glare, making me blind and dizzy with **luxuriousness**.

I knew my acquaintance to be wealthy. Report had spoken of his possessions in terms which I had even ventured to call terms of ridiculous exaggeration. But as I gazed about me, I could not bring myself to believe that the wealth of any subject in Europe could have supplied the princely magnificence which burned and blazed around.

Although, as I say, the sun had arisen, yet the room was still brilliantly lighted up. I judge from this

COUNTENANCE (<u>kown</u> tuh nuhns) *n.*
appearance, facial expression
Synonyms: face, features, visage
EMBELLISHMENT (ehm <u>behl</u> ihsh mihnt) *n.*
an ornament, a decorative detail
Synonyms: adornment, enhancement
DECORA (dih <u>kawr</u> uh) (dih <u>kohr</u> uh) *n.*
properness, tastefulness, a state of social correctness
Synonyms: politeness, courtesy, appropriateness
MELANCHOLY (mehl uhn <u>kahl</u> ee) *adj.*
sad, depressing
Synonyms: dejected, despondent, woeful, sorrowful
CONVOLUTE (kahn vuh <u>loot</u>) *adj.*
twisted, intricate; complicated, involved
Synonyms: coiled, elaborate; complex
MULTITUDINOUS (<u>muhl</u> tih too dih nihs) *adj.*
many, numerous
Synonyms: myriad, several, countless

RECONCILE (<u>reh</u> kuhn siel) *v.* **-ing,-ed.**
1. to accept
Synonyms: resign, submit, placate, pacify, appease
2. to resolve a dispute
Synonyms: agree, accommodate, rectify, reunite
SINGULAR (<u>sihn</u> gyuh luhr) *adj.*
uncommon, peculiar
Synonyms: unusual, odd, rare, unique, individual
LUDICROUS (<u>loo</u> dih kruhs) *adj.*
laughable, ridiculous
Synonyms: hilarious, absurd, foolish, silly,
preposterous

circumstance, as well as from an air of exhaustion in the **countenance** of my friend, that he had not retired to bed during the whole of the preceding night. In the architecture and **embellishments** of the chamber, the evident design had been to dazzle and astound. Little attention had been paid to the **decora** of what is technically called *keeping*, or to the proprieties of nationality. The eye wandered from object to object, and rested upon none—neither the *grotesques* of the Greek painters, nor the sculptures of the best Italian days, nor the huge carvings of untutored Egypt. Rich draperies in every part of the room trembled to the vibration of low, **melancholy** music, whose origin was not to be discovered. The senses were oppressed by mingled and conflicting perfumes, reeking up from strange **convolute** censers, together with **multitudinous** flaring and flickering tongues of emerald and violet fire. The rays of the newly risen sun poured in upon the whole, through windows formed each of a single pane of crimson-tinted glass. Glancing to and fro in a thousand reflections, from curtains which rolled from their cornices like cataracts of molten silver, the beams of natural glory mingled at length fitfully with the artificial light and lay weltering in subdued masses upon a carpet of rich, liquid-looking cloth of Chili gold.

"Ha, ha, ha! Ha, ha, ha!" laughed the proprietor, motioning me to a seat as I entered the room, and throwing himself back at full-length upon an ottoman. "I see," said he, perceiving that I could not immediately **reconcile** myself to the *bienséance*[13] of so **singular** a welcome, "I see you are astonished at my apartment—at my statues—my pictures—my originality of conception in architecture and upholstery! Absolutely drunk, eh, with my magnificence? But pardon me, my dear sir (here his tone of voice dropped to the very spirit of cordiality), pardon me for my uncharitable laughter. You appeared so *utterly* astonished. Besides, some things are so completely **ludicrous**, that a man *must* laugh or die. To die laughing must be the

CHAOS (<u>kay</u> ahs) *n.*
  extreme disorder
    Synonyms: incoherence, randomness, disorganization
LEGIBLE (<u>leh</u> juh buhl) *adj.*
  readable
    Synonyms: plain, clear
DIVINITY (dih <u>vihn</u> ih tee) *n.*
  a supreme being, a god
    Synonyms: deity, immortal, godhead
SINGULAR (<u>sihn</u> gyuh luhr) *adj.*
  uncommon, peculiar
    Synonyms: unusual, odd, rare, unique, individual
INSIPIDITY (ihn sih <u>pihd</u> ih tee) *n.*
  blandness, lack of flavor; lack of excitement
    Synonyms: dullness, flatness
PATRIMONY (<u>paa</u> trih moh nee) *n.*
  inheritance
    Synonyms: estate, possessions, endowment
PROFANATION (prah feh <u>nay</u> shuhn) *n.*
  the act of abusing or disrespecting sacred things
    Synonyms: desecration, sacrilege, blasphemy
IMPERIAL (ihm <u>peer</u> ee uhl) *adj.*
  majestic, sovereign
    Synonyms: executive, authoritative, supreme
CONSTRUE (kuhn <u>stroo</u>) *v.* **-ing,-ed.**
  to explain or interpret
    Synonyms: analyze, translate
SAUNTER (<u>sawn</u> tuhr) *v.* **-ing,-ed.**
  to walk leisurely or amble
    Synonyms: stroll, ramble, perambulate
DEFERENCE (<u>dehf</u> uhr uhnts) (<u>dehf</u> ruhnts) *n.*
  a submission in opinion, yielding to the views of
  another
    Synonyms: acquiescence, compliance, courtesy

most glorious of all glorious deaths! Sir Thomas More—
a very fine man was Sir Thomas More—Sir Thomas
More died laughing, you remember. Also in the
'Absurdities' of Ravisius Textor, there is a long list of
characters who came to the same magnificent end. Do
you know, however," continued he musingly, "that at
Sparta (which is now Palæochori), at Sparta, I say, to the
west of the citadel, among a **chaos** of scarcely visible
ruins, is a kind of socle upon which are still **legible** the letters AAZM. They are undoubtedly part of ΓΈΛΑΣΜΑ.
Now, at Sparta were a thousand temples and shrines to a
thousand different **divinities.** How exceedingly strange
that the altar of Laughter should have survived all the
others! But in the present instance," he resumed, with a
singular alteration of voice and manner, "I have no right
to be merry at your expense. You might well have been
amazed. Europe cannot produce anything so fine as this,
my little regal cabinet. My other apartments are by no
means of the same order—mere ultras of fashionable
insipidity. This is better than fashion, is it not? Yet this
has but to be seen to become the rage—that is, with those
who could afford it at the cost of their entire **patrimony.** I
have guarded, however, against any such **profanation.**
With one exception, you are the only human being
besides myself and my *valet* who has been admitted
within the mysteries of these **imperial** precincts, since they
have been bedizened[14] as you see!"

I bowed in acknowledgment, for the overpowering
sense of splendor and perfume and music, together with
the unexpected eccentricity of his address and manner,
prevented me from expressing in words my appreciation
of what I might have **construed** into a compliment.

"Here," he resumed, arising and leaning on my arm as
he **sauntered** around the apartment, "here are paintings
from the Greeks to Cimabue,[15] and from Cimabue to the
present hour. Many are chosen, as you see, with little
deference to the opinions of Virtu. They are all, however,

PERSPICACITY (puhr spih <u>kaa</u> sih tee) *n.*
  shrewdness, wisdom
    Synonyms: insight, intelligence, knowledge
PORE (pohr) *v.* **-ing,-ed.**
  to study closely or meditatively
    Synonyms: peruse, gaze, ponder
SURPASSING (suhr <u>paas</u> ihng) *adj.*
  superior
    Synonyms: transcending, exceeding, excellent
DIMINUTIVE (dih <u>mihn</u> yuh tihv) *adj.*
  small
    Synonyms: short, tiny, wee, minuscule
COQUETRY (<u>koh</u> keh tree) (koh <u>keh</u> tree) *n.*
  playful behavior, flirtation
    Synonyms: seduction, teasing, toying
QUINTESSENCE (kwihn <u>teh</u> sihns) *n.*
  concentrated essence; most typical example
    Synonyms: heart, root; paragon, epitome
AFFECTATION (aaf ehk <u>tay</u> shun) *n.*
  fakeness, phoniness, artificiality, false display
    Synonyms: insincerity, pose, pretension

DEMEANOR (dih <u>meen</u> uhr) *n.*
  one's behavior or conduct
    Synonyms: attitude, disposition, manner, presence
TEMPERAMENT (<u>tehm</u> puhr uh mehnt) *n.*
  an attitude, a manner of behaving
    Synonyms: disposition, mood, mentality

fitting tapestry for a chamber such as this. Here, too, are some *chef-d'oeuvres* of the unknown great, and here, unfinished designs by men, celebrated in their day, whose very names the **perspicacity** of the academies has left to silence and to me. What think you," said he, turning abruptly as he spoke, "what think you of this Madonna della Pietà?"

"It is Guido's own!" I said, with all the enthusiasm of my nature, for I had been **poring** intently over its **surpassing** loveliness. "It is Guido's own! How *could* you have obtained it? She is undoubtedly in painting what the Venus is in sculpture."

"Ha!" said he, thoughtfully. "The Venus? The beautiful Venus? The Venus of the Medici? She of the **diminutive** head and the gilded hair? Part of the left arm [here his voice dropped so as to be heard with difficulty], and all the right, are restorations, and in the **coquetry** of that right arm lies, I think, the **quintessence** of all **affectation**. Give *me* the Canova! The Apollo, too, is a copy—there can be no doubt of it—blind fool that I am, who cannot behold the boasted inspiration of the Apollo! I cannot help—pity me!—I cannot help preferring the Antinous. Was it not Socrates who said that the <u>statuary</u> found his statue in the block of marble? Then Michael Angelo was by no means original in his couplet:

'*Non ha l'ottimo artista atcun concetto*
Che un marmo solo in se non circunscriva.' "[16]

It has been, or should be remarked, that in the manner of the true gentleman, we are always aware of a difference from the bearing of the vulgar, without being at once precisely able to determine in what such difference consists. Allowing the remark to have applied in its full force to the outward **demeanor** of my acquaintance, I felt it, on that eventful morning, still more fully applicable to his moral **temperament** and character. Nor can I better define that

PERVADE (puhr <u>vayd</u>) *v.* **-ing,-ed.**
    to become diffused throughout every part of
        Synonyms: permeate, spread, fill, transfuse

LEVITY (<u>leh</u> vih tee) *n.*
    humor, frivolity, gaiety
        Synonyms: lightness, amusement, cheer
SOLEMNITY (suh <u>lehm</u> nih tee) *n.*
    dignified seriousness
        Synonyms: ceremoniousness, formality, observance
TREPIDATION (treh pih <u>day</u> shuhn) *n.*
    fear, anxiety
        Synonyms: alarm, dread, apprehension, fright

REVERY or REVERIE (<u>rehv</u> uh ree) *n.*
    a daydream
        Synonyms: dream, absorption, muse, meditation

TAINT (taynt) *v.* **-ing,-ed.**
    to spoil or infect
        Synonyms: contaminate, befoul, poison, pollute
NOVEL (<u>nah</u> vuhl) *adj.*
    new, original
        Synonyms: fresh, newfangled, innovative, unusual,
        different

peculiarity of spirit which seemed to place him so essentially apart from all other human beings, than by calling it a *habit* of intense and continual thought, **pervading** even his most trivial actions—intruding upon his moments of dalliance—and interweaving itself with his very flashes of merriment—like adders which writhe from out the eyes of the grinning masks in the cornices around the temples of Persepolis.

I could not help, however, repeatedly observing, through the mingled tone of **levity** and **solemnity** with which he rapidly descanted upon matters of little importance, a certain air of **trepidation**—a degree of nervous *unction* in action and in speech—an unquiet excitability of manner which appeared to me at all times unaccountable, and upon some occasions even filled me with alarm. Frequently, too, pausing in the middle of a sentence whose commencement he had apparently forgotten, he seemed to be listening in the deepest attention, as if either in momentary expectation of a visitor, or to sounds which must have had existence in his imagination alone.

It was during one of these **reveries** or pauses of apparent abstraction, that, in turning over a page of the poet and scholar Politian's beautiful tragedy, "The Orfeo" (the first native Italian tragedy), which lay near me upon an ottoman, I discovered a passage underlined in pencil. It was a passage toward the end of the third act—a passage of the most heart-stirring excitement—a passage which, although **tainted** with impurity, no man shall read without a thrill of **novel** emotion, no woman without a sigh. The whole page was blotted with fresh tears, and upon the opposite interleaf were the following English lines, written in a hand so very different from the peculiar characters of my acquaintance, that I had some difficulty in recognizing it as his own:

> Thou wast that all to me, love,
> For which my soul did pine—

SOLEMN (<u>sah</u> luhm) *adj.*
   quiet, deeply serious; somberly impressive
      Synonyms: earnest, brooding; dignified, ceremonial

ETHEREAL (ih <u>theer</u> ee uhl) *adj.*
   not earthly, spiritual, delicate
      Synonyms: intangible, diaphanous, airy, gossamer,
      sheer
BILLOW (<u>bih</u> loh) *n.*
   a great wave of sea water
      Synonyms: surge, flood

SINGULAR (<u>sihn</u> gyuh luhr) *adj.*
   uncommon, peculiar
      Synonyms: unusual, odd, rare, unique, individual

A green isle in the sea, love,
    A fountain and a shrine,
All wreathed with fairy fruits and flowers;
    And all the flowers were mine.

Ah, dream too bright to last!
    Ah, starry Hope, that didst arise
But to be overcast!
    A voice from out the Future cries,
"Onward!"—but o'er the Past
    (Dim gulf!) my spirit hovering lies.
Mute—motionless—aghast!

For alas! alas! with me
    The light of life is o'er.
No more—no more—no more,
    (Such language holds the **solemn** sea
To the sands upon the shore),
    Shall bloom the thunder-blasted tree,
Or the stricken eagle soar!

Now all my hours are trances;
    And all my nightly dreams
Are where thy dark eye glances,
    And where thy footstep gleams
In what **ethereal** dances,
    By what Italian streams.

Alas! for that accursed time
    They bore thee o'er the **billow**,
From Love to titled age and crime,
    And an unholy pillow!—
From me, and from our misty climate,
    Where weeps the silver willow!

That these lines were written in English—a language with which I had not believed their author acquainted—afforded me little matter of surprise. I was too well aware of the extent of his acquirements and of the **singular**

SCRUTINIZING (<u>skroot</u> niez ihng) *adj.*
   carefully observant
      Synonyms: examining, studying, surveying

DELINEATION (dih lihn ee <u>ay</u> shuhn) *n.*
   depiction, representation
      Synonyms: portrayal, illustration, picture,
   figuration
ETHEREAL (ih <u>theer</u> ee uhl) *adj.*
   not earthly, spiritual, delicate
      Synonyms: intangible, diaphanous, airy, gossamer,
   sheer
COUNTENANCE (<u>kown</u> tuh nuhns) *n.*
   appearance, facial expression
      Synonyms: face, features, visage
LURK (luhrk) *v.* **-ing,-ed.**
   to hide, to lie hidden or unsuspected; to prowl, sneak
      Synonyms: conceal; stalk, creep, skulk, slink
ANOMALY (uh <u>nah</u> moh lee) *n.*
   an irregularity or deviation from the norm
      Synonyms: oddity, aberration, deviance, peculiarity,
   abnormality
MELANCHOLY (<u>mehl</u> uhn kahl ee) *n.*
   sadness, depression
      Synonyms: dejection, despondency, woe, sorrow
DISCERNIBLE (dihs <u>uhrn</u> ih buhl) *adj.*
   able to be perceived or recognized
      Synonyms: observable, distinguishable, visible, evident

pleasure he took in concealing them from observation, to be astonished at any similar discovery; but the place of date, I must confess, occasioned me no little amazement. It had been originally London, and afterward carefully overscored—not, however, so effectually as to conceal the word from a **scrutinizing** eye. I say, this occasioned me no little amazement; for I well remember that, in a further conversation with my friend, I particularly inquired if he had at any time met in London the Marchesa di Mentoni (who for some years previous to her marriage had resided in that city), when his answer, if I mistake not, gave me to understand that he had never visited the metropolis of Great Britain. I might as well here mention that I have more than once heard (without, of course, giving credit to a report involving so many improbabilities), that the person of whom I speak, was not only by birth, but in education, an *Englishman*.

"There is one painting," said he, without being aware of my notice of the tragedy, "there is still one painting which you have not seen." And throwing aside a drapery, he discovered a full-length portrait of the Marchesa Aphrodite.

Human art could have done no more in the **delineation** of her superhuman beauty. The same **ethereal** figure which stood before me the preceding night upon the steps of the Ducal Palace, stood before me once again. But in the expression of the **countenance**, which was beaming all over with smiles, there still **lurked** (incomprehensible **anomaly**!) that fitful stain of **melancholy** which will ever be found inseparable from the perfection of the beautiful. Her right arm lay folded over her bosom. With her left she pointed downward to a curiously fashioned vase. One small fairy foot, alone visible, barely touched the earth; and, scarcely **discernible** in the brillant atmosphere which seemed to encircle and enshrine her loveliness, floated a

CHERUB (<u>cheh</u> ruhb) *n.*
  an adorable child; a winged angel
    Synonyms: baby, doll; guardian, heavenly being

SOLEMN (<u>sah</u> luhm) *adj.*
  quiet, deeply serious; somberly impressive
    Synonyms: earnest, brooding; dignified, ceremonial

EMBELLISHMENT (ehm <u>behl</u> ihsh mihnt) *n.*
  an ornament, a decorative detail
    Synonyms: adornment, enhancement

CHASTITY (<u>chaas</u> tih tee) *n.*
  purity, virginity
    Synonyms: celibacy, virtue

ANTEDILUVIAN (aan tih duh <u>loo</u> vee uhn) adj.
  ancient beyond measure
    Synonyms: old, archaic, antique

pair of the most delicately imagined wings. My glance fell from the painting to the figure of my friend, and the vigorous words of Chapman's *Bussy D'Ambois*, quivered instinctively upon my lips:

"He is up
There like a Roman statue! He will stand
Till Death hath made him marble!"

"Come," he said at length, turning toward a table of richly enamelled and massive silver, upon which were a few goblets fantastically stained, together with two large Etruscan vases, fashioned in the same extraordinary model as that in the foreground of the portrait, and filled with what I supposed to be Johannisberger. "Come," he said, abruptly, "let us drink! It is early—but let us drink. It is *indeed* early," he continued, musingly, as a cherub with a heavy golden hammer made the apartment ring with the first hour after sunrise. "It is *indeed* early—but what matters it? Let us drink! Let us pour out an offering to yon solemn sun which these gaudy lamps and censers are so eager to subdue!" And having made me pledge him in a bumper, he swallowed in rapid succession several goblets of the wine.

"To dream," he continued, resuming the tone of his desultory conversation as he held up to the rich light of a censer one of the magnificent vases, "to dream has been the business of my life. I have therefore framed for myself, as you see, a bower of dreams. In the heart of Venice could I have erected a better? You behold around you, it is true, a medley of architectural embellishments. The chastity of Ionia is offended by antediluvian devices, and the sphinxes of Egypt are outstretched upon carpets of gold. Yet the effect is incongruous to the timid alone. Proprieties of place and especially of time are the bugbears[17] which terrify mankind from the contemplation of the magnificent. Once I was myself a decorist, but that

THE ASSIGNATION

SUBLIMATION (suh blih <u>may</u> shuhn) *n.*
a restriction put upon oneself
    Synonyms: suppression, inhibition, reserve

EJACULATE (ih <u>jaak</u> yuh layt) *v.* **-ing,-ed.**
to exclaim suddenly
    Synonyms: blurt, shout, declare

INCOHERENT (ihn koh <u>hihr</u> uhnt) *adj.*
unable to think or express one's thoughts in a clear or
orderly manner
    Synonyms: incohesive, unintelligible

LIVID (<u>lih</u> vihd) *adj.*
pale; reddened with anger; discolored from a bruise
    Synonyms: ashen, pallid; furious; black-and-blue

sublimation of folly has <u>palled</u> upon my soul. All this is now the fitter for my purpose. Like these <u>arabesque censers</u>, my spirit is writhing in fire, and the delirium of this scene is fashioning me for the wilder visions of that land of real dreams whither I am now rapidly departing."

He here paused abruptly, bent his head to his bosom, and seemed to listen to a sound which I could not hear. At length, erecting his frame, he looked upwards, and **ejaculated** the lines of the Bishop of Chichester:

*"Stay for me there! I will not fail
To meet thee in that hollow vale."*

In the next instant, confessing the power of the wine, he threw himself at full length upon an ottoman.

A quick step was now heard upon the staircase, and a loud knock at the door rapidly succeeded. I was hastening to anticipate a second disturbance, when a page of Mentoni's household burst into the room and faltered out, in a voice choking with emotion, the **incoherent** words, "My mistress—my mistress! Poisoned—poisoned! Oh, beautiful—oh, beautiful Aphrodite!"

Bewildered, I flew to the ottoman and endeavored to arouse the sleeper to a sense of the startling intelligence. But his limbs were rigid—his lips were **livid**—his lately beaming eyes were riveted in *death*. I staggered back toward the table—my hand fell upon a cracked and blackened goblet—and a consciousness of the entire and terrible truth flashed suddenly over my soul.

SUMPTUOUSLY (<u>suhm</u> choo uhs lee) *adv.*
  lavishly, splendidly
    Synonyms: elaborately, luxuriously

INCIPIENT (ihn <u>sihp</u> ee uhnt) *adj.*
  beginning to exist or appear, in an initial stage
    Synonyms: dawning, nascent, inchoate
PERUSAL (puh <u>roos</u> uhl) *n.*
  a close examination
    Synonyms: scrutiny, inspection
PURPORT (puhr <u>pohrt</u>) *v.* **-ing,-ed.**
  to profess, suppose, claim
    Synonyms: pretend, mean, purpose, indicate
DEVOUTLY (dih <u>vowt</u> lee) *adv.*
  with much devotion, especially to religion
    Synonyms: piously, observantly, sincerely, earnestly,
    reverently

THE OVAL PORTRAIT

The château into which my valet had ventured to make forcible entrance, rather than permit me in my desperately wounded condition to pass a night in the open air, was one of those piles of commingled gloom and grandeur which have so long frowned among the Apennines, not less in fact than in the fancy of Mrs. Radcliffe. To all appearance it had been temporarily and very lately abandoned. We established ourselves in one of the smallest and least sumptuously furnished apartments. It lay in a remote turret of the building. Its decorations were rich, yet tattered and antique. Its walls were hung with tapestry and bedecked with manifold and multiform armorial trophies, together with an unusually great number of very spirited modern paintings in frames of rich golden arabesque. In these paintings, which depended from the walls not only in their main surfaces, but in very many nooks which the bizarre architecture of the château rendered necessary—in these paintings my incipient delirium, perhaps, had caused me to take deep interest, so that I bade Pedro to close the heavy shutters of the room—since it was already night—to light the tongues of a tall candelabrum which stood by the head of my bed, and to throw open far and wide the fringed curtains of black velvet which enveloped the bed itself. I wished all this done that I might resign myself, if not to sleep, at least alternately to the contemplation of these pictures and the perusal of a small volume which had been found upon the pillow, and which purported to criticize and describe them.

Long, long I read—and devoutly, devoutly I gazed. Rapidly and gloriously the hours flew by and the deep

NICHE (nihch) *n.*
recess in a wall; best position for something
Synonyms: alcove, cranny, crevice; place, station

IMPULSIVE (ihm <u>puhl</u> sihv) *adj.*
sudden, spontaneous
Synonyms: whimsical, unprompted, involuntary

SOBER (<u>soh</u> buhr) *adj.*
self-controlled; serious; not intoxicated
Synonyms: subdued, sedate; grave; dry, not drunk

DISSIPATE (<u>dihs</u> uh payt) *v.* **-ing,-ed.**
to scatter
Synonyms: disperse, dissolve

STUPOR (<u>stoo</u> puhr) *n.*
astonishment; a state of having numbed senses
Synonyms: bewilderment, amazement; daze, trance

EXECUTION (ehk sih <u>kyoo</u> shuhn) *n.*
1. the act of performing or carrying out a task
   Synonyms: operation, enactment, accomplishment, achievement
2. the act of putting to death
   Synonyms: killing, suicide, murder

COUNTENANCE (<u>kown</u> tuh nuhns) *n.*
appearance, facial expression
Synonyms: face, features, visage

VEHEMENTLY (<u>vee</u> huh muhnt lee) *adv.*
strongly, urgently
Synonyms: intensely, passionately, ardently

midnight came. The position of the candelabrum displeased me, and outreaching my hand with difficulty, rather than disturb my slumbering valet, I placed it so as to throw its rays more fully upon the book.

But the action produced an effect altogether unanticipated. The rays of the numerous candles (for there were many) now fell within a niche of the room which had hitherto been thrown into deep shade by one of the bedposts. I thus saw in vivid light a picture all unnoticed before. It was the portrait of a young girl just ripening into womanhood. I glanced at the painting hurriedly and then closed my eyes. Why I did this was not at first apparent even to my own perception. But while my lids remained thus shut, I ran over in mind my reason for so shutting them. It was an impulsive movement to gain time for thought—to make sure that my vision had not deceived me—to calm and subdue my fancy for a more sober and more certain gaze. In a very few moments I again looked fixedly at the painting.

That I now saw aright I could not and would not doubt, for the first flashing of the candles upon that canvas had seemed to dissipate the dreamy stupor which was stealing over my senses, and to startle me at once into waking life.

The portrait, I have already said, was that of a young girl. It was a mere head and shoulders, done in what is technically termed a *vignette* manner, much in the style of the favorite heads of Sully. The arms, the bosom, and even the ends of the radiant hair melted imperceptibly into the vague yet deep shadow which formed the background of the whole. The frame was oval, richly gilded and filigreed in *Moresque*.[18] As a thing of art nothing could be more admirable than the painting itself. But it could have been neither the execution of the work, nor the immortal beauty of the countenance, which had so suddenly and so vehemently moved me. Least of all, could it have been that my fancy, shaken from its half slumber,

THE OVAL PORTRAIT

DISPEL (dihs <u>pehl</u>) *v.* **-ling,-led.**
to drive out or scatter
Synonyms: disband, disperse

CONFOUND (kuhn <u>fownd</u>) *v.* **-ing,-ed.**
to baffle, perplex; to mistake something for another
Synonyms: overwhelm, disconcert, entangle,
muddle; confuse, misidentify

APPALL (uh <u>pahl</u>) *v.* **-ing,-ed.**
to overcome with shock or dismay
Synonyms: horrify, astound, petrify

REVERENT (<u>reh</u> vuhr ehnt) *adj.*
expressing deep respect, worshipful
Synonyms: venerating, adoring, admiring

AGITATION (aa gih <u>tay</u> shuhn) *n.*
uneasiness; commotion, excitement
Synonyms: restlessness, anxiety; disturbance

AUSTERE (aw <u>steer</u>) *adj.*
stern, strict, unadorned
Synonyms: dour, bare, ascetic

COUNTENANCE (<u>kown</u> tuh nuhns) *n.*
appearance, facial expression
Synonyms: face, features, visage

REVERY or REVERIE (<u>rehv</u> uh ree) *n.*
a daydream
Synonyms: dream, absorption, muse, meditation

had mistaken the head for that of a living person. I saw at once that the peculiarities of the design, of the *vignetting*, and of the frame, must have instantly dispelled such an idea—must have prevented even its momentary entertainment. Thinking earnestly upon these points, I remained, for an hour perhaps, half sitting, half reclining, with my vision riveted upon the portrait. At length, satisfied with the true secret of its effect, I fell back within the bed. I had found the spell of the picture in an absolute life-likeness of expression, which, at first startling, finally confounded, subdued, and appalled me. With deep and reverent awe I replaced the candelabrum in its former position. The cause of my deep agitation being thus shut from view, I sought eagerly the volume which discussed the paintings and their histories. Turning to the number which designated the oval portrait, I there read the vague and quaint words which follow:

"She was a maiden of rarest beauty, and not more lovely than full of glee. And evil was the hour when she saw, and loved, and wedded the painter. He, passionate, studious, austere, and having already a bride in his Art; she a maiden of rarest beauty, and not more lovely than full of glee, all light and smiles, and frolicsome as the young fawn, loving and cherishing all things, hating only the Art which was her rival, dreading only the palette and brushes and other untoward instruments which deprived her of the countenance of her lover. It was thus a terrible thing for this lady to hear the painter speak of his desire to portray even his young bride. But she was humble and obedient, and sat meekly for many weeks in the dark high turret-chamber where the light dripped upon the pale canvas only from overhead. But he, the painter, took glory in his work, which went on from hour to hour, and from day to day. And he was a passionate and wild and moody man, who became lost in reveries so that he would not see that the light which fell so ghastly in that lone turret withered the health and the spirits of his bride, who

THE OVAL PORTRAIT

RENOWN (rih <u>nown</u>) *n.*
  fame, widespread acclaim
    Synonyms: eminence, distinction, prestige,
    standing, celebrity

FERVID (<u>fuhr</u> vihd) *adj.*
  passionate, intense, zealous
    Synonyms: vehement, ardent, enthusiastic, avid,
    eager

DEPICT (dih <u>pihkt</u>) *v.* **-ing,-ed.**
  to represent, to describe
    Synonyms: portray, render, delineate, picture

SURPASSINGLY (suhr <u>paas</u> ihng lee) *adv.*
  superiorly
    Synonyms: exceptionally, exceedingly, excellently

ARDOR (<u>ahr</u> duhr) *n.*
  passion, enthusiasm
    Synonyms: intensity, vehemence

COUNTENANCE (<u>kown</u> tuh nuhns) *n.*
  appearance, facial expression
    Synonyms: face, features, visage

TREMULOUS (<u>treh</u> myoo luhs) *adj.*
  trembling, quivering; fearful, timid
    Synonyms: shaking, palsied; timorous, anxious

PALLID (<u>paa</u> lihd) *adj.*
  lacking color or liveliness
    Synonyms: pale, wan, ashen, blanched, ghostly

pined visibly to all but him. Yet she smiled on and still on, uncomplainingly, because she saw that the painter (who had high **renown**) took a **fervid** and burning pleasure in his task, and wrought day and night to **depict** her who so loved him, yet who grew daily more dispirited and weak. And in <u>sooth</u> some who beheld the portrait spoke of its resemblance in low words, as of a mighty marvel, and a proof not less of the power of the painter than of his deep love for her whom he **depicted** so **surpassingly** well. But at length, as the labor drew nearer to its conclusion, there were admitted none into the turret, for the painter had grown wild with the **ardor** of his work, and turned his eyes from the canvas rarely, even to regard the **countenance** of his wife. And he would not see that the tints which he spread upon the canvas were drawn from the cheeks of her who sat beside him. And when many weeks had passed, and but little remained to do, save one brush upon the mouth and one tint upon the eye, the spirit of the lady again flickered up as the flame within the socket of the lamp. And then the brush was given, and then the tint was placed; and for one moment, the painter stood entranced before the work which he had wrought. But in the next, while he yet gazed, he grew **tremulous** and very **pallid** and aghast, and crying with a loud voice, 'This is indeed *Life* itself!' turned suddenly to regard his beloved. *She was dead!*"

MELANCHOLY (<u>mehl</u> uhn kahl ee) *adj.*
  sad, gloomy
    Synonyms: depressed, despondent, woeful, sorrowful
PERVADE (puhr <u>vayd</u>) *v.* **-ing,-ed.**
  to become diffused throughout every part of
    Synonyms: permeate, spread, fill, transfuse
SENTIMENT (<u>sehn</u> tuh muhnt) *n.*
  an attitude, thought, or judgment prompted by
  feeling; a romantic or nostalgic feeling
    Synonyms: idea; emotion
DESOLATE (<u>deh</u> soh liht) *adj.*
  showing the effects of abandonment or neglect; devoid
  of warmth or comfort
    Synonyms: barren, bleak, forsaken, vacant;
    cheerless, somber, wretched
REVELLER (<u>reh</u> vuhl uhr) *n.*
  one who partakes in boisterous festivities
    Synonyms: merrymaker, partier, carouser
GOAD (gohd) *v.* **-ing,-ed.**
  to prod or urge
    Synonyms: impel, incite, stimulate, provoke, rouse
SUBLIME (suh <u>bliem</u>) *adj.*
  awe-inspiring; of high spiritual or moral value
    Synonyms: noble, majestic, supreme, ideal

THE FALL OF THE HOUSE OF USHER

Son cœur est un luth suspendu;
Sitôt qu'on le touche il résonne.
                        —*De Béranger*[19]

During the whole of a dull, dark, and soundless day in the autumn of the year, when the clouds hung oppressively low in the heavens, I had been passing alone, on horseback, through a singularly dreary tract of country, and at length found myself, as the shades of the evening drew on, within view of the **melancholy** House of Usher. I know not how it was, but with the first glimpse of the building, a sense of insufferable gloom **pervaded** my spirit. I say insufferable, for the feeling was unrelieved by any of that half-pleasurable, because poetic, **sentiment** with which the mind usually receives even the sternest natural images of the **desolate** or terrible. I looked upon the scene before me—upon the mere house and the simple landscape features of the domain—upon the bleak walls—upon the vacant eye-like windows—upon a few rank sedges—and upon a few white trunks of decayed trees with an utter depression of soul which I can compare to no earthly sensation more properly than to the after-dream of the **reveller** upon opium—the bitter lapse into every-day life—the hideous dropping off of the veil. There was an iciness, a sinking, a sickening of the heart, an unredeemed dreariness of thought which no **goading** of the imagination could torture into aught of the **sublime**. What was it—I paused to think—what was it that so unnerved me in the contemplation of the House of Usher? It was a mystery all insoluble, nor could I grapple with the shadowy fancies that crowded upon me as I

PONDER (<u>pahn</u> duhr) *v.* **-ing,-ed.**
  to consider or think about something in depth
    Synonyms: contemplate, reflect, ruminate

PRECIPITOUS (pree <u>sih</u> puh tuhs) *adj.*
  very steep; hasty, quickly, with too little caution
    Synonyms: high, craggy, sharp; impetuous,
    reckless, abrupt, rash

LURID (<u>loor</u> ihd) *adj.*
  harshly shocking, revolting; glowing
    Synonyms: ghastly, garish, gruesome, grisly,
    macabre

SOJOURN (<u>soh</u> juhrn) (soh <u>juhrn</u>) *n.*
  visit, stay
    Synonyms: call, residency, stop, tenancy

IMPORTUNATE (ihm <u>pohr</u> chuh niht) *adj.*
  extremely urgent, pleading
    Synonyms: craving, beseeching, earnest, imperative

AGITATION (aa gih <u>tay</u> shuhn) *n.*
  uneasiness; commotion, excitement
    Synonyms: restlessness, anxiety; disturbance

ACUTE (uh <u>kyoot</u>) *adj.*
  1. severe; sensitive, heightened; sharp, pointed
    Synonyms: intense, fierce; perceptive; piercing
  2. clever, shrewd
    Synonyms: ingenious, keen

ALLEVIATION (uh lee vee <u>ay</u> shuhn) *n.*
  relief, a partial improvement
    Synonyms: assuagement, mitigation, quelling

MALADY (<u>maal</u> uh dee) *n.*
  illness
    Synonyms: disease, disorder, ailment, affliction,
    infirmity

SINGULAR (<u>sihn</u> gyuh luhr) *adj.*
  uncommon, peculiar
    Synonyms: unusual, odd, rare, unique, individual

pondered. I was forced to fall back upon the unsatisfactory conclusion that while, beyond doubt, there *are* combinations of very simple natural objects which have the power of thus affecting us, still the analysis of this power lies among considerations beyond our depth. It was possible, I reflected, that a mere different arrangement of the particulars of the scene, of the details of the picture, would be sufficient to modify, or perhaps to annihilate its capacity for sorrowful impression; and, acting upon this idea, I reined my horse to the **precipitous** brink of a black and **lurid** <u>tarn</u> that lay in unruffled lustre by the dwelling, and gazed down—but with a shudder even more thrilling than before—upon the remodelled and inverted images of the gray <u>sedge</u>, and the ghastly tree-stems, and the vacant and eye-like windows.

Nevertheless, in this mansion of gloom I now proposed to myself a **sojourn** of some weeks. Its proprietor, Roderick Usher, had been one of my boon companions in boyhood but many years had elapsed since our last meeting. A letter, however, had lately reached me in a distant part of the country—a letter from him—which, in its wildly **importunate** nature, had admitted of no other than a personal reply. The MS. gave evidence of nervous **agitation**. The writer spoke of **acute** bodily illness—of a mental disorder which oppressed him—and of an earnest desire to see me, as his best and indeed his only personal friend, with a view of attempting, by the cheerfulness of my society, some **alleviation** of his **malady**. It was the manner in which all this and much more was said—it was the apparent *heart* that went with his request—which allowed me no room for hesitation. I accordingly obeyed forthwith what I still considered a very **singular** summons.

Although, as boys, we had been even intimate associates, I really knew little of my friend. His reserve had been always excessive and habitual. I was aware, however, that his very ancient family had been noted, time out of

TEMPERAMENT (<u>tehm</u> puhr uh mehnt) *n.*
  an attitude, a manner of behaving
    Synonyms: disposition, mood, mentality
EXALTED (ihg <u>zahlt</u> ihd) *adj.*
  praised, elevated
    Synonyms: important, high-ranking, superior
MANIFEST (<u>maan</u> uh fehst) *v.* **-ing,-ed.**
  to make evident or certain by display
    Synonyms: exhibit, showcase, expose
MUNIFICENT (myoo <u>nihf</u> ih suhnt) *adj.*
  generous, lavish
    Synonyms: liberal, bountiful
DESCENT (dih <u>sehnt</u>) (dee <u>sehnt</u>) *n.*
  1. one's ancestry
    Synonyms: heredity, lineage
  2. a decline; the passing from a higher place to a
    lower place
    Synonyms: slope; lowering, dismount, gravitation
TRIFLING (<u>trie</u> flihng) *adj.*
  of slight worth or little importance
    Synonyms: trivial, insignificant, worthless, silly
UNDEVIATING (uhn <u>dee</u> vee ay tihng) *adj.*
  direct, straightforward
    Synonyms: consistent, regular, unvarying
PATRIMONY (<u>paa</u> trih moh nee) *n.*
  inheritance
    Synonyms: estate, possessions, endowment
EQUIVOCAL (ih <u>kwihv</u> uh kuhl) *adj.*
  equal in name, but not in reality; ambiguous, open to
  more than one interpretation
    Synonyms: misleading; doubtful, uncertain
APPELLATION (aa puhl <u>ay</u> shuhn) *n.*
  a title or name
    Synonyms: denomination, designation, moniker, tag
SINGULAR (<u>sihn</u> gyuh luhr) *adj. (See page 132.)*
PARADOXICAL (paar uh <u>dahks</u> ih kuhl) *adj.*
  contradicting, incongruous; puzzling
    Synonyms: opposing; perplexing
SENTIMENT (<u>sehn</u> tuh muhnt) *n. (See page 130.)*

mind, for a peculiar sensibility of **temperament**, displaying itself, through long ages, in many works of **exalted** art, and **manifested**, of late, in repeated deeds of **munificent** yet unobtrusive charity, as well as in a passionate devotion to the intricacies, perhaps even more than to the <u>orthodox</u> and easily recognizable beauties of musical science. I had learned, too, the very remarkable fact that the stem of the Usher race, all time-honored as it was, had put forth, at no period, any enduring branch. In other words, the entire family lay in the direct line of **descent**, and had always, with very **trifling** and very temporary variation, so lain. It was this deficiency I considered while running over in thought the perfect keeping of the character of the premises with the accredited character of the people, and while speculating upon the possible influence which the one, in the long lapse of centuries, might have exercised upon the other—it was this deficiency, perhaps, of collateral issue, and the consequent **undeviating** transmission from sire to son, of the **patrimony** with the name, which had at length so identified the two as to merge the original title of the estate in the quaint and **equivocal appellation** of the "House of Usher," an **appellation,** which seemed to include, in the minds of the peasantry who used it, both the family and the family mansion.

I have said that the sole effect of my somewhat childish experiment—that of looking down within the <u>tarn</u>—had been to deepen the first **singular** impression. There can be no doubt that the consciousness of the rapid increase of my superstition—for why should I not so term it?—served mainly to accelerate the increase itself. Such, I have long known, is the **paradoxical** law of all **sentiments** having terror as a basis. And it might have been for this reason only that, when I again uplifted my eyes to the house itself, from its image in the pool, there grew in my mind a strange fancy—a fancy so ridiculous, indeed, that I but mention it to show the vivid force of the sensations

AFFINITY (uh <u>fih</u> nih tee) *n.*
similarity, likeness; fondness
Synonyms: inclination; partiality, penchant
PESTILENT (<u>peh</u> stihl ehnt) *adj.*
deadly, infected, poisonous
Synonyms: harmful, dangerous, noxious
DISCERNIBLE (dihs <u>uhrn</u> ih buhl) *adj.*
able to be perceived or recognized
Synonyms: observable, distinguishable, visible, evident
ANTIQUITY (aan <u>tih</u> kwih tee) *n.*
the quality of being very old; ancient times
Synonyms: hoariness, antiqueness; history
MINUTE (mie <u>noot</u>) (mih <u>noot</u>) *adj.*
very small; precise, detailed
Synonyms: tiny, diminutive, infinitesimal; attentive,
critical
DILAPIDATION (dih laap ih <u>day</u> shuhn) *n.*
disrepair
Synonyms: destruction, ruin, deterioration, decay
ADAPTATION (uh daap <u>tay</u> shuhn) *n.*
adjustment, transformation
Synonyms: preparedness, fit, accomodation
SCRUTINIZING (<u>skroot</u> niez ihng) *adj.*
observing carefully
Synonyms: examining, studying, surveying
SULLEN (<u>suh</u> luhn) *adj.*
brooding, gloomy
Synonyms: morose, sulky, somber, glum
STEALTHY (<u>stehl</u> thee) *adj.*
sly and cautious, sneaky
Synonyms: furtive, secretive, unperceived
SENTIMENT (<u>sehn</u> tuh muhnt) *n.*
an attitude, thought, or judgment prompted by
feeling; a romantic or nostalgic feeling
Synonyms: idea; emotion

which oppressed me. I had so worked upon my imagination as really to believe that about the whole mansion and domain there hung an atmosphere peculiar to themselves and their immediate vicinity—an atmosphere which had no **affinity** with the air of heaven, but which had reeked up from the decayed trees, and the gray wall, and the silent <u>tarn</u>—a **pestilent** and mystic vapor, dull, sluggish, faintly **discernible**, and leaden-hued.

Shaking off from my spirit what *must* have been a dream, I scanned more narrowly the real aspect of the building. Its principal feature seemed to be that of an excessive **antiquity**. The discoloration of ages had been great. **Minute** fungi overspread the whole exterior, hanging in a fine tangled web-work from the eaves. Yet all this was apart from any extraordinary **dilapidation**. No portion of the masonry had fallen and there appeared to be a wild inconsistency between its still perfect **adaptation** of parts, and the crumbling condition of the individual stones. In this there was much that reminded me of the <u>specious</u> totality of old wood-work, which has rotted for long years in some neglected vault, with no disturbance from the breath of the external air. Beyond this indication of extensive decay, however, the fabric gave little token of instability. Perhaps the eye of a **scrutinizing** observer might have discovered a barely perceptible <u>fissure</u>, which, extending from the roof of the building in front, made its way down the wall in a zigzag direction, until it became lost in the **sullen** waters of the <u>tarn</u>.

Noticing these things, I rode over a short causeway to the house. A servant in waiting took my horse, and I entered the Gothic archway of the hall. A valet of **stealthy** step thence conducted me in silence through many dark and intricate passages in my progress to the studio of his master. Much that I encountered on the way contributed, I know not how, to heighten the vague **sentiments** of which I have already spoken. While the objects around me—while the carvings of the ceilings, the

SOMBRE or SOMBER (<u>sahm</u> buhr) *adj.*
  dark and gloomy, melancholy, dismal
    Synonyms: serious, grave, mournful, lugubrious, funereal

COUNTENANCE (<u>kown</u> tuh nuhns) *n.*
  appearance, facial expression
    Synonyms: face, features, visage

ACCOST (uh <u>cahst</u>) (uh <u>kawst</u>) *v.* **-ing,-ed.**
  to approach and speak to someone, often in an aggressive way
    Synonyms: stop, address, detain, buttonhole

TREPIDATION (treh pih <u>day</u> shuhn) *n.*
  fear, anxiety
    Synonyms: alarm, dread, apprehension, fright

PROFUSE (pruh <u>fyoos</u>) *adj.*
  plentiful, copious; lavish, extravagant
    Synonyms: abundant; prodigal, prosperous, thriving

PERVADE (puhr <u>vayd</u>) *v.* **-ing,-ed.**
  to become diffused throughout every part of
    Synonyms: permeate, spread, fill, transfuse

VIVACIOUS (vie <u>vay</u> shuhs) *adj.*
  lively, spirited
    Synonyms: animated, dynamic, sprightly, vibrant, zesty

CONSTRAINED (kuhn <u>straynd</u>) *adj.*
  forced, impelled, not voluntary
    Synonyms: restricted, controlled, calculated

ENNUYÉ or ENNUI (ahn <u>wee</u>) (<u>ahn</u> wee) *adj.*
  bored, lacking interest or energy
    Synonyms: tedious, listless, world-weary

sombre tapestries of the walls, the ebon blackness of the floors, and the <u>phantasmagoric</u> armorial trophies which rattled as I strode, were but matters to which, or to such as which, I had been accustomed from my infancy—while I hesitated not to acknowledge how familiar was all this—I still wondered to find how unfamiliar were the fancies which ordinary images were stirring up. On one of the staircases, I met the physician of the family. His **countenance**, I thought, wore a mingled expression of low cunning and perplexity. He **accosted** me with **trepidation** and passed on. The valet now threw open a door and ushered me into the presence of his master.

The room in which I found myself was very large and lofty. The windows were long, narrow, and pointed, and at so vast a distance from the black oaken floor as to be altogether inaccessible from within. Feeble gleams of <u>encrimsoned</u> light made their way through the trellissed panes, and served to render sufficiently distinct the more prominent objects around. The eye, however, struggled in vain to reach the remoter angles of the chamber, or the recesses of the vaulted and <u>fretted</u> ceiling. Dark draperies hung upon the walls. The general furniture was **profuse**, comfortless, antique, and tattered. Many books and musical instruments lay scattered about, but failed to give any vitality to the scene. I felt that I breathed an atmosphere of sorrow. An air of stern, deep, and irredeemable gloom hung over and **pervaded** all.

Upon my entrance, Usher arose from a sofa on which he had been lying at full length and greeted me with a **vivacious** warmth which had much in it, I at first thought, of an overdone cordiality—of the **constrained** effort of the **ennuyé** man of the world. A glance, however, at his **countenance** convinced me of his perfect sincerity. We sat down and for some moments, while he spoke not, I gazed upon him with a feeling half of pity, half of awe. Surely, man had never before so terribly altered in so brief a period as had Roderick Usher! It was with difficulty that I

WAN (wahn) *adj. (See page 60.)*
LUMINOUS (<u>loo</u> muhn uhs) *adj. (See page 68.)*
PALLID (<u>paa</u> lihd) *adj. (See page 128.)*
SURPASSINGLY (suhr <u>paas</u> ihng lee) *adv. (See page 128.)*
TENUITY (tehn <u>yoo</u> ih tee) *n.*
　low density, thinness
　　Synonyms: weakness, delicacy, fineness, fragility
COUNTENANCE (<u>kown</u> tuh nuhns) *n. (See page 138.)*
PREVAILING (prih <u>vayl</u> ihng) *adj.*
　predominant; lasting
　　Synonyms: principle, main; persisting, enduring
INCOHERENCE (ihn koh <u>hihr</u> uhnts) *n.*
　the inability to express one's thoughts in a clear or
　orderly manner; lack of cohesion or connection
　　Synonyms: confusion; disorder, disarray
FUTILE (<u>fyoo</u> tuhl) (fyoo <u>tiel</u>) *adj.*
　hopeless, useless; serving no useful purpose
　　Synonyms: ineffective, worthless; unimportant
TREPIDANCY (<u>treh</u> pih daan see) *n.*
　fear and anxiety
　　Synonyms: alarm, dread, apprehension, fright, dread
AGITATION (aa gih <u>tay</u> shuhn) *n. (See page 132.)*
REMINISCENCE (reh muh <u>nihs</u> ehnts) *n.*
　remembrance of past events
　　Synonyms: memory, recollection, recall
TEMPERAMENT (<u>tehm</u> puhr uh mehnt) *n. (See pg. 134.)*
VIVACIOUS (vie <u>vay</u> shuhs) *adj. (See page 138.)*
SULLEN (<u>suh</u> luhn) *adj. (See page 136.)*
TREMULOUS (<u>treh</u> myoo luhs) *adj. (See page 128.)*
ABEYANCE (uh <u>bay</u> uhnts) *n.*
　temporary suppression or suspension, remission
　　Synonyms: delay, deferral, postponement, dormancy
ENUNCIATION (ih nuhn see <u>ay</u> shuhn) *n.*
　the act of pronouncing clearly, speaking
　　Synonyms: articulation, stating, utterance
MODULATED (<u>mah</u> juh lay tihd) *adj.*
　changed or adjusted, with regards to one's voice
　　Synonyms: intonated, inflected

could bring myself to admit the identity of the wan being before me with the companion of my early boyhood. Yet the character of his face had been at all times remarkable. A cadaverousness of complexion; an eye large, liquid, and luminous beyond comparison; lips somewhat thin and very pallid, but of a surpassingly beautiful curve; a nose of a delicate Hebrew model, but with a breadth of nostril unusual in similar formations; a finely moulded chin, speaking, in its want of prominence, of a want of moral energy; hair of a more than web-like softness and tenuity; these features, with an inordinate expansion above the regions of the temple, made up altogether a countenance not easily to be forgotten. And now in the mere exaggeration of the prevailing character of these features, and of the expression they were wont to convey, lay so much of change that I doubted to whom I spoke. The now ghastly pallor of the skin and the now miraculous lustre of the eye, above all things startled and even awed me. The silken hair, too, had been suffered to grow all unheeded, and as, in its wild gossamer texture, it floated rather than fell about the face, I could not, even with effort, connect its Arabesque expression with any idea of simple humanity.

In the manner of my friend I was at once struck with an incoherence, an inconsistency; and I soon found this to arise from a series of feeble and futile struggles to overcome an habitual trepidancy—an excessive nervous agitation. For something of this nature I had indeed been prepared, no less by his letter, than by reminiscences of certain boyish traits and by conclusions deduced from his peculiar physical confirmation and temperament. His action was alternately vivacious and sullen. His voice varied rapidly from a tremulous indecision (when the animal spirits seemed utterly in abeyance) to that species of energetic concision—that abrupt, weighty, unhurried, and hollow-sounding enunciation—that leaden, self-balanced, and perfectly modulated guttural utterance, which may be

SOLACE (<u>sah</u> lihs) *n.*
comfort in distress, consolation
Synonyms: succor, balm, cheer, condolence

MALADY (<u>maal</u> uh dee) *n.*
illness
Synonyms: disease, disorder, ailment, affliction, infirmity

CONSTITUTIONAL (kahn stih <u>too</u> shuh nuhl) *adj.*
having to do with the physical structure or health of something or someone
Synonyms: natural, inherent, innate

MORBID (<u>mohr</u> bihd) *adj.*
relating to disease; gruesome; abnormally gloomy
Synonyms: pathological, unhealthy; grisly, macabre, unwholesome; dismal

ACUTENESS (uh <u>kyoot</u> nehs) *n.*
sharpness, severity
Synonym: intensity

INSIPID (ihn <u>sihp</u> ihd) *adj.*
bland, lacking flavor; lacking excitement
Synonyms: lackluster, dull, flat, weak

ANOMALOUS (uh <u>nah</u> moh luhs) *adj.*
irregular or deviating from the norm
Synonyms: odd, aberrant, peculiar, abnormal

DEPLORABLE (dih <u>plohr</u> uh buhl) *adj.*
woeful; strongly regrettable or condemnable
Synonyms: unfortunate, lamentable, pitiful; wretched

AGITATION (aa gih <u>tay</u> shuhn) *n.*
commotion, excitement; uneasiness
Synonyms: disturbance; restlessness, anxiety

ABHORRENCE (uhb <u>hohr</u> ehnts) *n.*
loathing, detestation
Synonyms: hatred, condemnation, abomination

EQUIVOCAL (ih <u>kwihv</u> uh kuhl) *adj.*
ambiguous, open to more than one interpretation; equal in name, but not in reality
Synonyms: doubtful, uncertain; misleading

SINGULAR (<u>sihn</u> gyuh luhr) *adj.* *(See page 132.)*

observed in the lost drunkard, or the irreclaimable eater of opium, during the periods of his most intense excitement.

It was thus that he spoke of the object of my visit, of his earnest desire to see me, and of the **solace** he expected me to afford him. He entered, at some length, into what he conceived to be the nature of his **malady**. It was, he said, a **constitutional** and a family evil, and one for which he despaired to find a remedy—a mere nervous affection, he immediately added, which would undoubtedly soon pass off. It displayed itself in a host of unnatural sensations. Some of these, as he detailed them, interested and bewildered me; although, perhaps, the terms and the general manner of their narration had their weight. He suffered much from a **morbid acuteness** of the senses; the most **insipid** food was alone endurable. He could wear only garments of certain texture; the odors of all flowers were oppressive; his eyes were tortured by even a faint light; and there were but peculiar sounds, and these from stringed instruments, which did not inspire him with horror.

To an **anomalous** species of terror I found him a bound slave. "I shall perish," said he, "I *must* perish in this **deplorable** folly. Thus, thus, and not otherwise, shall I be lost. I dread the events of the future, not in themselves, but in their results. I shudder at the thought of any, even the most trivial incident, which may operate upon this intolerable **agitation** of soul. I have indeed no **abhorrence** of danger, except in its absolute effect—in terror. In this unnerved, in this pitiable, condition I feel that the period will sooner or later arrive when I must abandon life and reason together, in some struggle with the grim phantasm, Fear."

I learned, moreover, at intervals, and through broken and **equivocal** hints, another **singular** feature of his mental condition. He was enchained by certain superstitious impressions in regard to the dwelling which he tenanted, and whence, for many years, he had never ventured forth—in regard to an influence whose supposititious

AFFLICT (uh <u>flihkt</u>) *v.* **-ing,-ed.**
   to distress severely so as to cause persistent anguish
      Synonyms: torment, hurt, trouble
PALPABLE (<u>paalp</u> uh buhl) *adj.*
   obvious, real, tangible
      Synonyms: perceptible, appreciable, discernable,
      concrete, material

STUPOR (<u>stoo</u> puhr) *n.*
   astonishment; a state of having numbed senses
      Synonyms: bewilderment, amazement; daze, trance
COUNTENANCE (<u>kown</u> tuh nuhns) *n.*
   appearance, facial expression
      Synonyms: face, features, visage
WANNESS (<u>wahn</u> nehs) *n.*
   sickly paleness
      Synonyms: pallor, lividity
EMACIATED (ih <u>may</u> shee ay tihd) *adj.*
   very thin due to hunger or disease; feeble
      Synonyms: bony, gaunt, haggard, skeletal
APATHY (<u>aa</u> pah thee) *n.*
   lack of feeling or emotion
      Synonyms: indifference, insouciance, disregard,
      unconcern
TRANSIENT (<u>traan</u> see uhnt) *adj.*
   temporary, short-lived, fleeting
      Synonyms: ephemeral, momentary, evanescent
MALADY (<u>maal</u> uh dee) *n.*
   illness
      Synonyms: disease, disorder, ailment, affliction,
      infirmity

force was conveyed in terms too shadowy here to be re-stated—an influence which some peculiarities in the mere form and substance of his family mansion had, by <u>dint</u> of long sufferance, he said, obtained over his spirit—an effect which the physique of the gray walls and turrets, and of the dim <u>tarn</u> into which they all looked down, had, at length, brought about upon the morale of his existence.

He admitted, however, although with hesitation, that much of the peculiar gloom, which thus **afflicted** him could be traced to a more natural and far more **palpable** origin—to the severe and long-continued illness—indeed to the evidently approaching <u>dissolution</u> of a tenderly beloved sister, his sole companion for long years, his last and only relative on earth.

"Her decease," he said, with a bitterness which I can never forget, "would leave him (him, the hopeless and the frail) the last of the ancient race of the Ushers." While he spoke, the lady Madeline (for so was she called) passed through a remote portion of the apartment and, without having noticed my presence, disappeared. I regarded her with an utter astonishment not unmingled with dread; and yet I found it impossible to account for such feelings. A sensation of **stupor** oppressed me as my eyes followed her retreating steps. When a door, at length, closed upon her, my glance sought instinctively and eagerly the **counte-nance** of the brother, but he had buried his face in his hands, and I could only perceive that a far more than ordinary **wanness** had overspread the **emaciated** fingers through which trickled many passionate tears.

The disease of the lady Madeline had long baffled the skill of her physicians. A settled **apathy**, a gradual wasting away of the person, and frequent although **transient** affections of a partially <u>cataleptical</u> character were the unusual diagnosis. Hitherto she had steadily borne up against the pressure of her **malady**, and had not betaken herself finally to bed. But on the closing in of the evening of my arrival at the house, she <u>succumbed</u> (as her brother

AGITATION (aa gih <u>tay</u> shuhn) *n.*
uneasiness; commotion, excitement
Synonyms: restlessness, anxiety; disturbance
PROSTRATING (<u>prah</u> stray tihng) *adj.*
causing debilitation and weakness
Synonyms: incapacitating, destructive, ruinous
ALLEVIATE (uh <u>lee</u> vee ayt) *v.* **-ing,-ed.**
to relieve, improve partially
Synonyms: allay, assuage, palliate, mitigate, quell
MELANCHOLY (<u>mehl</u> uhn kahl ee) *n.*
sadness, gloom
Synonyms: depression, despondence, woe, sorrow
FUTILITY (fyoo <u>tihl</u> ih tee) *n.*
uselessness; lack of importance
Synonyms: worthlessness, waste
SOLEMN (<u>sah</u> luhm) *adj.*
deeply serious; somberly impressive
Synonyms: dignified, earnest, ceremonial
IDEALITY (ie dee <u>aal</u> ih tee) *n.*
a state of being perfect or ideal, an unobtainable idea
Synonyms: impracticality, quixoticism,
romanticism
DIRGE (duhrj) *n.*
funeral hymn
Synonyms: elegy, threnody, lament
SINGULAR (<u>sihn</u> gyuh luhr) *adj.*
uncommon, peculiar
Synonyms: unusual, odd, rare, unique, individual
PERVERSION (puhr <u>vuhrs</u> zhuhn) *n.*
corruption; deliberate disobedience or misbehavior
Synonyms: immorality, irrationality; unruliness
AMPLIFICATION (aam pluh fih <u>kay</u> shuhn) *n.*
an increase or intensification
Synonyms: augmentation, escalation, magnification
BROOD (brood) *v.* **-ing,-ed.**
to think gloomily about; to cluster, breed
Synonyms: ponder, worry, obsess; incubate, cover

told me at night with inexpressible **agitation**) to the **prostrating** power of the destroyer; and I learned that the glimpse I had obtained of her person would thus probably be the last I should obtain—that the lady, at least while living, would be seen by me no more.

For several days ensuing, her name was unmentioned by either Usher or myself; and during this period I was busied in earnest endeavors to **alleviate** the **melancholy** of my friend. We painted and read together, or I listened as if in a dream, to the wild improvisations of his speaking guitar. And thus, as a closer and still closer intimacy admitted me more unreservedly into the recesses of his spirit, the more bitterly did I perceive the **futility** of all attempts at cheering a mind from which darkness, as if an inherent positive quality, poured forth upon all objects of the moral and physical universe in one unceasing radiation of gloom.

I shall ever bear about me a memory of the many **solemn** hours I thus spent alone with the master of the House of Usher. Yet I should fail in any attempt to convey an idea of the exact character of the studies, or of the occupations, in which he involved me, or led me the way. An excited and highly distempered **ideality** threw a sulphurous lustre over all. His long improvised **dirges** will ring forever in my ears. Among other things, I hold painfully in mind a certain **singular perversion** and **amplification** of the wild air of the last waltz of Von Weber. From the paintings over which his elaborate fancy **brooded**, and which grew, touch by touch, into vaguenesses at which I shuddered the more thrillingly, because I shuddered knowing not why—from these paintings (vivid as their images now are before me) I would in vain endeavor to educe' more than a small portion which should lie within the compass of merely written words. By the utter simplicity, by the nakedness of his designs, he arrested and overawed attention. If ever mortal painted an idea, that mortal was Roderick Usher. For me at least,

HYPOCHONDRIAC (hie puh <u>kahn</u> dree aak) *n.*
  one who often falsely believes himself to be ill
    Synonyms: valetudinarian
CONTRIVE (kuhn <u>triev</u>) *v.* **-ing,-ed.**
  to devise, plan, or manage; to form in an artistic manner
    Synonyms: concoct, scheme; create, design
REVERY or REVERIE (<u>rehv</u> uh ree) *n.*
  a daydream
    Synonyms: dream, absorption, muse, meditation
DISCERNIBLE (dihs <u>uhrn</u> ih buhl) *adj.*
  able to be perceived or recognized
    Synonyms: observable, distinguishable, visible, evident
MORBID (<u>mohr</u> bihd) *adj.*
  relating to disease; gruesome; abnormally gloomy
    Synonyms: pathological, unhealthy; grisly, macabre,
    unwholesome; dismal
AUDITORY (<u>aw</u> dih tohr ee) *adj.*
  having to do with hearing
    Synonyms: aural, otic
FERVID (<u>fuhr</u> vihd) *adj.*
  passionate, intense, zealous
    Synonyms: vehement, ardent, enthusiastic, avid,
    eager
FACILITY (faa <u>sihl</u> ih tee) *n.*
  ease, proficiency
    Synonyms: simplicity, dexterity, poise, assuredness
IMPROMPTU (ihm <u>prahmp</u> too) (ihm <u>prahmp</u> tyoo) *n.*
  a spontaneous, unrehearsed performance
    Synonyms: improvisation, invention
ALLUDE (uh <u>lood</u>) *v.* **-ing,-ed.**
  to make an indirect reference
    Synonyms: intimate, suggest, hint
RHAPSODY (<u>raap</u> suh dee) *n.*
  an emotional literary or musical work
    Synonyms: dithyramb, paean

in the circumstances then surrounding me, there arose out of the pure abstractions which the **hypochondriac contrived** to throw upon his canvas, an intensity of intolerable awe, no shadow of which felt I ever yet in the contemplation of the certainly glowing yet too concrete **reveries** of Fuseli.[20]

One of the <u>phantasmagoric</u> conceptions of my friend, partaking not so rigidly of the spirit of abstraction, may be shadowed forth, although feebly, in words. A small picture presented the interior of an immensely long and rectangular vault or tunnel, with low walls, smooth, white, and without interruption or device. Certain accessory points of the design served well to convey the idea that this <u>excavation</u> lay at an exceeding depth below the surface of the earth. No outlet was observed in any portion of its vast extent, and no torch or other artificial source of light was **discernible**; yet a flood of intense rays rolled throughout, and bathed the whole in a ghastly and inappropriate splendor.

I have just spoken of that **morbid** condition of the **auditory** nerve which rendered all music intolerable to the sufferer with the exception of certain effects of stringed instruments. It was, perhaps, the narrow limits to which he thus confined himself upon the guitar which gave birth, in great measure, to the fantastic character of his performances. But the **fervid facility** of his **impromptus** could not be so accounted for. They must have been, and were, in the notes, as well as in the words of his wild fantasies (for he not unfrequently accompanied himself with rhymed verbal improvisations), the result of that intense mental collectedness and concentration to which I have previously **alluded** as observable only in particular moments of the highest artificial excitement. The words of one of these **rhapsodies** I have easily remembered. I was, perhaps, the more forcibly impressed with it as he gave it, because in the under or mystic current of its meaning I fancied that I perceived, and for the first time, a

THE FALL OF THE HOUSE OF USHER

TOTTERING (<u>tah</u> tuhr ihng) *n.*
   instability, imbalance, uncertainty
      Synonyms: unsteadiness, wobbling, fluctuation

SERAPH (<u>seh</u> ruhf) *n.*
   angel, guardian
      Synonyms: heavenly being, cherub, spirit

PALLID (<u>paa</u> lihd) *adj.*
   lacking color or liveliness
      Synonyms: pale, wan, ashen, blanched, ghostly

LUMINOUS (<u>loo</u> muhn uhs) *adj.*
   bright, brilliant, glowing
      Synonyms: radiant, incandescent, effulgent

full consciousness on the part of Usher of the **tottering** of his lofty reason upon her throne. The verses, which were entitled "The Haunted Palace," ran very nearly, if not accurately, thus:

I.

In the greenest of our valleys,
    By good angels tenanted,
Once a fair and stately palace—
    Radiant palace—reared its head.
In the monarch Thought's dominion—
    It stood there!
Never **seraph** spread a <u>pinion</u>
    Over fabric half so fair.

II.

Banners yellow, glorious, golden,
    On its roof did float and flow
(This—all this—was in the olden
    Time long ago);
And every gentle air that dallied,
    In that sweet day,
Along the <u>ramparts</u> plumed and **pallid**,
    A winged odor went away.

III.

Wanderers in that happy valley
    Through two **luminous** windows saw
Spirits moving musically
    To a lute's well-tuned law;
Round about a throne, where sitting
    (Porphyrogene!)[21]
In state his glory well befitting,
    The ruler of the realm was seen.

IV.

And all with pearl and ruby glowing
    Was the fair palace door,
Through which came flowing, flowing, flowing

SURPASSING (suhr <u>paas</u> ihng) *adj.*
   superior
      Synonyms: transcending, exceeding, excellent
ASSAIL (uh <u>sayl</u>) *v.* **-ing,-ed.**
   to attack, assault
      Synonyms: beset, storm, strike
DESOLATE (<u>deh</u> soh liht) *adj.*
   showing the effects of abandonment or neglect; devoid
   of warmth or comfort
      Synonyms: barren, bleak, forsaken, vacant;
      cheerless, somber, wretched

DISCORDANT (dihs <u>kohr</u> duhnt) *adj.*
   inharmonious; disagreeing
      Synonyms: cacophonous; dissonant
MANIFEST (<u>maan</u> uh fehst) *v.* **-ing,-ed.**
   to make evident or certain by display
      Synonyms: exhibit, showcase, expose
NOVELTY (<u>nah</u> vuhl tee) *n.*
   something new and original
      Synonyms: surprise, change, innovation
PERTINACITY (puhr tih <u>naa</u> sih tee) *n.*
   stubborn persistence
      Synonyms: obstinacy, diligence
SENTIENCE (<u>sehn</u> shuhnts) *n.*
   awareness, consciouness, perception
      Synonyms: thinking, feeling, intelligence
ABANDON (uh <u>baan</u> duhn) *n.*
   total lack of inhibition
      Synonyms: exuberance, enthusiasm

And sparkling evermore,
A troop of Echoes whose sweet duty
    Was but to sing,
In voices of **surpassing** beauty,
    The wit and wisdom of their king.

V.

But evil things, in robes of sorrow,
    assailed the monarch's high estate;
(Ah, let us mourn, for never morrow
    Shall dawn upon him, **desolate**!)
And, round about his home, the glory
    That blushed and bloomed
Is but a dim-remembered story
    Of the old time entombed.

VI.

And travellers now within that valley,
    Through the red-litten windows see
Vast forms that move fantastically
    To a **discordant** melody;
While, like a rapid ghastly river,
    Through the pale door;
A hideous <u>throng</u> rush out forever,
    And laugh—but smile no more.

I well remember that suggestions arising from this ballad led us into a train of thought wherein there became **manifest** an opinion of Usher's which I mention not so much on account of its **novelty** (for other men have thought thus), as on account of the **pertinacity** with which he maintained it. This opinion, in its general form, was that of the **sentience** of all vegetable things. But, in his disordered fancy, the idea had assumed a more daring character, and trespassed, under certain conditions, upon the kingdom of inorganization. I lack words to express the full extent, or the earnest **abandon** of his persuasion. The belief, however, was connected (as I have previously

SENTIENCE (<u>sehn</u> shuhnts) *n.*
    awareness, consciouness, perception
        Synonyms: thinking, feeling, intelligence
IMPORTUNATE (ihm <u>pohr</u> chuh niht) *adj.*
    1. troublesome, difficult
        Synonyms: annoying, disturbing
    2. extremely urgent, pleading
        Synonyms: craving, beseeching, earnest, imperative

PORE (pohr) *v.* **-ing,-ed.**
    to study closely or meditatively
        Synonyms: peruse, gaze, ponder
SUBTERRANEAN (suhb tuh <u>ray</u> nee uhn) *adj.*
    hidden, secret; underground
        Synonyms: concealed; buried, sunken, covered

PERUSAL (puh <u>roos</u> uhl) *n.*
    a close examination
        Synonyms: scrutiny, inspection
HYPOCHONDRIAC (hie puh <u>kahn</u> dree aak) *n.*
    one who often falsely believes himself to be ill
        Synonyms: valetudinarian

hinted) with the gray stones of the home of his forefathers. The conditions of the sentence had been here, he imagined, fulfilled in the method of <u>collocation</u> of these stones—in the order of their arrangement, as well as in that of the many *fungi* which overspread them, and of the decayed trees which stood around—above all, in the long undisturbed endurance of this arrangement, and in its reduplication in the still waters of the <u>tarn</u>. Its evidence—the evidence of the **sentience**—was to be seen, he said (and I here started as he spoke), in the gradual yet certain condensation of an atmosphere of their own about the waters and the walls. The result was discoverable, he added, in that silent yet **importunate** and terrible influence which for centuries had moulded the destinies of his family, and which made *him* what I now saw him—what he was. Such opinions need no comment, and I will make none.

Our books—the books which, for years, had formed no small portion of the mental existence of the invalid—were, as might be supposed, in strict keeping with this character of phantasm. We **pored** together over such works as the "Ververt et Chartreuse" of Gresset; the "Belphegor" of Machiavelli; the "Heaven and Hell" of Swedenborg; the "**Subterranean** Voyage of Nicholas Klimm" of Holberg; the "<u>Chiromancy</u>" of Robert Flud, of Jean D'Indaginé, and of Dela Chambre; the "Journey into the Blue Distance" of Tieck; and the "City of the Sun" of Campanella. One favorite volume was a small octavo edition of the "Directorium Inquisitorium," by the Dominican Eymeric de Gironne; and there were passages in Pomponius Mela, about the old African Satyrs and Œgipans, over which Usher would sit dreaming for hours. His chief delight, however, was found in the **perusal** of an exceedingly rare and curious book in quarto Gothic—the manual of a forgotten church—the *Vigiliæ Mortuorum Secundum Chorum Ecclesiæ Maguntinæ.*

I could not help thinking of the wild ritual of this work, and of its probable influence upon the **hypochondriac**,

INTERMENT (ihn <u>tuhr</u> mehnt) *n.*
  burial
    Synonyms: entombment, inhumation
SINGULAR (<u>sihn</u> gyuh luhr) *adj.*
  uncommon, peculiar
    Synonyms: unusual, odd, rare, unique, individual
RESOLUTION (reh suh <u>loo</u> shuhn) *n.*
  a firm decision
    Synonyms: determination, will, explanation
MALADY (<u>maal</u> uh dee) *n.*
  illness
    Synonyms: disease, disorder, ailment, affliction,
    infirmity
COUNTENANCE (<u>kown</u> tuh nuhns) *n.*
  appearance, facial expression
    Synonyms: face, features, visage

when, one evening, having informed me abruptly that the lady Madeline was no more, he stated his intention of preserving her corpse for a <u>fortnight</u> (previously to its final **interment**), in one of the numerous vaults within the main walls of the building. The worldly reason, however, assigned for this **singular** proceeding, was one which I did not feel at liberty to dispute. The brother had been led to his **resolution** (so he told me) by consideration of the unusual character of the **malady** of the deceased, of certain obtrusive and eager inquiries on the part of her medical men, and of the remote and exposed situation of the burial-ground of the family. I will not deny that when I called to mind the sinister **countenance** of the person whom I met upon the staircase, on the day of my arrival at the house, I had no desire to oppose what I regarded as at best but a harmless, and by no means an unnatural, precaution.

At the request of Usher, I personally aided him in the arrangements for the temporary entombment. The body having been encoffined, we two alone bore it to its rest. The vault in which we placed it (and which had been so long unopened that our torches, half smothered in its oppressive atmosphere, gave us little opportunity for investigation) was small, damp, and entirely without means of admission for light; lying, at great depth, immediately beneath that portion of the building in which was my own sleeping apartment. It had been used, apparently, in remote feudal times, for the worst purposes of a donjon-keep, and, in later days, as a place of deposit for powder, or some other highly combustible substance, as a portion of its floor and the whole interior of a long archway through which we reached it were carefully sheathed with copper. The door of massive iron had been, also, similarly protected. Its immense weight caused an unusually sharp, grating sound, as it moved upon its hinges.

Having deposited our mournful burden upon tressels within this region of horror, we partially turned aside the

THE FALL OF THE HOUSE OF USHER

SIMILITUDE (sih <u>mih</u> lih tood) *n.*
similarity, likeness
Synonym: resemblance
DIVINE (dih <u>vien</u>) *v.* **-ing,-ed.**
to foretell or know by inspiration
Synonyms: predict, intuit, auger, foresee, presage

MALADY (<u>maal</u> uh dee) *n.*
illness
Synonyms: disease, disorder, ailment, affliction,
infirmity

COUNTENANCE (<u>kown</u> tuh nuhns) *n.*
appearance, facial expression
Synonyms: face, features, visage
LUMINOUSNESS (<u>loo</u> muhn uhs nehs) *n.*
brightness, brilliance, glow
Synonyms: radiance, incandescence, effulgence
AGITATED (<u>aa</u> gih tay tihd) *adj.*
upset or uneasy
Synonyms: disturbed, flustered, bothered
OBLIGE (uh <u>bliej</u>) *v.* **-ing,-ed.**
to be obligated or forced to comply
Synonyms: compel, constrain, bind, favor
RESOLVE (rih <u>sahlv</u>) *v.* **-ing,-ed.**
to determine or to make a firm decision about
Synonyms: solve, decide
PROFOUND (pruh <u>fownd</u>) (proh <u>fownd</u>) *adj.*
deep, infinite; intelligent; difficult to understand
Synonyms: bottomless, unending; smart; thorough,
weighty

yet unscrewed lid of the coffin, and looked upon the face of the tenant. A striking **similitude** between the brother and sister now first arrested my attention; and Usher, **divining**, perhaps, my thoughts, murmured out some few words from which I learned that the deceased and himself had been twins, and that sympathies of a scarcely intelligible nature had always existed between them. Our glances, however, rested not long upon the dead—for we could not regard her unawed. The disease which had thus entombed the lady in the maturity of youth, had left, as usual in all **maladies** of a strictly cataleptical character, the mockery of a faint blush upon the bosom and the face, and that suspiciously lingering smile upon the lip which is so terrible in death. We replaced and screwed down the lid, and, having secured the door of iron, made our way, with toil, into the scarcely less gloomy apartments of the upper portion of the house.

And now, some days of bitter grief having elapsed, an observable change came over the features of the mental disorder of my friend. His ordinary manner had vanished. His ordinary occupations were neglected or forgotten. He roamed from chamber to chamber with hurried, unequal, and objectless step. The pallor of his **countenance** had assumed, if possible, a more ghastly hue—but the **luminousness** of his eye had utterly gone out. The once occasional huskiness of his tone was heard no more, and a tremendous quaver, as if of extreme terror, habitually characterized his utterance. There were times indeed when I thought his unceasingly **agitated** mind was laboring with some oppressive secret, to divulge which he struggled for the necessary courage. At times, again, I was **obliged** to **resolve** all into the mere inexplicable vagaries of madness, for I beheld him gazing upon vacancy for long hours, in an attitude of the **profoundest** attention, as if listening to some imaginary sound. It was no wonder that his condition terrified—that it infected me. I felt creeping upon me,

WANE (wayn) *v.* **-ing,-ed.**
   to decrease gradually
      Synonyms: dwindle, flag, fade, shrink, diminish

TEMPEST (<u>tehm</u> pehst) *n.*
   a storm; rage or fury
      Synonyms: inclemency; tumult, turbulence, torrent

PERVADE (puhr <u>vayd</u>) *v.* **-ing,-ed.**
   to become diffused throughout every part of
      Synonyms: permeate, spread, fill, transfuse

SENTIMENT (<u>sehn</u> tuh muhnt) *n.*
   an attitude, thought, or judgment prompted by
   feeling; a romantic or nostalgic feeling
      Synonyms: idea; emotion

COUNTENANCE (<u>kown</u> tuh nuhns) *n.*
   appearance, facial expression
      Synonyms: face, features, visage

WAN (wahn) *adj.*
   sickly pale
      Synonyms: ashen, pallid, blanched, pasty

RESTRAINED (rih <u>straynd</u>) *adj.*
   controlled, repressed, restricted
      Synonyms: hampered, bridled, curbed, checked

DEMEANOR (dih <u>meen</u> uhr) *n.*
   one's behavior or conduct
      Synonyms: attitude, disposition, manner, presence

APPALL (uh <u>pahl</u>) *v.* **-ing,-ed.**
   to overcome with shock or dismay
      Synonyms: horrify, astound, petrify

by slow yet certain degrees, the wild influences of his own fantastic yet impressive superstitions.

It was especially upon retiring to bed late in the night of the seventh or eighth day after the placing of the lady Madeline within the <u>donjon</u>, that I experienced the full power of such feelings. Sleep came not near my couch—while the hours **waned** and **waned** away. I struggled to reason off the nervousness which had dominion over me. I endeavored to believe that much, if not all of what I felt, was due to the bewildering influence of the gloomy furniture of the room—of the dark and tattered draperies, which, tortured into motion by the breath of a rising **tempest**, swayed fitfully to and fro upon the walls, and rustled uneasily about the decorations of the bed. But my efforts were fruitless. An irrepressible tremor gradually **pervaded** my frame; and, at length, there sat upon my very heart an <u>incubus</u> of utterly causeless alarm. Shaking this off with a gasp and a struggle, I uplifted myself upon the pillows and, peering earnestly within the intense darkness of the chamber, <u>hearkened</u>—I know not why, except that an instinctive spirit prompted me—to certain low and indefinite sounds which came, through the pauses of the storm at long intervals, I knew not whence. Overpowered by an intense **sentiment** of horror, unaccountable yet unendurable, I threw on my clothes with haste (for I felt that I should sleep no more during the night), and endeavored to arouse myself from the pitiable condition into which I had fallen by pacing rapidly to and fro through the apartment.

I had taken but few turns in this manner, when a light step on an adjoining staircase arrested my attention. I presently recognized it as that of Usher. In an instant afterward he rapped, with a gentle touch, at my door, and entered, bearing a lamp. His **countenance** was as usual, <u>cadaverously</u> **wan**—but, moreover, there was a species of mad hilarity in his eyes—an evidently **restrained** *hysteria* in his whole **demeanor**. His air **appalled** me—but any

IMPETUOUS (ihm <u>peh</u> choo uhs) *adj.*
  forceful, rapid; quick to act without thinking
    Synonyms: fierce, raging; impulsive, passionate
TEMPESTUOUS (tehm <u>pehs</u> tyoo uhs) *adj.*
  stormy, raging, furious
      Synonyms: tumultuous, blustery, inclement,
      turbulent, torrential
SINGULAR (<u>sihn</u> gyuh luhr) *adj.*
  uncommon, peculiar
      Synonyms: unusual, odd, rare, unique, individual

AGITATED (<u>aa</u> gih tay tihd) *adj.*
  upset or uneasy
      Synonyms: disturbed, flustered, bothered
TERRESTRIAL (tuh <u>reh</u> stree uhl) *adj.*
  commonplace; down-to-earth, earthly
      Synonyms: mundane; tellurian, terrene,
      earthbound, sublunary
LUMINOUS (<u>loo</u> muhn uhs) *adj.*
  bright, brilliant, glowing
      Synonyms: radiant, incandescent, effulgent
ENSHROUD or SHROUD (ehn <u>shrowd</u>) *v.* **-ing,-ed.**
  to wrap up, to hide from sight
      Synonyms: blanket, obscure, conceal, cloak,
      envelop
MIASMA (mie <u>aaz</u> muh) (mee <u>aaz</u> muh) *n.*
  a polluted or poisonous atmosphere
      Synonyms: mist, haze, smog, vapor

thing was preferable to the solitude which I had so long endured, and I even welcomed his presence as a relief.

"And you have not seen it?" he said abruptly, after having stared about him for some moments in silence. "You have not then seen it? But, stay! You shall." Thus speaking and having carefully shaded his lamp, he hurried to one of the <u>casements</u>, and threw it freely open to the storm.

The **impetuous** fury of the entering gust nearly lifted us from our feet. It was, indeed, a **tempestuous** yet sternly beautiful night, and one wildly **singular** in its terror and its beauty. A whirlwind had apparently collected its force in our vicinity; for there were frequent and violent alterations in the direction of the wind; and the exceeding density of the clouds (which hung so low as to press upon the turrets of the house) did not prevent our perceiving the life-like velocity with which they flew <u>careering</u> from all points against each other, without passing away into the distance. I say that even their exceeding density did not prevent our perceiving this—yet we had no glimpse of the moon or stars, nor was there any flashing forth of the lightning. But the under surfaces of the huge masses of **agitated** vapor, as well as all **terrestrial** objects immediately around us, were glowing in the unnatural light of a faintly **luminous** and distinctly visible gaseous exhalation which hung about and **enshrouded** the mansion.

"You must not—you shall not behold this!" said I, shuddering, to Usher, as I led him with a gentle violence from the window to a seat. "These appearances which bewilder you are merely electrical phenomena not uncommon—or it may be that they have their ghastly origin in the <u>rank</u> **miasma** of the <u>tarn</u>. Let us close this <u>casement</u>. The air is chilling and dangerous to your frame. Here is one of your favorite romances. I will read, and you shall listen—and so we will pass away this terrible night together."

UNCOUTH (uhn <u>kooth</u>) *adj.*
lacking in refinement, awkward and uncultivated in
appearance or manner
Synonyms: crude, clumsy, ungraceful

IDEALITY (ie dee <u>aal</u> ih tee) *n.*
a state of being perfect or ideal
Synonyms: impracticality, quixoticism,
romanticism

INDULGE (ihn <u>duhlj</u>) *v.* **-ing,-ed.**
to give in, as to a craving or desire
Synonyms: humor, gratify, allow, pamper

AGITATE (<u>aa</u> gih tayt) *v.* **-ing,-ed.**
to upset or excite, to make uneasy
Synonyms: disturb, fluster, bother

HYPOCHONDRIAC (hie puh <u>kahn</u> dree aak) *n.*
one who often falsely believes himself to be ill
Synonyms: valetudinarian

ANOMALY (uh <u>nah</u> moh lee) *n.*
an irregularity or deviation from the norm
Synonyms: oddity, aberration, deviance, peculiarity,
abnormality

VIVACITY (vih <u>vahs</u> ih tee) *n.*
liveliness, spiritedness
Synonyms: vibrance, zest

OBSTINATE (<u>ahb</u> stih nuht) *adj.*
stubborn
Synonyms: headstrong, stiff-necked, bullheaded,
pigheaded, mulish

MALICEFUL (<u>maal</u> ihs fuhl) *adj.*
having feeling of animosity, spite, or hatred
Synonyms: malevolent, cruel, rancorous, hostile

TEMPEST (<u>tehm</u> pehst) *n.*
a storm; rage or fury
Synonyms: inclemency; tumult, turbulence, torrent

The antique volume which I had taken up was the "Mad Trist" of Sir Launcelot Canning, but I had called it a favorite of Usher's more in sad jest than in earnest. For, in truth, there is little in its **uncouth** and unimaginative prolixity which could have had interest for the lofty and spiritual **ideality** of my friend. It was, however, the only book immediately at hand; and I **indulged** a vague hope that the excitement which now **agitated** the **hypochondriac** might find relief (for the history of mental disorder is full of similar **anomalies**) even in the extremeness of the folly which I should read. Could I have judged, indeed, by the wild overstrained air of **vivacity** with which he hearkened, or apparently hearkened, to the words of the tale, I might well have congratulated myself upon the success of my design.

I had arrived at that well-known portion of the story where Ethelred, the hero of the Trist, having sought in vain for peaceable admission into the dwelling of the hermit, proceeds to make good an entrance by force. Here, it will be remembered, the words of the narrative run thus:

"And Ethelred, who was by nature of a doughty heart, and who was now mighty withal, on account of the powerfulness of the wine which he had drunken, waited no longer to hold parley with the hermit, who, in sooth, was of an **obstinate** and **maliceful** turn. But, feeling the rain upon his shoulders, and fearing the rising of the **tempest**, uplifted his mace outright, and, with blows, made quickly room in the plankings of the door for his gauntleted hand; and now pulling therewith sturdily, he so cracked, and ripped, and tore all asunder, that the noise of the dry and hollow-sounding wood alarumed[22] and reverberated throughout the forest."

At the termination of this sentence I started and for a moment paused; for it appeared to me (although I at once concluded that my excited fancy had deceived me)—it appeared to me that, from some very remote portion of the mansion, there came, indistinctly to my ears, what

STIFLED (<u>stie</u> fuhld) *adj.*
   suppressed or held back; smothered or suffocated
     Synonyms: muted, muffled, restrained; deadened

MALICEFUL (<u>maal</u> ihs fuhl) *adj.*
   having feeling of animosity, spite, or hatred
     Synonyms: malevolent, cruel, rancorous, hostile
PRODIGIOUS (pruh <u>dih</u> juhs) *adj.*
   vast, enormous, extraordinary
     Synonyms: huge, gigantic, impressive, marvelous
DEMEANOR (dih <u>meen</u> uhr) *n.*
   one's behavior or conduct
     Synonyms: attitude, disposition, manner, presence

PROTRACTED (proh <u>traak</u> tihd) *adj.*
   prolonged, drawn out, extended
     Synonyms: lengthy, elongated, stretched
CONJURE (<u>kahn</u> juhr) *v.* **-ing,-ed.**
   to summon a devil or spirit by invocation; to affect or
   effect as if by magic; to bring to mind
     Synonyms: materialize; invoke, arouse; recollect

166

might have been, in its exact similarity of character, the echo (but a **stifled** and dull one certainly) of the very cracking and ripping sound which Sir Launcelot had so particularly described. It was, beyond doubt, the coincidence alone which had arrested my attention; for amid the rattling of the sashes of the casements, and the ordinary <u>commingled</u> noises of the still increasing storm, the sound in itself had nothing, surely, which should have interested or disturbed me. I continued the story:

"But the good champion Ethelred, now entering within the door, was sore enraged and amazed to perceive no signal of the **maliceful** hermit; but, in the stead thereof, a dragon of a scary and **prodigious demeanor**, and of a fiery tongue, which <u>sate</u> in guard before a palace of gold, with a floor of silver; and upon the wall there hung a shield of shining brass with this legend enwritten—

Who entereth herein, a conqueror hath bin;
Who slayeth the dragon, the shield he shall win.

And Ethelred uplifted his mace and struck upon the head of the dragon, which fell before him, and gave up his pesty breath, with a shriek so horrid and harsh, and withal so piercing, that Ethelred had <u>fain</u> to close his ears with his hands against the dreadful noise of it, the like whereof was never before heard."

Here again I paused abruptly, and now with a feeling of wild amazement—for there could be no doubt whatever that, in this instance, I did actually hear (although from what direction it proceeded I found it impossible to say) a low and apparently distant, but harsh, **protracted**, and most unusual screaming or grating sound—the exact counterpart of what my fancy had already **conjured** up for the dragon's unnatural shriek as described by the romancer.

Oppressed, as I certainly was, upon the occurrence of this second and most extraordinary coincidence, by a

RETAIN (rih <u>tayn</u>) *v.* **-ing,-ed.**
to hold, keep possession of
Synonyms: withhold, reserve, maintain, remember

DEMEANOR (dih <u>meen</u> uhr) *n.*
one's behavior or conduct
Synonyms: attitude, disposition, manner, presence

INAUDIBLY (ihn <u>aw</u> dih blee) *adv.*
in a manner not capable of being heard
Synonyms: faintly, unclearly, imperceptibly

UNIFORM (<u>yoo</u> nuh fohrm) *adj.*
consistent and unchanging; identical
Synonyms: unvarying, steady, even, homogeneous;
indistinguishable
BRAZEN (<u>bray</u> zihn) *adj.*
1. made of or looking like brass
Synonym: flashy
2. shameless, defiant
Synonyms: brash, audacious, forward
VALOROUSLY (<u>vaa</u> luhr ihs lee) *adv.*
bravely, courageously
Synonyms: heroically, intrepidly, gallantly, valiantly

COUNTENANCE (<u>kown</u> tuh nuhns) *n.*
appearance, facial expression
Synonyms: face, features, visage

thousand conflicting sensations, in which wonder and extreme terror were predominant, I still **retained** sufficient presence of mind to avoid exciting, by any observation, the sensitive nervousness of my companion. I was by no means certain that he had noticed the sounds in question; although, assuredly, a strange alteration had, during the last few minutes, taken place in his **demeanor**. From a position fronting my own, he had gradually brought round his chair, so as to sit with his face to the door of the chamber; and thus I could but partially perceive his features, although I saw that his lips trembled as if he were murmuring **inaudibly**. His head had dropped upon his breast—yet I knew that he was not asleep, from the wide and rigid opening of the eye as I caught a glance of it in profile. The motion of his body, too, was at variance with this idea—for he rocked from side to side with a gentle yet constant and **uniform** sway. Having rapidly taken notice of all this, I resumed the narrative of Sir Launcelot, which thus proceeded:

"And now, the champion, having escaped from the terrible fury of the dragon, bethinking himself of the **brazen** shield, and of the breaking up of the enchantment which was upon it, removed the carcass from out of the way before him, and approached **valorously** over the silver pavement of the castle to where the shield was upon the wall; which in <u>sooth</u> <u>tarried</u> not for his full coming, but fell down at his feet upon the silver floor with a mighty great and terrible ringing sound."

No sooner had these syllables passed my lips, than—as if a shield of brass had indeed, at the moment, fallen heavily upon a floor of silver—I became aware of a distinct, hollow, metallic, and <u>clangorous</u>, yet apparently muffled, reverberation. Completely unnerved, I leaped to my feet; but the measured rocking movement of Usher was undisturbed. I rushed to the chair in which he sat. His eyes were bent fixedly before him and throughout his whole **countenance** there reigned a stony rigidity. But, as I

ACUTE (uh <u>kyoot</u>) *adj.*
1. sensitive, heightened; sharp, pointed; severe
   Synonyms: perceptive; piercing; intense, fierce
2. clever, shrewd
   Synonyms: ingenious, keen

UPBRAID (uhp <u>brayd</u>) *v.* **-ing,-ed.**
to scold sharply
   Synonyms: berate, tax, reproach, rebuke, chide

PONDEROUS (<u>pahn</u> duhr uhs) *adj.*
weighty, heavy, large
   Synonyms: hefty, massive, cumbersome, unwieldy
ENSHROUD or SHROUD (ehn <u>shrowd</u>) *v.* **-ing,-ed.**
to wrap up, hide from sight
   Synonyms: blanket, obscure, conceal, cloak,
   envelop
EMACIATED (ih <u>may</u> shee ay tihd) *adj.*
very thin due to hunger or disease; feeble
   Synonyms: bony, gaunt, haggard, skeletal

placed my hand upon his shoulder, there came a strong shudder over his whole person; a sickly smile quivered about his lips, and I saw that he spoke in a low, hurried, and gibbering murmur, as if unconscious of my presence. Bending closely over him, I at length drank in the hideous import of his words.

"Now hear it?—yes, I hear it, and *have* heard it. Long—long—long—many minutes, many hours, many days, have I heard it—yet I dared not—oh, pity me, miserable wretch that I am—I dared not—I *dared* not speak! *We have put her living in the tomb!* Said I not that my senses were **acute**? I *now* tell you that I heard her first feeble movements in the hollow coffin. I heard them, many, many days ago—yet I dared not—*I dared not speak*! And now—to-night—Ethelred—ha! ha!—the breaking of the hermit's door, and the death-cry of the dragon, and the clangor of the shield—say, rather, the rending of her coffin, and the grating of the iron hinges of her prison, and her struggles within the coppered archway of the vault! Oh! Whither shall I fly? Will she not be here anon? Is she not hurrying to **upbraid** me for my haste? Have I not heard her footstep on the stair? Do I not distinguish that heavy and horrible beating of her heart? Madman!"—here he sprang furiously to his feet and shrieked out his syllables as if in the effort he were giving up his soul—"*Madman! I tell you that she now stands outside the door!*"

As if in the superhuman energy of his utterance there had been found the potency of a spell, the huge antique panels to which the speaker pointed threw slowly back, upon the instant, their **ponderous** and ebony jaws. It was the work of the rushing gust—but then without those doors there *did* stand the lofty and **enshrouded** figure of the lady Madeline of Usher. There was blood upon her white robes, and the evidence of some bitter struggle upon every portion of her **emaciated** frame. For a moment she remained trembling and reeling to and fro upon the threshold—then, with a low moaning cry, fell

WRATH (raath) *n.*
anger, rage
Synonyms: fury, ire, resentment, indignation

DISCERNIBLE (dihs <u>uhrn</u> ih buhl) *adj.*
able to be perceived
Synonyms: observable, recognizable, distinguishable

TUMULTUOUS (tuh <u>muhl</u> choo uhs) *adj.*
noisy; confused and disordered
Synonyms: boisterous; turbulent, excited

SULLENLY (<u>suh</u> luhn lee) *adv.*
in a brooding and gloomy manner
Synonyms: morosely, somberly, glumly

heavily inward upon the person of her brother, and in her violent and now final death-agonies, bore him to the floor a corpse, and a victim to the terrors he had anticipated.

From that chamber, and from that mansion, I fled aghast. The storm was still abroad in all its **wrath** as I found myself crossing the old causeway. Suddenly there shot along the path a wild light, and I turned to see whence a gleam so unusual could have issued; for the vast house and its shadows were alone behind me. The radiance was that of the full, setting, and blood-red moon, which now shone vividly through that once barely **discernible** <u>fissure</u> of which I have before spoken as extending from the roof of the building, in a zigzag direction, to the base. While I gazed, this <u>fissure</u> rapidly widened—there came a fierce breath of the whirlwind— the entire <u>orb</u> of the satellite burst at once upon my sight—my brain reeled as I saw the mighty walls rushing asunder—there was a long **tumultuous** shouting sound like the voice of a thousand waters—and the deep and <u>dank</u> <u>tarn</u> at my feet closed **sullenly** and silently over the fragments of the "*House of Usher.*"

CONJECTURE (kuhn <u>jehk</u> shuhr) *n.*
  speculation, prediction
    Synonyms: postulation, hypothesis, supposition, guess
DISCOURSE (<u>dihs</u> kohrs) *v.* **-ing,-ed.**
  to talk or converse
    Synonyms: speak, discuss, lecture
SUSCEPTIBLE (suh <u>sehp</u> tuh buhl) *adj.*
  vulnerable, unprotected
    Synonyms: sensitive, impressionable, prone, subject
EXULT (ihg <u>suhlt</u>) *v.* **-ing,-ed.** *(See page 56.)*
DERIVE (dih <u>riev</u>) *v.* **-ing,-ed.** *(See page 64.)*
ENIGMA (eh <u>nihg</u> muh) *n.*
  a puzzle; an inexplicable event
    Synonyms: brainteaser, riddle; mystery
CONUNDRUM (kuh <u>nuhn</u> druhm) *n.*
  riddle, puzzle, or problem with no solution
    Synonyms: enigma, mystery, paradox
ACUMEN (<u>aak</u> yuh muhn) (uh <u>kyoo</u> muhn) *n.*
  sharpness of insight
    Synonyms: sagacity, discernment, shrewdness
APPREHENSION (aa prih <u>hehn</u> shuhn) *n.*
  the act of perceiving or comprehending; a legal
  seizure; suspicion or fear of future or unknown evil
    Synonyms: understanding; capture; concern, worry
PRETERNATURAL (pree tuhr <u>naach</u> uh ruhl) *adj.*
  extraordinary, unnatural
    Synonyms: abnormal, mysterious, odd, unearthly
INTUITION (ihn too <u>ih</u> shihn) *n.*
  instinct, innate knowledge that is not learned
    Synonyms: insight, clairvoyance, premonition
FACULTY (<u>faa</u> kuhl tee) *n. (See page 40.)*
RESOLUTION (reh suh <u>loo</u> shuhn) *n. (See page 156.)*
INVIGORATE (ihn <u>vih</u> guh rayt) *v.* **-ing,-ed.**
  to give life or energy to
    Synonyms: stimulate, strengthen, revitalize
RETROGRADE (<u>reh</u> troh grayd) *adj.*
  having a backward motion or direction
    Synonyms: inverted, reversed
PREFACE (<u>preh</u> fuhs) *v.* **-ing,-ed.**
  to give or present an introduction or opening remarks
    Synonyms: introduce, begin, precede, open

THE MURDERS IN THE RUE[23] MORGUE

What song the Syrens[24] sang, or what name Achilles[25] assumed when he hid himself among women, although puzzling questions, are not beyond *all* **conjecture**.
—*Sir Thomas Browne*

The mental features **discoursed** of as the analytical, are, in themselves, but little **susceptible** of analysis. We appreciate them only in their effects. We know of them, among other things, that they are always to their possessor, when inordinately possessed, a source of the liveliest enjoyment. As the strong man **exults** in his physical ability, delighting in such exercises as call his muscles into action, so glories the analyst in that moral activity which *disentangles*. He **derives** pleasure from even the most trivial occupations bringing his talent into play. He is fond of **enigmas**, of **conundrums**, hieroglyphics; exhibiting in his solutions of each a degree of **acumen** which appears to the ordinary **apprehension preternatural**. His results, brought about by the very soul and essence of method, have, in truth, the whole air of **intuition**.

The **faculty** of **resolution** is possibly much **invigorated** by mathematical study, and especially by that highest branch of it which, unjustly, and merely on account of its **retrograde** operations, has been called, as if *par excellence*, analysis. Yet to calculate is not in itself to analyze. A chess player, for example, does the one without effort at the other. It follows that the game of chess, in its effects upon mental character, is greatly misunderstood. I am not now writing a treatise, but simply **prefacing** a somewhat peculiar narrative by observations very much at random. I will, therefore, take occasion to assert that the

UNOSTENTATIOUS (uhn <u>ah</u> stehn tay shuhs) *adj.*
  not showy, simple
    Synonyms: ordinary, plain, familiar, unassuming
FRIVOLITY (frih <u>vahl</u> ih tee) *n.*
  triviality, silliness
    Synonyms: lightness, childishness, nonsense
PROFOUND (pruh <u>fownd</u>) (proh <u>fownd</u>) *adj.*
  deep, infinite; difficult to understand; intelligent
    Synonyms: bottomless, unending; thorough,
    weighty; smart
FLAG (flaag) *v.* **-ging,-ged.**
  to decline in vigor, strength, or interest
    Synonyms: wane, subside, ebb, dwindle, slacken
ACUTE (uh <u>kyoot</u>) *adj.*
  1. clever, shrewd
    Synonyms: ingenious, keen
  2. sharp, pointed, severe
    Synonyms: intense, fierce
INADVERTENCE (ihn uhd <u>vuhr</u> tnts) *n.*
  inattention, disrespect; an unintentional act
    Synonyms: indifference; accident, error
ACUMEN (<u>aak</u> yuh muhn) (uh <u>kyoo</u> muhn) *n.*
  sharpness of insight
    Synonyms: sagacity, discernment, shrewdness
ESCHEW (ehs <u>choo</u>) *v.* **-ing,-ed.**
  to abstain from, avoid based on principles
    Synonyms: shun, sidestep, elude
FRIVOLOUS (<u>frihv</u> uh luhs) *adj.*
  petty, trivial, flippant, silly
    Synonyms: frothy, light, vapid
FACULTY (<u>faa</u> kuhl tee) *n.*
  the ability to act or do
    Synonyms: aptitude, capability, sense, skill
PROFICIENCY (proh <u>fihsh</u> ehn see) *n.*
  expertise, skill in a certain subject
    Synonyms: adeptness, experience, competence

higher powers of the reflective intellect are more decid-edly and more usefully tasked by the **unostentatious** game of Draughts than by all the elaborate **frivolity** of chess. In this latter, where the pieces have different and bizarre motions, with various and variable values, what is only complex, is mistaken (a not unusual error) for what is **profound**. The *attention* is here called powerfully into play. If it **flags** for an instant, an oversight is committed, result-ing in injury or defeat. The possible moves being not only manifold, but involute, the chances of such oversights are multiplied; and in nine cases out of ten, it is the more con-centrative rather than the more **acute** player who con**quers**. In Draughts, on the contrary, where the moves are *unique* **and have but** little variation, the probabilities of **inadvertence** are diminished and the mere attention being left comparatively unemployed, what advantages are obtained by either party are obtained by superior **acumen**. To be less abstract, let us suppose a game of Draughts where the pieces are reduced to four kings, and where, of course, no oversight is to be expected. It is obvi-ous that here the victory can be decided (the players being at an equal) only by some *recherché* movement, the result of some strong exertion of the intellect. Deprived of ordi-nary resources, the analyst throws himself into the spirit of his opponent, identifies himself therewith, and not unfrequently sees thus, at a glance, the sole methods (sometimes indeed absurdly simple ones) by which he may seduce into error or hurry into miscalculation.

Whist has long been known for its influence upon what is termed the calculating power, and men of the highest order of intellect have been known to take appar-ently unaccountable delight in it, while **eschewing** chess as **frivolous**. Beyond doubt there is nothing of a similiar nature so greatly tasking the **faculty** of analysis. The best chess player in Christendom *may* be little more than the best player of chess; but **proficiency** in Whist implies capacity for success in all these more important

PROFICIENCY (proh <u>fihsh</u> ehn see) *n.*
expertise, skill in a certain subject
Synonyms: adeptness, experience, competence

DERIVE (dih <u>riev</u>) *v.* **-ing,-ed.**
to receive from a source, to originate
Synonyms: infer, descend, deduce, come (from)

EVINCE (ih <u>vihns</u>) *v.* **-ing,-ed.**
to show clearly or display
Synonyms: express, exhibit, demonstrate, manifest

COUNTENANCE (<u>kown</u> tuh nuhns) *n.*
appearance, facial expression
Synonyms: face, features, visage

BESTOW (bih <u>stoh</u>) *v.* **-ing,-ed.**
to apply or devote time or effort; to give as a gift
Synonyms: allocate, dedicate; endow, confer, present

CHAGRIN (shuh <u>grihn</u>) *n.*
shame, embarrassment, humiliation
Synonyms: mortification, discomfiture

INADVERTENT (ihn uhd <u>vuhr</u> tnt) *adj.*
unintentional
Synonyms: accidental, involuntary

undertakings where mind struggles with mind. When I say **proficiency**, I mean that perfection in the game which includes a comprehension of *all* the sources whence legitimate advantage may be **derived**. These are not only <u>manifold</u>, but multiform, and lie frequently among recesses of thought altogether inaccessible to the ordinary understanding. To observe attentively is to remember distinctly; and, so far, the concentrative chess-player will do very well at Whist; while the rules of Hoyle (themselves based upon the mere mechanism of the game) are sufficiently and generally comprehensible. Thus to have a retentive memory and proceed by "the book" are points commonly regarded as the sum total of good playing. But it is in matters beyond the limits of mere rule that the skill of the analyst is **evinced**. He makes, in silence, a host of observations and inferences. So, perhaps, do his companions; and the difference in the extent of the information obtained, lies not so much in the validity of the inference as in the quality of the observation. The necessary knowledge is that of *what* to observe. Our player confines himself not at all; nor, because the game is the object, does he reject deductions from things external to the game. He examines the **countenance** of his partner, comparing it carefully with that of each of his opponents. He considers the mode of assorting the cards in each hand; often counting trump by trump, and honor by honor, through the glances **bestowed** by their holders upon each. He notes every variation of face as the play progresses, gathering a fund of thought from the differences in the expression of certainty, of surprise, of triumph, or **chagrin**. From the manner of gathering up a trick he judges whether the person taking it, can make another in the suit. He recognizes what is played through <u>feint</u>, by the manner with which it is thrown upon the table. A casual or **inadvertent** word; the accidental dropping or turning of a card, with the accompanying anxiety or carelessness in

TREPIDATION (treh pih <u>day</u> shuhn) *n.*
  fear, anxiety
    Synonyms: alarm, dread, apprehension, fright
INTUITIVE (ihn <u>too</u> ih tihv) *adj.*
  instinctive, untaught
    Synonyms: visceral, innate
CONFOUND (kuhn <u>fownd</u>) *v.* **-ing,-ed.**
  to mistake something for another; to baffle, perplex
    Synonyms: confuse, misidentify; overwhelm,
    disconcert, entangle
INGENUITY (ihn jeh <u>noo</u> ih tee) *n.*
  cleverness
    Synonyms: inventiveness, imagination, creativity
INGENIOUS (ih <u>jeen</u> yuhs) *adj.*
  original, clever, inventive
    Synonyms: shrewd, cunning, imaginative
MANIFEST (<u>maan</u> uh fehst) *v.* **-ing,-ed.**
  to make evident or certain by display
    Synonyms: exhibit, showcase, expose
ERRONEOUSLY (eh <u>roh</u> nee uhs lee) *adv.*
  mistakenly
    Synonyms: incorrectly, falsely
FACULTY (<u>faa</u> kuhl tee) *n.*
  the ability to act or do
    Synonyms: aptitude, capability, sense, skill
ANALOGOUS (uh <u>naal</u> uh guhs) *adj.*
  drawing a likeness, parallel
    Synonyms: akin, corresponding, correlative,
    homologous, similar
ILLUSTRIOUS (ih <u>luhs</u> tree uhs) *adj.*
  famous, renowned
    Synonyms: noted, celebrated, eminent
RETRIEVAL (rih <u>tree</u> vuhl) *n.*
  the act of reclaiming; the act of bringing or fetching
    Synonyms: recovery, salvage; acquiring
PATRIMONY (<u>paa</u> trih moh nee) *n.*
  inheritance
    Synonyms: estate, possessions, endowment

regard to its concealment; the counting of the tricks, with the order of their arrangement; embarrassment, hesitation, eagerness, or trepidation—all afford, to his apparently intuitive perception, indications of the true state of affairs. The first two or three rounds having been played, he is in full possession of the contents of each hand, and thenceforward puts down his cards with as absolute a precision of purpose as if the rest of the party had turned outward the faces of their own.

The analytical power should not be confounded with simple ingenuity; for while the analyst is necessarily ingenious, the ingenious man is often remarkably incapable of analysis. The constructive or combining power, by which ingenuity is usually manifested, and to which the phrenologists (I believe erroneously) have assigned a separate organ, supposing it a primitive faculty, has been so frequently seen in those whose intellect bordered otherwise upon idiocy, as to have attracted general observation among writers on morals. Between ingenuity and the analytic ability there exists a difference far greater, indeed, than that between the fancy and the imagination, but of a character very strictly analogous. It will be found, in fact, that the ingenious are always fanciful, and the truly imaginative never otherwise than analytic.

The narrative which follows will appear to the reader somewhat in the light of a commentary upon the propositions just advanced.

Residing in Paris during the spring and part of the summer of 18—, I there became acquainted with a Monsieur C. Auguste Dupin. This young gentleman was of an excellent, indeed of an illustrious family, but, by a variety of untoward events, had been reduced to such poverty that the energy of his character succumbed beneath it, and he ceased to bestir himself in the world or to care for the retrieval of his fortunes. By courtesy of his creditors, there still remained in his possession a small remnant of his patrimony; and upon the income arising

PROCURE (proh <u>kyoor</u>) *v.* **-ing,-ed.**
to obtain
Synonyms: acquire, secure, get, gain

SUPERFLUITY (soo puhr <u>floo</u> ih tee) *n.*
something that is extra or more than necessary
Synonyms: excess, spare, surplus

LUXURY (<u>luhg</u> zhoor ee) *n.*
something done or had purely for enjoyment
Synonyms: comfort, indulgence, splendor, frill

OBSCURE (uhb <u>skyoor</u>) *adj.*
not well known; dim, unclear
Synonyms: remote, minor; dark, faint

CANDOR (<u>kaan</u> dohr) *n.*
honest expression
Synonyms: frankness, sincerity, bluntness

INDULGE (ihn <u>duhlj</u>) *v.* **-ing,-ed.**
to give in, as to a craving or desire
Synonyms: humor, gratify, allow, pamper

ENKINDLE (ehn <u>kihn</u> duhl) *v.* **-ing,-ed.**
to excite or inspire; to set fire to or ignite
Synonyms: arouse, awaken; light, spark

FERVOUR or FERVOR (<u>fuhr</u> vuhr) *n.*
passion, intensity, zeal
Synonyms: vehemence, eagerness, enthusiasm

TOTTER (<u>tah</u> tuhr) *v.* **-ing,-ed.**
to stand with much unsteadiness
Synonyms: wobble, sway, reel, stagger

DESOLATE (<u>deh</u> soh liht) *adj.*
showing the effects of abandonment or neglect;
devoid of warmth or comfort
Synonyms: barren, bleak, vacant; dreary, dismal

SECLUSION (sih <u>cloo</u> zhuhn) *n.*
isolation, detachment
Synonyms: separation, privacy, solitude

from this, he managed, by means of a rigorous economy, to procure the necessities of life without troubling himself about its superfluities. Books, indeed, were his sole luxuries, and in Paris these are easily obtained.

Our first meeting was at an obscure library in the Rue Montmartre, where the accident of our both being in search of the same very rare and very remarkable volume, brought us into closer communion. We saw each other again and again. I was deeply interested in the little family history which he detailed to me with all that candor which a Frenchman indulges whenever mere self is the theme. I was astonished, too, at the vast extent of his reading and, above all, I felt my soul enkindled within me by the wild fervor and the vivid freshness of his imagination. Seeking in Paris the objects I then sought, I felt that the society of such a man would be to me a treasure beyond price; and this feeling I frankly confided to him. It was at length arranged that we should live together during my stay in the city; and as my worldly circumstances were somewhat less embarrassed than his own, I was permitted to be at the expense of renting, and furnishing in a style which suited the rather fantastic gloom of our common temper, a time-eaten and grotesque mansion, long deserted through superstitions into which we did not inquire, and tottering to its fall in a retired and desolate portion of the Faubourg St. Germain.

Had the routine of our life at this place been known to the world, we should have been regarded as madmen—although, perhaps, as madmen of a harmless nature. Our seclusion was perfect. We admitted no visitors. Indeed the locality of our retirement had been carefully kept a secret from my own former associates; and it had been many years since Dupin had ceased to know or be known in Paris. We existed within ourselves alone.

It was a freak of fancy in my friend (for what else shall I call it?) to be enamored of the night for her own sake; and into this *bizarrerie*, as into all his others, I quietly fell;

WHIM (wihm) *n.*
a playful or fanciful idea
Synonyms: caprice, impulse, dream, vision, fantasy
ABANDON (uh <u>baan</u> duhn) *n.*
total lack of inhibition
Synonyms: exuberance, enthusiasm
DIVINITY (dih <u>vihn</u> ih tee) *n.*
a supreme being, a god
Synonyms: deity, immortal, godhead

IDEALITY (ie dee <u>aal</u> ih tee) *n.*
a state of being perfect or ideal, an unobtainable idea
Synonyms: impracticality, quixoticism,
romanticism
DERIVE (dih <u>riev</u>) *v.* **-ing,-ed.**
to receive from a source, to originate
Synonyms: infer, descend, deduce, come (from)

PETULANT (<u>peh</u> chuh luhnt) *adj.*
rude, peevish
Synonyms: irritable, querulous, testy, fretful
ENUNCIATION (ih nuhn see <u>ay</u> shuhn) *n.*
the act of pronouncing clearly, speaking
Synonyms: articulation, stating, utterance
RESOLVENT (rih <u>sahlv</u> ihnt) *adj.*
determined, stubborn
Synonyms: decisive, persevering

giving myself up to his wild **whims** with a perfect **abandon**. The <u>sable</u> **divinity** would not herself dwell with us always; but we could counterfeit her presence. At the first dawn of the morning we closed all the massy shutters of our old building; lighted a couple of tapers which, strongly perfumed, threw out only the ghastliest and feeblest of rays. By the aid of these we then busied our souls in dreams—reading, writing, or conversing, until warned by the clock of the <u>advent</u> of true Darkness. Then we <u>sallied</u> forth into the streets, arm in arm, continuing the topics of the day, or roaming far and wide until a late hour, seeking, amid the wild lights and shadows of the populous city, that infinity of mental excitement which quiet observation can afford.

At such times I could not help remarking and admiring (although from his rich **ideality** I had been prepared to expect it) a peculiar analytic ability in Dupin. He seemed, too, to take an eager delight in its exercise—if not exactly in its display—and did not hesitate to confess the pleasure thus **derived**. He boasted to me, with a low chuckling laugh, that most men, in respect to himself, wore windows in their bosoms, and was wont to follow up such assertions by direct and very startling proofs of his ultimate knowledge of my own. His manner at these moments was frigid and abstract; his eyes were vacant in expression; while his voice, usually a rich tenor, rose into a <u>treble</u> which would have sounded **petulant** but for the deliberateness and entire distinctness of the **enunciation**. Observing him in these moods, I often dwelt meditatively upon the old philosophy of the Bi-Part Soul, and amused myself with the fancy of a double Dupin—the creative and the **resolvent**.

Let it not be supposed, from what I have just said, that I am detailing any mystery or penning any romance. What I have described in the Frenchman was merely the result of an excited, or perhaps of a diseased, intelligence. But of the character of his remarks at the periods in question, an example will best convey the idea.

UNWITTINGLY (uhn <u>wih</u> ting lee) *adv.*
unconsciously, unintentionally
Synonyms: obliviously, inadvertently

PROFOUND (pruh <u>fownd</u>) (proh <u>fownd</u>) *adj.*
deep, infinite; intelligent; difficult to understand
Synonyms: bottomless, unending; smart; thorough, weighty

ASCERTAIN (aa suhr <u>tayn</u>) *v.* **-ing,-ed.**
to determine, discover, make certain of
Synonyms: verify, calculate, detect

DIMINUTIVE (dih <u>mihn</u> yuh tihv) *adj.*
small
Synonyms: short, tiny, wee, minuscule

NOTORIOUSLY (noh <u>tohr</u> ee uhs lee) *adv.*
in an unfavorable and public way
Synonyms: infamously, disgracefully, dishonorably

FATHOM (<u>faath</u> uhm) *v.* **-ing,-ed.**
to understand fully; to measure the depth of, gauge
Synonyms: comprehend; sound

We were strolling one night down a long dirty street, in the vicinity of the Palais Royal. Being both apparently occupied with thought, neither of us had spoken a syllable for fifteen minutes at least. All at once Dupin broke forth with these words:

"He is a very little fellow, that's true, and would do better for the *Théâtre des Variétés*." [26]

"There can be no doubt of that," I replied, **unwittingly**, and not at first observing (so much had I been absorbed in reflection) the extraordinary manner in which the speaker had chimed in with my meditations. In an instant afterward I recollected myself, and my astonishment was **profound**.

"Dupin," said I, gravely, "this is beyond my comprehension. I do not hesitate to say that I am amazed, and can scarcely credit my senses. How was it possible you should know I was thinking of—" Here I paused, to **ascertain** beyond a doubt whether he really knew of whom I thought.

"—of Chantilly," said he. "Why do you pause? You were remarking to yourself that his **diminutive** figure unfitted him for tragedy."

This was precisely what had formed the subject of my reflections. Chantilly was a *quondam* cobbler of the Rue St. Denis, who, becoming stage-mad, had attempted the *rôle* of Xerxes, in Crébillon's tragedy [27] so called, and been **notoriously** pasquinaded [28] for his pains.

"Tell me, for Heaven's sake," I exclaimed, "the method—if method there is—by which you have been enabled to **fathom** my soul in this matter." In fact, I was even more startled than I would have been willing to express.

"It was the fruiterer," replied my friend, "who brought you to the conclusion that the mender of soles was not of sufficient height for Xerxes *et id genus omne*." [29]

"The fruiterer! You astonish me—I know no fruiterer whomsoever."

ILLIMITABLE (ih lih <u>miht</u> uh buhl) *adj.*
   not having a limit or boundary, endless
      Synonyms: infinite, vast, immeasurable
INCOHERENCE (ihn koh <u>hihr</u> uhnts) *n.*
   lack of cohesion or connection; the inability to express
   one's thoughts in a clear or orderly manner
      Synonyms: disorder, disarray; confusion

VEXED (vehksd) *adj.*
   irritated, annoyed; confused, puzzled
      Synonyms: bothered, plagued, afflicted, irked;
      perplexed, perturbed

"The man who ran up against you as we entered the street—it may have been fifteen minutes ago."

I now remembered that, in fact, a fruiterer, carrying upon his head a large basket of apples, had nearly thrown me down, by accident, as we passed from the Rue C—— into the thoroughfare where we stood; but what this had to do with Chantilly I could not possibly understand.

There was not a particle of *charlatânerie*[30] about Dupin. "I will explain," he said, "and that you may comprehend all clearly, we will first retrace the course of your meditations, from the moment in which I spoke to you until that of the *rencontre* with the fruiterer in question. The larger links of the chain run thus—Chantilly, Orion, Dr. Nichols, Epicurus,[31] <u>Stereotomy</u>, the street stones, the fruiterer."

There are few persons who have not, at some period of their lives, amused themselves in retracing the steps by which particular conclusions of their own minds have been attained. The occupation is often full of interest; and he who attempts it for the first time is astonished by the apparently **illimitable** distance and **incoherence** between the starting-point and the goal. What, then, must have been my amazement, when I heard the Frenchman speak what he had just spoken, and when I could not help acknowledging that he had spoken the truth. He continued:

"We had been talking of horses, if I remember aright, just before leaving the Rue C——. This was the last subject we discussed. As we crossed into this street, a fruiterer with a large basket upon his head, brushing quickly past us, thrust you upon a pile of paving-stones collected at a spot where the causeway is undergoing repair. You stepped upon one of the loose fragments, slipped, slightly strained your ankle, appeared **vexed** or sulky, muttered a few words, turned to look at the pile, and then proceeded in silence. I was not particularly attentive to what you did; but observation has become with me, of late, a species of necessity.

PETULANT (<u>peh</u> chuh luhnt) *adj.*
  rude, peevish
    Synonyms: irritable, querulous, testy, fretful

COUNTENANCE (<u>kown</u> tuh nuhns) *n.*
  appearance, facial expression
    Synonyms: face, features, visage

NEBULAR (<u>neh</u> byoo luhr) *adj.*
  relating to a cloud of interstellar gas or dust; vague,
  cloudy
    Synonyms: galactic; misty, hazy, fuzzy, unclear
TIRADE (<u>tie</u> rayd) (tie <u>rayd</u>) *n.*
  long, violent speech, a verbal assault
    Synonyms: diatribe, fulmination, harangue,
    jeremiad, philippic
ALLUSION (uh <u>loo</u> zhuhn) *n.*
  indirect reference
    Synonyms: intimation, suggestion
PUNGENCY (<u>puhn</u> juhn see) *n.*
  strength or sharpness, as in smell or taste
    Synonyms: acridity, bite, piquancy, keenness
GAIT (gayt) *n.*
  the way one moves on foot, a manner of walking
    Synonyms: tread, walk, march, pace
DRAW *v.* **-ing, drew, drawn**
  to pull, drag; to lead, to bring about on purpose;
  to attract or be attracted to
    Synonyms: haul, tow, yank; provoke, elicit; lure,
    entice

"You kept your eyes upon the ground—glancing, with a **petulant** expression, at the holes and ruts in the pavement (so that I saw you were still thinking of the stones), until we reached the little alley called Lamartine, which has been paved, by way of experiment, with the overlapping and riveted blocks. Here your **countenance** brightened up, and, perceiving your lips move, I could not doubt that you murmured the word 'stereotomy,' a term very affectedly applied to this species of pavement. I knew that you could not say to yourself 'stereotomy' without being brought to think of atomies, and thus of the theories of Epicurus;[31] and since, when we discussed this subject not very long ago, I mentioned to you how singularly, yet with how little notice, the vague guesses of that noble Greek had met with confirmation in the late **nebular** cosmogony, I felt that you could not avoid casting your eyes upward to the great *nebula* in Orion, and I certainly expected that you would do so. You did look up; and I was now assured that I had correctly followed your steps. But in that bitter **tirade** upon Chantilly, which appeared in yesterday's '*Musée*,' the satirist, making some disgraceful **allusions** to the cobbler's change of name upon assuming the buskin,[32] quoted a Latin line about which we have often conversed. I mean the line

Perdidit antiquum litera prima sonum.[33]

"I had told you that this was in reference to Orion, formerly written Urion; and, from certain **pungencies** connected with this explanation, I was aware that you could not have forgotten it. It was clear, therefore, that you would not fail to combine the two ideas of Orion and Chantilly. That you did combine them I saw by the character of the smile which passed over your lips. You thought of the poor cobbler's immolation. So far, you had been stooping in your **gait**; but now I saw you **draw** yourself up to your full height. I was then sure that you

DIMINUTIVE (dih <u>mihn</u> yuh tihv) *adj.*
  small
    Synonyms: short, tiny, wee, minuscule

PROCURE (proh <u>kyoor</u>) *v.* **-ing,-ed.**
  to obtain
    Synonyms: acquire, secure, get, gain

CONTENTION (kuhn <u>tehn</u> shuhn) *n.*
  a quarrel or disagreement; competition
    Synonyms: controversy, argument; rivalry

reflected upon the **diminutive** figure of Chantilly. At this point I interrupted your meditations to remark that as, in fact, he was a very little fellow—that Chantilly—he would do better at the *Théâtre des Variétés*."

Not long after this, we were looking over an evening edition of the *Gazette des Tribunaux*, when the following paragraphs arrested our attention.

"EXTRAORDINARY MURDERS—This morning, about three o'clock, the inhabitants of the Quartier St. Roch were roused from sleep by a succession of terrific shrieks, issuing, apparently, from the fourth story of a house in the Rue Morgue, known to be in the sole occupancy of one Madame L'Espanaye, and her daughter, Mademoiselle Camille L'Espanaye. After some delay, occasioned by a fruitless attempt to **procure** admission the usual manner, the gateway was broken in with a crowbar, and eight or ten of the neighbors entered, accompanied by two *gendarmes*.[34] By this time the cries had ceased; but, as the party rushed up the first flight of stairs, two or more rough voices, in angry **contention**, were distinguished, and seemed to proceed from the upper part of the house. As the second landing was reached, these sounds, also, had ceased and every thing remained perfectly quiet. The party spread themselves and hurried from room to room. Upon arriving at a huge back chamber in the fourth story (the door of which, being found locked with the key inside, was forced open), a spectacle presented itself which struck every one present not less with horror than with astonishment.

"The apartment was in the wildest disorder—the furniture broken and thrown about in all directions. There was only one bedstead, and from this the bed had been removed and thrown into the middle of the floor. On a chair lay a razor, besmeared with blood. On the hearth were two or three long and thick tresses of gray human hair, also dabbled with blood, and seeming to have been pulled out by the roots. Upon the floor were found four

RETAIN (rih <u>tayn</u>) *v.* **-ing,-ed.**
    to hold, keep possession of
        Synonyms: withhold, reserve, maintain, remember

LEVITY (<u>leh</u> vih tee) *n.*
    humor, frivolity, gaiety
        Synonyms: lightness, amusement, cheer

Napoleons, an ear-ring of topaz, three large silver spoons, three smaller of *métal d'Alger*, and two bags, containing nearly four thousand francs in gold. The drawers of a *bureau*, which stood in one corner, were open, and had been, apparently, rifled, although many articles still remained in them. A small iron safe was discovered under the bed (not under the bedstead). It was open, with the key still in the door. It had no contents beyond a few old letters, and other papers of little consequence.

"Of Madame L'Espanaye no traces were here seen; but an unusual quantity of soot being observed in the fire-place, a search was made in the chimney, and (horrible to relate!) the corpse of the daughter, head downward, was dragged therefrom; it having been thus forced up the narrow <u>aperture</u> for a considerable distance. The body was quite warm. Upon examining it, many <u>excoriations</u> were perceived, no doubt occasioned by the violence with which it had been thrust up and disengaged. Upon the face were many severe scratches, and, upon the throat, dark bruises, and deep indentations of finger nails, as if the deceased had been throttled to death.

"After a thorough investigation of every portion of the house without farther discovery, the party made its way into a small paved yard in the rear of the building, where lay the corpse of the old lady, with her throat so entirely cut that, upon an attempt to raise her, the head fell off. The body, as well as the head, was fearfully mutilated—the former so much so as scarcely to **retain** any semblance of humanity.

"To this horrible mystery there is not as yet, we believe, the slightest clue."

The next day's paper had these additional particulars:

"*The Tragedy in the Rue Morgue*—Many individuals have been examined in relation to this most extraordinary and frightful affair," [the word '*affaire*' has not yet, in France, that **levity** of import which it conveys with us]

ELICIT (ih <u>lih</u> siht) *v.* **-ing,-ed.**
  to draw out, provoke
    Synonyms: evoke, educe, wring, extract, tap
DEPOSE (dih <u>pohs</u>) *v.* **-ing,-ed.**
  to testify; to remove from a high position
    Synonyms: declare, charge, affirm; dethrone,
    overthrow, displace

"but nothing whatsoever has transpired to throw light upon it. We give below all the material testimony **elicited**.

"*Pauline Dubourg*, laundress, **deposes** that she has known both the deceased for three years, having washed for them during that period. The old lady and her daughter seemed on good terms—very affectionate toward each other. They were excellent pay. Could not speak in regard to their mode or means of living. Believe that Madame L. told fortunes for a living. Was reputed to have money put by. Never met any person in the house when she called for the clothes or took them home. Was sure that they had no servant in employ. There appeared to be no furniture in any part of the building except in the fourth story.

"*Pierre Moreau*, tobacconist, **deposes** that he has been in the habit of selling small quantities of tobacco and snuff to Madame L'Espanaye for nearly four years. Was born in the neighborhood, and has always resided there. The deceased and her daughter had occupied the house in which the corpses were found, for more than six years. It was formerly occupied by a jeweller, who underlet the upper rooms to various persons. The house was the property of Madame L. She became dissatisfied with the abuse of the premises by her tenant, and moved into them herself, refusing to let any portion. The old lady was childish. Witness had seen the daughter some five or six times during the six years. The two lived an exceedingly retired life—were reputed to have money. Had heard it said among the neighbors that Madame L. told fortunes—did not believe it. Had never seen any person enter the door except the old lady and her daughter, a porter once or twice, and a physician some eight or ten times.

"Many other persons and neighbors gave evidence to the same effect. No one was spoken of as frequenting the house. It was not known whether there were any living connections of Madame L. and her daughter. The shutters of the front windows were seldom opened. Those in the rear were always closed, with the exception of the

DEPOSE (dih <u>pohs</u>) *v.* **-ing,-ed.**
to testify; to remove from a high position
Synonyms: declare, charge, affirm; dethrone,
overthrow, displace

CONTENTION (kuhn <u>tehn</u> shuhn) *n.*
a quarrel or disagreement; competition
Synonyms: controversy, argument; rivalry

CORROBORATE (kuh <u>rahb</u> uhr ayt) *v.* **-ing,-ed.**
to confirm, verify
Synonyms: prove, substantiate, warrant

large back room, fourth story. The house was a good house—not very old.

"*Isidore Musèt, gendarme,*[34] **deposes** that he was called to the house about three o'clock in the morning and found some twenty or thirty persons at the gateway, endeavoring to gain admittance. Forced it open, at length, with a bayonet—not with a crowbar. Had but little difficulty in getting it open, on account of its being a double or folding gate, and bolted neither at bottom nor top. The shrieks were continued until the gate was forced—and then suddenly ceased. They seemed to be screams of some person (or persons) in great agony—were loud and drawn out, not short and quick. Witness led the way up stairs. Upon reaching the first landing, heard two voices in loud and angry **contention**—the one a gruff voice, the other much shriller—a very strange voice. Could distinguish some words of the former, which was that of a Frenchman. Was positive that it was not a woman's voice. Could distinguish the words '*sacré*' and '*diable.*'[35] The shrill voice was that of a foreigner. Could not be sure whether it was the voice of a man or of a woman. Could not make out what was said, but believed the language to be Spanish. The state of the room and of the bodies was described by this witness as we described them yesterday.

"*Henri Duval*, a neighbor, and by trade a silver-smith, **deposes** that he was one of the party who first entered the house. **Corroborates** the testimony of Musèt in general. As soon as they forced an entrance, they reclosed the door, to keep out the crowd, which collected very fast, notwithstanding the lateness of the hour. The shrill voice, this witness thinks, was that of an Italian. Was certain it was not French. Could not be sure that it was a man's voice. It might have been a woman's. Was not acquainted with the Italian language. Could not distinguish the words, but was convinced by the intonation that the speaker was an Italian. Knew Madame L. and her daugh-

CORROBORATE (kuh <u>rahb</u> uhr ayt) *v.* **-ing,-ed.**
  to confirm, verify
    Synonyms: prove, substantiate, warrant

DEPOSE (dih <u>pohs</u>) *v.* **-ing,-ed.**
  to testify; to remove from a high position
    Synonyms: declare, charge, affirm; dethrone,
    overthrow, displace

ASCEND (uh <u>sehnd</u>) *v.* **-ing,-ed.**
  to rise to another level or climb; to move upward
    Synonyms: elevate, escalate, mount; hoist, lift
CONTENTION (kuhn <u>tehn</u> shuhn) *n.*
  a quarrel or disagreement; competition
    Synonyms: controversy, argument; rivalry

ter. Had conversed with both frequently. Was sure that the shrill voice was not that of either of the deceased.

"*Odenheimer, restaurateur*—This witness volunteered his testimony. Not speaking French, was examined through an interpreter. Is a native of Amsterdam. Was passing the house at the time of the shrieks. They lasted for several minutes—probably ten. They were long and loud—very awful and distressing. Was one of those who entered the building. **Corroborated** the previous evidence in every respect but one. Was sure that the shrill voice was that of a man—of a Frenchman. Could not distinguish the words uttered. They were loud and quick—unequal—spoken apparently in fear as well as in anger. The voice was harsh—not so much shrill as harsh. Could not call it a shrill voice. The gruff voice said repeatedly, '*sacré*,' '*diable*,'[35] and once '*mon Dieu*.'[36]

"*Jules Mignaud*, banker, of the firm of Mignaud et Fils, Rue Deloraine. Is the elder Mignaud. Madame L'Espanaye had some property. Had opened an account with his banking house in the spring of the year —— (eight years previously). Made frequent deposits in small sums. Had checked for nothing until the third day before her death, when she took out in person the sum of 4000 francs. This sum was paid in gold, and a clerk sent home with the money.

"*Adolphe Le Bon*, clerk to Mignaud et Fils, **deposes** that on the day in question, about noon, he accompanied Madame L'Espanaye to her residence with the 4000 francs, put up in two bags. Upon the door being opened, Mademoiselle L. appeared and took from his hands one of the bags, while the old lady relieved him of the other. He then bowed and departed. Did not see any person in the street at the time. It is a by-street—very lonely.

"*William Bird*, tailor, **deposes** that he was one of the party who entered the house. Is an Englishman. Has lived in Paris two years. Was one of the first to **ascend** the stairs. Heard the voices in **contention**. The gruff voice was

DEPOSE (dih pohs) *v.* **-ing,-ed.**
  to testify; to remove from a high position
    Synonyms: declare, charge, affirm; dethrone,
    overthrow, displace

CONTENTION (kuhn tehn shuhn) *n.*
  a quarrel or disagreement; competition
    Synonyms: controversy, argument; rivalry
APPREHENSIVE (aa prih hehn sihv) *adj.*
  suspicious or fearful of future or unknown evil
    Synonyms: concerned, worried
AGITATION (aa gih tay shuhn) *n.*
  uneasiness; commotion, excitement
    Synonyms: restlessness, anxiety; disturbance

that of a Frenchman. Could make out several words, but cannot now remember all. Heard distinctly '*sacré*'[35] and '*mon Dieu*.'[36] There was a sound at the moment as if of several persons struggling—a scraping and scuffling sound. The shrill voice was very loud—louder than the gruff one. Is sure that it was not the voice of an Englishman. Appeared to be that of a German. Might have been a woman's voice. Does not understand German.

"Four of the above-named witnesses, being recalled, **deposed** that the door of the chamber in which was found the body of Mademoiselle L. was locked on the inside when the party reached it. Every thing was perfectly silent—no groans or noises of any kind. Upon forcing the door no person was seen. The windows, both of the back and front room, were down and firmly fastened from within. A door between the two rooms was closed but not locked. The door leading from the front room into the passage was locked, with the key on the inside. A small room in the front of the house, on the fourth story, at the head of the passage, was open, the door being ajar. This room was crowded with old beds, boxes, and so forth. These were carefully removed and searched. There was not an inch of any portion of the house which was not carefully searched. Sweeps were sent up and down the chimneys. The house was a four-story one, with <u>garrets</u> (*mansardes*). A trap-door on the roof was nailed down very securely—did not appear to have been opened for years. The time elapsing between the hearing of the voices in **contention** and the breaking open of the room door was variously stated by the witnesses. Some made it as short as three minutes—some as long as five. The door was opened with difficulty.

"*Alfonzo Garcio*, undertaker, **deposes** that he resides in the Rue Morgue. Is a native of Spain. Was one of the party who entered the house. Did not proceed up stairs. Is nervous, and was **apprehensive** of the consequences of **agitation**. Heard the voices in **contention**. The gruff voice

DEPOSE (dih <u>pohs</u>) *v.* **-ing,-ed.**
    to testify; to remove from a high position
        Synonyms: declare, charge, affirm; dethrone,
        overthrow, displace

ASCEND (uh <u>sehnd</u>) *v.* **-ing,-ed.**
    to rise to another level or climb; to move upward
        Synonyms: elevate, escalate, mount; hoist, lift

EXPOSTULATE (ihk <u>spahs</u> chuh layt) *v.* **-ing,-ed.**
    to reason earnestly with another; to discuss or examine
        Synonyms: argue, protest, dissuade; debate

CORROBORATE (kuh <u>rahb</u> uhr ayt) *v.* **-ing,-ed.**
    to confirm, verify
        Synonyms: prove, substantiate, warrant

DESCEND (dih <u>sehnd</u>) (dee <u>sehnd</u>) *v.* **-ing,-ed.**
    to pass from a higher place to a lower place
        Synonyms: fall, dismount, gravitate

LIVID (<u>lih</u> vihd) *adj.*
    discolored from a bruise; pale; reddened with anger
        Synonyms: black-and-blue; ashen, pallid; furious

was that of a Frenchman. Could not distinguish what was said. The shrill voice was that of an Englishman—is sure of this. Does not understand the English language, but judges by the intonation.

"*Alberto Montani*, confectioner, **deposes** that he was among the first to **ascend** the stairs. Heard the voices in question. The gruff voice was that of a Frenchman. Distinguished several words. The speaker appeared to be **expostulating**. Could not make out the words of the shrill voice. Spoke quick and unevenly. Thinks it the voice of a Russian. **Corroborates** the general testimony. Is an Italian. Never conversed with a native of Russia.

"Several witnesses, recalled, here testified that the chimneys of all the rooms on the fourth story were too narrow to admit the passage of a human being. By 'sweeps' were meant cylindrical sweeping-brushes, such as are employed by those who clean chimneys. These brushes were passed up and down every flue in the house. There is no back passage by which any one could have **descended** while the party proceeded up stairs. The body of Mademoiselle L'Espanaye was so firmly wedged in the chimney that it could not be got down until four or five of the party united their strength.

"*Paul Dumas*, physician, **deposes** that he was called to view the bodies about daybreak. They were both then lying on the sacking of the bedstead in the chamber where Mademoiselle L. was found. The corpse of the young lady was much bruised and excoriated. The fact that it had been thrust up the chimney would sufficiently account for these appearances. The throat was greatly chafed. There were several deep scratches just below the chin, together with a series of **livid** spots which were evidently the impression of fingers. The face was fearfully discolored, and the eyeballs protruded. The tongue had been partially bitten through. A large bruise was discovered upon the pit of the stomach, produced, apparently, by the pressure of a knee. In the opinion of M. Dumas,

OBTUSE (uhb <u>toos</u>) *adj.*
   dull; insensitive, stupid, lacking intellect
     Synonyms: blunt; slow, dense, dim

CORROBORATE (kuh <u>rahb</u> uhr ayt) *v.* **-ing,-ed.**
   to confirm, verify
     Synonyms: prove, substantiate, warrant
ELICIT (ih <u>lih</u> siht) *v.* **-ing,-ed.**
   to draw out, provoke
     Synonyms: evoke, educe, wring, extract, tap

Mademoiselle L'Espanaye had been throttled to death by some person or persons unknown. The corpse of the mother was horribly mutilated. All the bones of the right leg and arm were more or less shattered. The left tibia much splintered, as well as all the ribs of the left side. Whole body dreadfully bruised and discolored. It was not possible to say how the injuries had been inflicted. A heavy club of wood, or a broad bar of iron—a chair—any large, heavy, and obtuse weapon would have produced such results, if wielded by the hands of a very powerful man. No woman could have inflicted the blows with any weapon. The head of the deceased, when seen by witness, was entirely separated from the body, and was also greatly shattered. The throat had evidently been cut with some very sharp instrument—probably with a razor.

"*Alexandre Etienne*, surgeon, was called with M. Dumas to view the bodies. Corroborated the testimony, and the opinions of M. Dumas.

"Nothing further of importance was elicited, although several other persons were examined. A murder so mysterious, and so perplexing in all its particulars, was never before committed in Paris—if indeed a murder has been committed at all. The police are entirely at fault—an unusual occurrence in affairs of this nature. There is not, however, the shadow of a clue apparent."

The evening edition of the paper stated that the greatest excitement still continued in the Quartier St. Roch—that the premises in question had been carefully re-searched, and fresh examinations of witnesses instituted, but all to no purpose. A postscript, however, mentioned that Adolphe Le Bon had been arrested and imprisoned—although nothing appeared to criminate him beyond the facts already detailed.

Dupin seemed singularly interested in the progress of this affair—at least so I judged from his manner, for he made no comments. It was only after the announcement

EXTOL (ihk <u>stohl</u>) *v.* **-ling,-led.**
to praise
Synonyms: acclaim, commend, laud, exalt, eulogize
ACUMEN (<u>aak</u> yuh muhn) (uh <u>kyoo</u> muhn) *n.*
sharpness of insight
Synonyms: sagacity, discernment, shrewdness
ILL-ADAPTED (ihl uh <u>daap</u> tihd) *adj.*
unaccustomed, poorly equipped
Synonyms: unprepared, unfit, unaccomodating
DILIGENCE (<u>dihl</u> uh juhns) *n.*
steady, earnest application of effort
Synonyms: perseverance, attentiveness
UNAVAILING (uhn uh <u>vayl</u> ihng) *adj.*
of no use or advantage
Synonyms: futile, ineffectual, worthless
PERSEVERING (pehr suh <u>veer</u> ihng) *adj.*
determined, steadfast
Synonyms: persistent, enduring, plodding
IMPAIR (ihm <u>payr</u>) *v.* **-ing,-ed.**
to damage, injure
Synonyms: harm, hurt, mar, spoil
PROFOUND (pruh <u>fownd</u>) (proh <u>fownd</u>) *adj.*
deep, infinite; intelligent; difficult to understand
Synonyms: bottomless, unending; smart; thorough,
weighty
SUPERFICIAL (soo puhr <u>fihsh</u> uhl) *adj.*
located near the surface; trivial; shallow and phony
Synonyms: outward, external; insignificant; false
SUSCEPTIBLE (suh <u>sehp</u> tuh buhl) *adj.*
vulnerable, unprotected
Synonyms: sensitive, impressionable, prone, subject

that Le Bon had been imprisoned, that he asked me my opinion respecting the murders.

I could merely agree with all Paris in considering them an <u>insoluble</u> mystery. I saw no means by which it would be possible to trace the murderer.

"We must not judge of the means," said Dupin, "by this shell of an examination. The Parisian police, so much **extolled** for **acumen**, are cunning, but no more. There is no method in their proceedings, beyond the method of the moment. They make a vast parade of measures; but, not unfrequently, these are so **ill-adapted** to the objects proposed, as to put us in mind of Monsieur Jourdain's calling for his *robe-de-chambre—pour mieux entendre la musique.*[37] The results attained by them are not unfrequently surprising, but, for the most part, are brought about by simple **diligence** and activity. When these qualities are **unavailing**, their schemes fail. Vidocq,[38] for example, was a good guesser, and a **persevering** man. But, without educated thought, he erred continually by the very intensity of his investigations. He **impaired** his vision by holding the object too close. He might see, perhaps, one or two points with unusual clearness, but in so doing he, necessarily, lost sight of the matter as a whole. Thus there is such a thing as being too **profound**. Truth is not always in a well. In fact, as regards the more important knowledge, I do believe that she is invariably **superficial**. The depth lies in the valleys where we seek her, and not upon the mountain-tops where she is found. The modes and sources of this kind of error are well typified in the contemplation of the heavenly bodies. To look at a star by glances—to view it in a side-long way, by turning toward it the exterior portions of the *retina* (more **susceptible** of feeble impressions of light than the interior), is to behold the star distinctly—is to have the best appreciation of its lustre—a lustre which grows dim just in proportion as we turn our vision *fully* upon it. A greater number of rays actually fall upon the eye in the latter case, but in the

PROFUNDITY (pruh <u>fuhn</u> dih tee) *n.*
  depth, infinity; intelligence, insight
    Synonyms: intensity, deepness; wisdom, knowledge
SCRUTINY (<u>skroot</u> nee) *n.*
  careful observation
    Synonyms: examination, study, surveillance
SUSTAIN (suh <u>stayn</u>) *v.* **-ing,-ed.**
  to support, uphold; endure, undergo
    Synonyms: maintain, prop, confirm, encourage;
    withstand

MINUTENESS (mie <u>noot</u> nehs) (mih <u>noot</u> nehs) *n.*
  precision, attention to detail; the state of being tiny
    Synonyms: accuracy, exactness, carefulness; smallness

former, there is the more refined capacity for comprehension. By undue **profundity** we perplex and <u>enfeeble</u> thought; and it is possible to make even Venus herself vanish from the <u>firmament</u> by a **scrutiny** too **sustained**, too concentrated, or too direct.

"As for these murders, let us enter into some examinations for ourselves, before we make up an opinion respecting them. An inquiry will afford us amusement," [I thought this an odd term, so applied, but said nothing] "and besides, Le Bon once rendered me a service for which I am not ungrateful. We will go and see the premises with our own eyes. I know G——, the Prefect of Police, and shall have no difficulty in obtaining the necessary permission."

The permission was obtained, and we proceeded at once to the Rue Morgue. This is one of those miserable thoroughfares which intervene between the Rue Richelieu and the Rue St. Roch. It was late in the afternoon when we reached it, as this quarter is at a great distance from that in which we resided. The house was readily found; for there were still many persons gazing up at the closed shutters, with an objectless curiosity, from the opposite side of the way. It was an ordinary Parisian house, with a gateway, on one side of which was a glazed watch-box, with a sliding panel in the window, indicating a *loge de concierge*.[39] Before going in we walked up the street, turned down an alley, and then, again turning, passed in the rear of the building—Dupin, meanwhile, examining the whole neighborhood, as well as the house, with a **minuteness** of attention for which I could see no possible object.

Retracing our steps we came again to the front of the dwelling, rang, and, having shown our credentials, were admitted by the agents in charge. We went up stairs—into the chamber where the body of Mademoiselle L'Espanaye had been found, and where both the deceased still lay. The disorders of the room had, as usual, been suffered to exist. I saw nothing beyond what had been

SCRUTINIZE (<u>skroot</u> niez) *v.* **-ing,-ed.**
  to observe carefully
    Synonyms: examine, study, survey

WHIM (wihm) *n.*
  a playful or fanciful idea
    Synonyms: caprice, impulse, dream, vision, fantasy

ATROCITY (uh <u>trah</u> sih tee) *n.*
  revolting wickedness, cruelty
    Synonyms: horror, barbarity, abomination, outrage
CONFOUND (kuhn <u>fownd</u>) *v.* **-ing,-ed.**
  to baffle, perplex; to mistake something for another
    Synonyms: overwhelm, disconcert, entangle,
    muddle; confuse, misidentify
RECONCILE (<u>reh</u> kuhn siel) *v.* **-ing,-ed.**
  1. to solve a puzzle or relieve confusion; resolve a dispute
    Synonyms: decipher; agree, accommodate, rectify,
    reunite
  2. to accept
    Synonyms: resign, submit, placate, pacify, appease
CONTENTION (kuhn <u>tehn</u> shuhn) *n.*
  a quarrel or disagreement; competition
    Synonyms: controversy, argument; rivalry
EGRESS (<u>ee</u> grehs) *n.*
  the act of leaving or the ability to leave; an exit
    Synonyms: emergence, departure; escape, doorway
ASCEND (uh <u>sehnd</u>) *v.* **-ing,-ed.**
  to rise to another level or climb; to move upward
    Synonyms: elevate, escalate, mount; hoist, lift
ACUMEN (<u>aak</u> yuh muhn) (uh <u>kyoo</u> muhn) *n.*
  sharpness of insight
    Synonyms: sagacity, discernment, shrewdness

stated in the *Gazette des Tribunaux*. Dupin **scrutinized** every thing—not excepting the bodies of the victims. We then went into the other rooms, and into the yard; a *gendarme*[34] accompanying us throughout. The examination occupied us until dark, when we took our departure. On our way home my companion stepped in for a moment at the office of one of the daily papers.

I have said that the **whims** of my friend were <u>manifold</u>, and that *Je les ménageais*—for this phrase there is no English equivalent.[40] It was his humor, now, to decline all conversation on the subject of the murder, until about noon the next day. He then asked me, suddenly, if I had observed any thing *peculiar* at the scene of the **atrocity**.

There was something in his manner of emphasizing the word "*peculiar*," which caused me to shudder, without knowing why.

"No, nothing *peculiar*," I said. "Nothing more, at least, than we both saw stated in the paper."

"The *Gazette*," he replied, "has not entered, I fear, into the unusual horror of the thing. But dismiss the idle opinions of this print. It appears to me that this mystery is considered <u>insoluble</u>, for the very reason which should cause it to be regarded as easy of solution—I mean for the *outré*[73] character of its features. The police are **confounded** by the seeming absence of motive—not for the murder itself—but for the **atrocity** of the murder. They are puzzled, too, by the seeming impossibility of **reconciling** the voices heard in **contention**, with the facts that no one was discovered upstairs but the assassinated Mademoiselle L'Espanaye, and that there were no means of **egress** without the notice of the party **ascending**. The wild disorder of the room; the corpse thrust, with the head downward, up the chimney; the frightful mutilation of the body of the old lady; these considerations, with those just mentioned, and others which I need not mention, have sufficed to paralyze the powers, by putting completely at fault the boasted *acumen*, of the

CONFOUND (kuhn <u>fownd</u>) *v.* **-ing,-ed.**
 to mistake something for another; to baffle, perplex
  Synonyms: confuse, misidentify; overwhelm,
  disconcert, entangle, muddle
DEVIATION (dee vee <u>ay</u> shuhn) *n.*
 the act of straying or wandering from a path or norm
  Synonyms: divergence, digression, diversion
FACILITY (fuh <u>sihl</u> ih tee) *n.*
 ease, proficiency
  Synonyms: simplicity, dexterity, poise, assuredness
PERPETRATOR (<u>puhr</u> peh tray tuhr) *n.*
 one who commits a crime; one who carries out or does
  Synonyms: culprit; performer
IMPLICATE (<u>ihm</u> pluh kayt) *v.* **-ing,-ed.**
 to involve in a crime, incriminate
  Synonyms: embroil, ensnare
PERPETRATION (puhr peh <u>tray</u> shuhn) *n.*
 the act of committing a crime, an evil action
  Synonyms: wrongdoing, action, job, performance

DETAIN (dih <u>tayn</u>) (dee <u>tayn</u>) *v.* **-ing,-ed.**
 to hold as if in custody; to restrain from continuing on
  Synonyms: keep, apprehend; delay, inhibit
SOLILOQUY (suh <u>lih</u> luh kwee) *n.*
 literary or dramatic speech by one character, not
 addressed to others
  Synonyms: monologue, solo
DISCOURSE (<u>dihs</u> kohrs) *n.*
 a formal, orderly, and extended expression of thought;
 the verbal interchange of ideas
  Synonyms: oration, lecture; dialogue, discussion
CONTENTION (kuhn <u>tehn</u> shuhn) *n.*
 a quarrel or disagreement; competition
  Synonyms: controversy, argument; rivalry

government agents. They have fallen into the gross but common error of **confounding** the unusual with the <u>abstruse</u>. But it is by these **deviations** from the plane of the ordinary, that reason feels its way, if at all, in its search for the true. In investigations such as we are now pursuing, it should not be so much asked 'what has occurred,' as 'what has occurred that has never occurred before.' In fact, the **facility** with which I shall arrive, or have arrived, at the solution of this mystery, is in the direct ratio of its apparent insolubility in the eyes of the police."

I stared at the speaker in mute astonishment.

"I am now awaiting," continued he, looking toward the door of our apartment, "I am now awaiting a person who, although perhaps not the **perpetrator** of these butcheries, must have been in some measure **implicated** in their **perpetration**. Of the worst portion of the crimes committed, it is probable that he is innocent. I hope that I am right in this <u>supposition</u>; for upon it I build my expectation of reading the entire riddle. I look for the man here—in this room—every moment. It is true that he may not arrive; but the probability is that he will. Should he come, it will be necessary to **detain** him. Here are pistols; and we both know how to use them when occasion demands their use."

I took the pistols, scarcely knowing what I did, or believing what I heard, while Dupin went on, very much as if in a **soliloquy**. I have already spoken of his abstract manner at such times. His **discourse** was addressed to myself; but his voice, although by no means loud, had that <u>intonation</u> which is commonly employed in speaking to some one at a great distance. His eyes, vacant in expression, regarded only the wall.

"That the voices heard in **contention**," he said, "by the party upon the stairs, were not the voices of the women themselves, was fully proved by the evidence. This relieves us of all doubt upon the question whether the old lady could have first destroyed the daughter, and afterward have

PRECLUDE (prih <u>clood</u>) *v.* **-ing,-ed.**
   to rule out
      Synonyms: prevent, avert, obviate, forestall, deter
CONTENTION (kuhn <u>tehn</u> shuhn) *n.*
   a quarrel or disagreement; competition
      Synonyms: controversy, argument; rivalry

committed suicide. I speak of this point chiefly for the sake of method; for the strength of Madame L'Espanaye would have been utterly unequal to the task of thrusting her daughter's corpse up the chimney as it was found; and the nature of the wounds upon her own person entirely **precludes** the idea of self-destruction. Murder, then, has been committed by some third party, and the voices of this third party were those heard in **contention**. Let me now advert—not to the whole testimony respecting these voices—but to what was *peculiar* in that testimony. Did you observe any thing peculiar about it?"

I remarked that, while all the witnesses agreed in supposing the gruff voice to be that of a Frenchman, there was much disagreement in regard to the shrill, or, as one individual termed it, the harsh voice.

"That was the evidence itself," said Dupin, "but it was not the peculiarity of the evidence. You have observed nothing distinctive. Yet there *was* something to be observed. The witnesses, as you remark, agreed about the gruff voice; they were here unanimous. But in regard to the shrill voice, the peculiarity is—not that they disagreed—but that, while an Italian, an Englishman, a Spaniard, a Hollander, and a Frenchman attempted to describe it, each one spoke of it as that *of a foreigner.* Each is sure that it was not the voice of one of his own countrymen. Each likens it—not to the voice of an individual of any nation with whose language he is conversant—but the converse. The Frenchman supposes it the voice of a Spaniard, and 'might have distinguished some words *had he been acquainted with the Spanish.*' The Dutchman maintains it to have been that of a Frenchman; but we find it stated that '*not understanding French this witness was examined through an interpreter.*' The Englishman thinks it the voice of a German, and '*does not understand German.*' The Spaniard '*is sure*' that it was that of an Englishman, but 'judges by the intonation' altogether, '*as he has no knowledge of the*

COGNIZANT (<u>kahg</u> nih zehnt) *adj.*
  having knowledge or awareness
    Synonyms: conscious, familiar, informed

ELICIT (ih <u>lih</u> siht) *v.* **-ing,-ed.**
  to draw out, provoke
    Synonyms: evoke, educe, wring, extract, tap

ENGENDER (ehn <u>gehn</u> duhr) *v.* **-ing,-ed.**
  to produce, cause, bring about
    Synonyms: procreate, propagate, originate, generate

INEVITABLY (ihn <u>ehv</u> ih tuh blee) *adv.*
  certainly, unavoidably
    Synonyms: inescapably, surely, predictably

EGRESS (<u>ee</u> grehs) *n.*
  the act of leaving or the ability to leave; an exit
    Synonyms: emergence, departure; escape, doorway

PRETERNATURAL (pree tuhr <u>naach</u> uh ruhl) *adj.*
  extraordinary or unnatural
    Synonyms: abnormal, mysterious, odd, unearthly

English.' The Italian believes it the voice of a Russian, but *'has never conversed with a native of Russia.'* A second Frenchman differs, moreover, with the first, and is positive that the voice was that of an Italian; but *not being cognizant of that tongue*, is like the Spaniard, 'convinced by the <u>intonation</u>.' Now, how strangely unusual must that voice have really been, about which such testimony as this *could* have been **elicited**!—in whose *tones*, even <u>denizens</u> of the five great divisions of Europe could recognize nothing familiar! You will say that it might have been the voice of an Asiatic—of an African. Neither Asiatics nor Africans abound in Paris; but, without denying the inference, I will now merely call your attention to three points. The voice is termed by one witness 'harsh rather than shrill.' It is represented by two others to have been 'quick and *unequal*.' No words—no sounds resembling words— were by any witness mentioned as distinguishable.

"I know not," continued Dupin, "what impression I may have made, so far, upon your own understanding; but I do not hesitate to say that legitimate deductions even from this portion of the testimony—the portion respecting the gruff and shrill voices—are in themselves sufficient to **engender** a suspicion which should give direction to all farther progress in the investigation of the mystery. I said 'legitimate deductions', but my meaning is not thus fully expressed. I designed to imply that the deductions are the *sole* proper ones, and that the suspicion arises *inevitably* from them as a single result. What the suspicion is, however, I will not say just yet. I merely wish you to bear in mind that, with myself, it was sufficiently forcible to give a definite form—a certain tendency—to my inquiries to the chamber.

"Let us now transport ourselves, in fancy, to this chamber. What shall we first seek here? The means of **egress** employed by the murderers. It is not too much to say that neither of us believes in **preternatural** events. Madame and Mademoiselle L'Espanaye were not

EGRESS (<u>ee</u> grehs) *n.*
the act of leaving or the ability to leave; an exit
Synonyms: emergence, departure; escape, doorway
ASCEND (uh <u>sehnd</u>) *v.* **-ing,-ed.**
to rise to another level or climb; to move upward
Synonyms: elevate, escalate, mount; hoist, lift

VIGILANCE (<u>vih</u> juh lehnts) *n.*
attention, watchfulness
Synonyms: alertness, awareness, care

UNEQUIVOCAL (uhn ih <u>kwihv</u> uh kuhl) *adj.*
unambiguous, not open to more than one
interpretation
Synonyms: certain, clear, evident, definitive

destroyed by spirits. The doers of the deed were material and escaped materially. Then how? Fortunately there is but one mode of reasoning upon the point, and that mode *must* lead us to a definite decision. Let us examine, each by each, the possible means of **egress**. It is clear that the assassins were in the room where Mademoiselle L'Espanaye was found, or at least in the room adjoining, when the party **ascended** the stairs. It is then, only from these two apartments that we have to seek issues. The police have laid bare the floors, the ceiling, and the masonry of the walls, in every direction. No *secret* issues could have escaped their **vigilance**. But, not trusting to *their* eyes, I examined with my own. There were, then, *no* secret issues. Both doors leading from the rooms into the passage were securely locked, with the keys inside. Let us turn to the chimneys. These, although of ordinary width for some eight or ten feet above the hearths, will not admit, throughout their extent, the body of a large cat. The impossibility of **egress**, by means already stated, being thus absolute, we are reduced to the windows. Through those of the front room no one could have escaped without notice from the crowd in the street. The murderers *must* have passed, then, through those of the back room. Now, brought to this conclusion in so **unequivocal** a manner as we are, it is not our part, as reasoners, to reject it on account of apparent impossibilities. It is only left for us to prove that these apparent 'impossibilities' are, in reality, not such.

"There are two windows in the chamber. One of them is unobstructed by furniture, and is wholly visible. The lower portion of the other is hidden from view by the head of the unwieldy bedstead which is thrust close up against it. The former was found securely fastened from within. It resisted the utmost force of those who endeavored to raise it. A large gimlet-hole had been pierced in its frame to the left, and a very stout nail was found fitted therein, nearly to the head. Upon examining the other

EGRESS (<u>ee</u> grehs) *n.*
    the act of leaving or the ability to leave; an exit
        Synonyms: emergence, departure; escape, doorway

SCRUTINY (<u>skroot</u> nee) *n.*
    careful observation
        Synonyms: examination, study, surveillance

CORROBORATION (kuh rahb uhr <u>ay</u> shuhn) *n.*
    confirmation, verification
        Synonyms: proof, substantiation, certification

FORBEAR (fohr <u>bayr</u>) *v.* **-ing,-bore.**
    to refrain or resist; to tolerate or put up with
        Synonym: avoid, withhold, inhibit; endure, suffer

window, a similar nail was seen similarly fitted in it; and a vigorous attempt to raise this sash failed also. The police were now entirely satisfied that **egress** had not been in these directions. And *therefore*, it was thought a matter of supererogation to withdraw the nails and open the windows.

"My own examination was somewhat more particular, and was so for the reason I have just given—because here it was, I knew, that all apparent impossibilities *must* be proved to be not such in reality.

"I proceeded to think thus—*a posteriori.*[41] The murderers *did* escape from one of these windows. This being so, they could not have re-fastened the sashes from the inside, as they were found fastened—the consideration which put a stop, through its obviousness, to the **scrutiny** of the police in this quarter. Yet the sashes *were* fastened. They *must*, then, have the power of fastening themselves. There was no escape from this conclusion. I stepped to the unobstructed casement, withdrew the nail with some difficulty, and attempted to raise the sash. It resisted all my efforts, as I had anticipated. A concealed spring must, I now knew, exist; and this **corroboration** of my idea convinced me that my premises, at least, were correct, however mysterious still appeared the circumstances attending the nails. A careful search soon brought to light the hidden spring. I pressed it, and, satisfied with the discovery, **forbore** to upraise the sash.

"I now replaced the nail and regarded it attentively. A person passing out through this window might have reclosed it, and the spring would have caught—but the nail could not have been replaced. The conclusion was plain, and again narrowed in the field of my investigations. The assassins *must* have escaped through the other window. Supposing, then, the springs upon each sash to be the same, as was probable, there *must* be found a difference between the nails, or at least between the modes of their fixture. Getting upon the sacking of the bedstead,

MINUTELY (mie <u>noot</u> lee) (mih <u>noot</u> lee) *adv.*
    precisely, in a detailed manner
        Synonyms: attentively, critically

INDUCTION (ihn <u>duhk</u> shuhn) *n.*
    1. a conclusion based on facts and evidence
        Synonyms: inference, reasoning, conjecture
    2. a ceremony conducted to admit or reward someone
        Synonyms: installation, inauguration, initiation

NULLITY (<u>nuh</u> lih tee) *n.*
    a worthless or unimportant point of reasoning,
    something which has no legal validity
        Synonyms: untruth, negation, contradiction

I looked over the head-board **minutely** at the second <u>casement</u>. Passing my hand down behind the board, I readily discovered and pressed the spring, which was, as I had supposed, identical in character with its neighbor. I now looked at the nail. It was as stout as the other, and apparently fitted in the same manner—driven in nearly up to the head.

"You will say that I was puzzled; but, if you think so, you must have misunderstood the nature of the **inductions**. To use a sporting phrase, I had not been once 'at fault.' The scent had never for an instant been lost. There was no flaw in any link of the chain. I had traced the secret to its ultimate result—and that result was *the nail*. It had, I say, in every respect, the appearance of its fellow in the other window; but this fact was an absolute **nullity** (conclusive as it might seem to be) when compared with the consideration that here, at this point, terminated the clue. 'There *must* be something wrong,' I said, 'about the nail.' I touched it; and the head, with about a quarter of an inch of the shank, came off in my fingers. The rest of the shank was in the gimlet-hole, where it had been broken off. The fracture was an old one (for its edges were incrusted with rust), and had apparently been accomplished by the blow of a hammer, which had partially imbedded, in the top of the bottom sash, the head portion of the nail. I now carefully replaced this head portion in the indentation whence I had taken it, and the resemblance to a perfect nail was complete—the <u>fissure</u> was invisible. Pressing the spring, I gently raised the sash for a few inches; the head went up with it, remaining firm in its bed. I closed the window, and the semblance of the whole nail was again perfect.

"This riddle, so far, was now unriddled. The assassin had escaped through the window which looked upon the bed. Dropping of its own accord upon his exit (or perhaps purposely closed), it had become fastened by the spring; and it was the retention of this spring which had

DESCENT (dih <u>sehnt</u>) (dee <u>sehnt</u>) *n.*
  1. the passing from a higher place to a lower place;
a decline
    Synonyms: lowering, dismount, gravitation; slope
  2. one's ancestry
    Synonyms: heredity, lineage

TENEMENT (<u>teh</u> nuh muhnt) *n.*
  a house used as a dwelling, any form of livable
property that is leased by one person to another
    Synonyms: apartment, rental, residence

EGRESS (<u>ee</u> grehs) *n.*
  the act of leaving or the ability to leave; an exit
    Synonyms: emergence, departure; escape, doorway

BESTOW (bih <u>stoh</u>) *v.* **-ing,-ed.**
  to apply or devote time or effort; to give as a gift
    Synonyms: allocate, dedicate; endow, confer, present

CURSORY (<u>kuhr</u> suh ree) *adj.*
  hastily done, superficial
    Synonyms: shallow, careless

been mistaken by the police for that of the nail, farther inquiry being thus considered unnecessary.

"The next question is that of the mode of **descent**. Upon this point I had been satisfied in my walk with you around the building. About five feet and a half from the casement in question there runs a lightning-rod. From this rod it would have been impossible for any one to reach the window itself, to say nothing of entering it. I observed, however, that the shutters of the fourth story were of the peculiar kind called by Parisian carpenters *ferrades*—a kind rarely employed at the present day, but frequently seen upon very old mansions at Lyons and Bordeaux. They are in the form of an ordinary door (a single, not a folding door), except that the lower half is latticed or worked in open trellis—thus affording an excellent hold for the hands. In the present instance these shutters are fully three feet and a half broad. When we saw them from the rear of the house, they were both about half open—that is to say they stood off at right angles from the wall. It is probable that the police, as well as myself, examined the back of the **tenement**; but, if so, in looking at these *ferrades* in the line of their breadth (as they must have done), they did not perceive this great breadth itself, or, at all events, failed to take it into due consideration. In fact, having once satisfied themselves that no **egress** could have been made in this quarter, they would naturally **bestow** here a very **cursory** examination. It was clear to me, however, that the shutter belonging to the window at the head of the bed, would, if swung fully back to the wall, reach to within two feet of the lightning-rod. It was also evident that, by exertion of a very unusual degree of activity and courage, an entrance into the window, from the rod, might have been thus effected. By reaching to the distance of two feet and a half (we now suppose the shutter open to its whole extent) a robber might have taken a firm grasp upon the trellis-work. Letting go, then, his hold upon the rod, placing his feet

REQUISITE (<u>reh</u> kwih ziht) *adj.*
 essential, necessary
  Synonyms: required, indispensable

PRETERNATURAL (pree tuhr <u>naach</u> uh ruhl) *adj.*
 extraordinary, unnatural
  Synonyms: abnormal, mysterious, odd, unearthly
AGILITY (uh <u>jihl</u> ih tee) *n.*
 great coordination, nimbleness
  Synonyms: spryness, dexterity, litheness

JUXTAPOSITION (juk stuh puh <u>zihsh</u> uhn) *n.*
 side-by-side placement
  Synonyms: comparison, contrast

DISCOURSE (<u>dihs</u> kohrs) *n.*
 a formal, orderly, and extended expression of thought;
 the verbal interchange of ideas
  Synonyms: oration, lecture; dialogue, discussion
EGRESS (<u>ee</u> grehs) *n.*
 the act of leaving or the ability to leave; an exit
  Synonyms: emergence, departure; escape, doorway
INGRESS (<u>ihn</u> grehs) *n.*
 the act of going in or the ability to enter; an entrance
  Synonyms: access, admittance, permission; entry,
  doorway
REVERT (rih <u>vuhrt</u>) *v.* **-ing,-ed.**
 to backslide, regress
  Synonyms: return, recur, degenerate, deteriorate

securely against the wall, and springing boldly from it, he might have swung the shutter so as to close it, and, if we imagine the window open at the time, might even have swung himself into the room.

"I wish you to bear especially in mind that I have spoken of a very unusual degree of activity as **requisite** to success in so hazardous and so difficult a feat. It is my design to show you first, that the thing might possibly have been accomplished. But secondly and *chiefly*, I wish to impress upon your understanding the *very extraordinary*—the almost **preternatural** character of that **agility** which could have accomplished it.

"You will say, no doubt, using the language of the law, that 'to make out my case, I should rather undervalue than insist upon a full estimation of the activity required in this matter.' This may be the practice in law, but it is not the usage of reason. My ultimate object is only the truth. My immediate purpose is to lead you to place in **juxtaposition**, that very unusual activity of which I have just spoken, with that very peculiar shrill (or harsh) and *unequal* voice, about whose nationality no two persons could be found to agree, and in whose utterance no syllabification could be detected."

At these words a vague and half-formed conception of the meaning of Dupin flitted over my mind. I seemed to be upon the verge of comprehension, without power to comprehend—as men, at times, find themselves upon the brink of remembrance, without being able, in the end, to remember. My friend went on with his **discourse**.

"You will see," he said, "that I have shifted the question from the mode of **egress** to that of **ingress**. It was my design to convey the idea that both were effected in the same manner, at the same point. Let us now **revert** to the interior of the room. Let us survey the appearances here. The drawers of the bureau, it is said, had been rifled, although many articles of apparel still remained within them. The conclusion here is absurd. It is a mere guess—a

ENCUMBER (ehn <u>kuhm</u> buhr) *v.* **-ing,-ed.**
    to hinder, burden, restrict motion
        Synonyms: impede, handicap, saddle, inconvenience
ENGENDER (ehn <u>gehn</u> duhr) *v.* **-ing,-ed.**
    to produce, to cause
        Synonyms: propagate, originate, generate

CORROBORATIVE (kuh <u>rahb</u> uh ruh tihv) *adj.*
    strengthening, verifying
        Synonyms: supportive, substantiative, confirmatory
PERPETRATOR (<u>puhr</u> peh tray tuhr) *n.*
    one who commits a crime; one who carries out or does
        Synonyms: culprit; performer
VACILLATING (<u>vaa</u> sihl ay tihng) *adj.*
    wavering, showing indecision
        Synonyms: swaying, oscillating, hesitant, faltering
DRAW *v.* **-ing, drew, drawn**
    to lead, to bring about on purpose; to attract or be
    attracted to; to pull, drag
        Synonyms: provoke, elicit; lure, entice; haul, tow, yank
AGILITY (uh <u>jihl</u> ih tee) *n.*
    great coordination, nimbleness
        Synonyms: spryness, dexterity, litheness
ATROCIOUS (uh <u>troh</u> shuhs) *adj.*
    revolting, shockingly bad, wicked
        Synonyms: horrible, appalling, deplorable, direful

very silly one—and no more. How are we to know that the articles found in the drawers were not all these drawers had originally contained? Madame L'Espanaye and her daughter lived an exceedingly retired life—saw no company—seldom went out—had little use for numerous changes of <u>habiliment</u>. Those found were at least of as good quality as any likely to be possessed by these ladies. If a thief had taken any, why did he not take the best— why did he not take all? In a word, why did he abandon four thousand francs in gold to **encumber** himself with a bundle of linen? The gold was abandoned. Nearly the whole sum mentioned by Monsieur Mignaud, the banker, was discovered, in bags, upon the floor. I wish you therefore, to discard from your thoughts the blundering idea of *motive*, **engendered** in the brains of the police by that portion of the evidence which speaks of money delivered at the door of the house. Coincidences ten times as remarkable as this (the delivery of the money, and murder committed within three days upon the party receiving it), happen to all of us every hour of our lives, without attracting even momentary notice. Coincidences, in general, are great stumbling-blocks in the way of that class of thinkers who have been educated to know nothing of the theory of probabilities—that theory to which the most glorious objects of human research are indebted for the most glorious of illustration. In the present instance, had the gold been gone, the fact of its delivery three days before would have formed something more than a coincidence. It would have been **corroborative** of this idea of motive. But, under the real circumstances of the case, if we are to suppose gold the motive of this outrage, we must also imagine the **perpetrator** so **vacillating** an idiot as to have abandoned his gold and his motive together.

"Keeping now steadily in mind the points to which I have **drawn** your attention—that peculiar voice, that unusual **agility**, and that startling absence of motive in a murder so singularly **atrocious** as this—let us glance at the

MANUAL (<u>maan</u> yoo uhl) *adj.*
   by hand; hand-operated
      Synonyms: physical; mechanical
DISPOSE (dih <u>spohz</u>) *v.* **-ing,-ed.**
   to get rid of; to put in place, to settle; to incline or give
   a tendency to
      Synonyms: discard; organize, position;
      determine, motivate
IRRECONCILABLE (eer reh kuhn <u>siel</u> uh buhl) *adj.*
   unable to be accepted or resolved
      Synonyms: unappeasable, inconsistent, conflicting
DEPRAVED (dih <u>prayvd</u>) *adj.*
   sinful, morally corrupted
      Synonyms: wicked, evil

PRODIGIOUS (pruh <u>dih</u> juhs) *adj.*
   vast, enormous, extraordinary
      Synonyms: huge, gigantic, impressive, marvelous

OBTUSE (uhb <u>toos</u>) *adj.*
   dull; insensitive, stupid, lacking intellect
      Synonyms: blunt; slow, dense, dim

HERMETICALLY (huhr <u>meh</u> tih klee) *adv.*
   in a tightly sealed or airtight manner
      Synonym: imperviously

butchery itself. Here is a woman strangled to death by **manual** strength, and thrust up a chimney head downward. Ordinary assassins employ no such mode of murder as this. Least of all, do they thus **dispose** of the murdered. In the manner of thrusting the corpse up the chimney, you will admit that there was something *excessively outré*[73]—something altogether **irreconcilable** with our common notions of human action, even when we suppose the actors the most **depraved** of men. Think, too, how great must have been that strength which could have thrust the body *up* such an <u>aperture</u> so forcibly that the united vigor of several persons was found barely sufficient to drag it *down*!

"Turn, now, to other indications of the employment of a vigor most marvellous. On the hearth were thick tresses—very thick tresses—of gray human hair. These had been torn out by the roots. You are aware of the great force necessary in tearing thus from the head even twenty or thirty hairs together. You saw the locks in question as well as myself. Their roots (a hideous sight!) were clotted with fragments of the flesh of the scalp—sure token of the **prodigious** power which had been exerted in uprooting perhaps half a million of hairs at a time. The throat of the old lady was not merely cut, but the head absolutely severed from the body; the instrument was a mere razor. I wish you also to look at the *brutal* ferocity of these deeds. Of the bruises upon the body of Madame L'Espanaye I do not speak. Monsieur Dumas, and his worthy coadjutor Monsieur Etienne, have pronounced that they were inflicted by some **obtuse** instrument; and so far these gentlemen are very correct. The **obtuse** instrument was clearly the stone pavement in the yard, upon which the victim had fallen from the window which looked in upon the bed. This idea, however simple it may now seem, escaped the police for the same reason that the breadth of the shutters escaped them—because, by the affair of the nails, their perceptions had been **hermetically** sealed

AGILITY (uh jihl ih tee) *n.*
    great coordination, nimbleness
        Synonyms: spryness, dexterity, litheness

DEVOID (dih voyd) *adj.*
    being without, lacking
        Synonyms: destitute, empty, vacant, null, bare

INCOHERENT (ihn koh hihr uhnt) *adj.*
    unable to think or express one's thoughts in a clear or
    orderly manner
        Synonyms: unintelligible, incohesive
COHERENCE (koh heer uhnts) *n.*
    uniformity, lucidity, the state of being understandable
        Synonyms: order, logic, consistency

LIVID (lih vihd) *adj.*
    discolored from a bruise; pale; reddened with anger
        Synonyms: black-and-blue; ashen, pallid; furious

against the possibility of the windows having ever been opened at all.

"If now, in addition to all these things, yon have properly reflected upon the odd disorder of the chamber, we have gone so far as to combine the ideas of an **agility** astounding, a strength superhuman, a ferocity brutal, a butchery without motive, a grotesquerie[42] in horror absolutely alien from humanity, and a voice foreign in tone to the ears of men of many nations, and **devoid** of all distinct or intelligible syllabification. What result, then, has <u>ensued</u>? What impression have I made upon your fancy?"

I felt a creeping of the flesh as Dupin asked me the question. "A madman," I said, "has done this deed—some raving maniac escaped from a neighboring *Maison de Santé.*"[43]

"In some respects," he replied, "your idea is not irrelevant. But the voices of madmen, even in their wildest <u>paroxysms</u>, are never found to tally with that peculiar voice heard upon the stairs. Madmen are of some nation, and their language, however **incoherent** in its words, has always the **coherence** of syllabification. Besides, the hair of a madman is not such as I now hold in my hand. I disentangled this little tuft from the rigidly clutched fingers of Madame L'Espanaye. Tell me what you can make of it."

"Dupin!" I said, completely unnerved, "this hair is most unusual—this is no *human* hair."

"I have not asserted that it is," said he, "but, before we decide this point, I wish you to glance at the little sketch I have here traced upon this paper. It is a <u>*facsimile*</u> drawing of what has been described in one portion of the testimony as 'dark bruises and deep indentations of finger nails' upon the throat of Mademoiselle L'Espanaye, and in another (by Messrs. Dumas and Etienne) as a 'series of **livid** spots, evidently the impression of fingers.'

"You will perceive," continued my friend, spreading out the paper upon the table before us, "that this drawing

RETAIN (rih <u>tayn</u>) *v.* **-ing,-ed.**
to hold, keep possession of
Synonyms: withhold, reserve, maintain, remember

MINUTE (mie <u>noot</u>) (mih <u>noot</u>) *adj.*
precise, detailed; very small
Synonyms: attentive, critical; tiny, diminutive, infinitesimal
PRODIGIOUS (pruh <u>dih</u> juhs) *adj.*
vast, enormous, extraordinary
Synonyms: huge, gigantic, impressive, marvelous
PROPENSITY (pruh <u>pehn</u> suh tee) *n.*
inclination, tendency
Synonyms: predilection, bias, leaning, penchant, proclivity

CONTENTION (kuhn <u>tehn</u> shuhn) *n.*
a quarrel or disagreement; competition
Synonyms: controversy, argument; rivalry

gives the idea of a firm and fixed hold. There is no *slipping* apparent. Each finger has **retained**—possibly until the death of the victim—the fearful grasp by which it originally imbedded itself. Attempt, now, to place all your fingers, at the same time, in the respective impressions as you see them."

I made the attempt in vain.

"We are possibly not giving this matter a fair trial," he said. "The paper is spread out upon a plane surface, but the human throat is cylindrical. Here is a billet of wood, the circumference of which is about that of the throat. Wrap the drawing around it, and try the experiment again."

I did so, but the difficulty was even more obvious than before. "This," I said, "is the mark of no human hand."

"Read now," replied Dupin, "this passage from Cuvier."

It was a **minute** anatomical and generally descriptive account of the large <u>fulvous</u> Ourang-Outang of the East Indian Islands. The gigantic stature, the **prodigious** strength and activity, the wild ferocity, and the imitative **propensities** of these mammalia are sufficiently well known to all. I understood the full horrors of the murder at once.

"The description of the digits," said I, as I made an end of the reading, "is in exact accordance with this drawing. I see that no animal but an Ourang-Outang, of the species here mentioned, could have impressed the indentations as you have traced them. This tuft of tawny hair, too, is identical in character with that of the beast of Cuvier. But I cannot possibly comprehend the particulars of this frightful mystery. Besides, there were two voices heard in **contention**, and one of them was unquestionably the voice of a Frenchman."

"True, and you will remember an expression attributed almost unanimously, by the evidence, to this voice— the expression, '*mon Dieu!*'[36] This, under the circumstances,

237

THE MURDERS IN THE RUE MORGUE

REMONSTRANCE (reh <u>mahn</u> strehnts) *n.*
the presentation and urging of reasons in opposition, protestation
Synonyms: objection, complaint, expostulation

EXPOSTULATION (ihk spahs chuh <u>lay</u> shuhn) *n.*
an expression of opposition; reasoning
Synonyms: argument, dissuasion, remonstration; assertion

COGNIZANT (<u>kahg</u> nih zehnt) *adj.*
having knowledge or awareness
Synonyms: conscious, familiar, informed

AGITATING (<u>aa</u> gih tay tihng) *adj.*
upsetting, distressing, agonizing
Synonyms: disturbing, flustering, bothersome

ATROCITY (uh <u>trah</u> sih tee) *n.*
revolting wickedness, cruelty
Synonyms: horror, barbarity, abomination, outrage

ASCERTAIN (aa suhr <u>tayn</u>) *v.* **-ing,-ed.**
to determine, discover, make certain of
Synonyms: verify, calculate, detect

has been justly characterized by one of the witnesses (Montani, the confectioner) as an expression of **remonstrance** or **expostulation**. Upon these two words, therefore, I have mainly built my hopes of a full solution of the riddle. A Frenchman was **cognizant** of the murder. It is possible—indeed it is far more than probable—that he was innocent of all participation in the bloody transactions which took place. The Ourang-Outang may have escaped from him. He may have traced it to the chamber; but, under the **agitating** circumstances which ensued, he could never have recaptured it. It is still at large. I will not pursue these guesses for I have no right to call them more—since the shades of reflection upon which they are based are scarcely of sufficient depth to be appreciable by my own intellect, and since I could not pretend to make them intelligible to the understanding of another. We will call them guesses, then, and speak of them as such. If the Frenchman in question is indeed, as I suppose, innocent of this **atrocity**, this advertisement, which I left last night, upon our return home, at the office of *Le Monde* (a paper devoted to the shipping interest, and much sought by sailors), will bring him to our residence."

He handed me a paper, and I read thus:

"CAUGHT—*In the Bois de Boulogne, early in the morning of the —— inst.* (the morning of the murder), *a very large, tawny Ourang-Outang of the Bornese species. The owner (who is **ascertained** to be a sailor, belonging to a Maltese vessel) may have the animal again, upon identifying it satisfactorily, and paying a few charges arising from its capture and keeping. Call at No. —— Rue ——, Faubourg St. Germain—au troisième.*"

"How was it possible," I asked, "that you should know the man to be a sailor, and belonging to a Maltese vessel?"

"I do *not* know it," said Dupin. "I am not *sure* of it. Here, however, is a small piece of ribbon, which from its

INDUCTION (ihn <u>duhk</u> shuhn) *n.*
1. a conclusion based on facts and evidence
   Synonyms: inference, reasoning, conjecture
2. a ceremony conducted to admit or reward someone
   Synonyms: installation, inauguration, initiation

COGNIZANT (<u>kahg</u> nih zehnt) *adj.*
having knowledge or awareness
   Synonyms: conscious, familiar, informed

APPREHENSION (aa prih <u>hehn</u> shuhn) *n.*
suspicion or fear of future or unknown evil; the act of
perceiving or comprehending; a legal seizure
   Synonyms: concern, worry; understanding; capture

PROCURE (proh <u>kyoor</u>) *v.* **-ing,-ed.**
to obtain
   Synonyms: acquire, secure, get, gain

IMPLICATE (<u>ihm</u> pluh kayt) *v.* **-ing,-ed.**
to involve in a crime, incriminate
   Synonyms: embroil, ensnare

COGNIZANCE (<u>kahg</u> nih zehnce) *n.*
knowledge or awareness
   Synonyms: consciousness, familiarity, experience

form, and from its greasy appearance, has evidently been used in tying the hair in one of those long *queues* of which sailors are so fond. Moreover, this knot is one which few besides sailors can tie, and is peculiar to the Maltese. I picked the ribbon up at the foot of the lightning-rod. It could not have belonged to either of the deceased. Now if, after all, I am wrong in my **induction** from this ribbon, that the Frenchman was a sailor belonging to a Maltese vessel, still I can have done no harm in saying what I did in the advertisement. If I am in error, he will merely suppose that I have been misled by some circumstance into which he will not take the trouble to inquire. But if I am right, a great point is gained. **Cognizant** although innocent of the murder, the Frenchman will naturally hesitate about replying to the advertisement—about demanding the Ourang-Outang. He will reason thus: I am innocent; I am poor; my Ourang-Outang is of great value—to one in my circumstance a fortune of itself—why should I lose it through idle **apprehensions** of danger? Here it is, within my grasp. It was found in the Bois de Boulogne—at a vast distance from the scene of that butchery. How can it ever be suspected that a brute beast should have done the deed? The police are at fault—they have failed to **procure** the slightest clue. Should they even trace the animal, it would be impossible to prove me **cognizant** of the murder, or to **implicate** me in guilt on account of that **cognizance**. Above all, *I am known*. The advertiser designates me as the possessor of the beast. I am not sure to what limit his knowledge may extend. Should I avoid claiming a property of so great value, which it is known that I possess, I will render the animal at least, liable to suspicion. It is not my policy to attract attention either to myself or to the beast. I will answer the advertisement, get the Ourang-Outang, and keep it close until this matter has blown over."

At this moment we heard a step upon the stairs.

"Be ready," said Dupin, "with your pistols, but neither use them nor show them until at a signal from myself."

DESCEND (dih <u>sehnd</u>) (dee <u>sehnd</u>) *v.* **-ing,-ed.**
to pass from a higher place to a lower place
Synonyms: fall, dismount, gravitate

COUNTENANCE (<u>kown</u> tuh nuhns) *n.*
appearance, facial expression
Synonyms: face, features, visage

The front door of the house had been left open, and the visitor had entered, without ringing, and advanced several steps upon the staircase. Now, however, he seemed to hesitate. Presently we heard him **descending**. Dupin was moving quickly to the door, when we again heard him coming up. He did not turn back a second time, but stepped up with decision, and rapped at the door of our chamber.

"Come in," said Dupin, in a cheerful and hearty tone.

A man entered. He was a sailor, evidently,—a tall, stout, and muscular-looking person, with a certain dare-devil expression of **countenance**, not altogether unprepossessing. His face, greatly sunburnt, was more than half hidden by whisker and *mustachio*. He had with him a huge oaken cudgel, but appeared to be otherwise unarmed. He bowed awkwardly, and bade us "good evening," in French accents, which, although somewhat Neufchâtelish, were still sufficiently indicative of a Parisian origin.

"Sit down, my friend," said Dupin. "I suppose you have called about the Ourang-Outang. Upon my word, I almost envy you the possession of him; a remarkably fine, and no doubt a very valuable animal. How old do you suppose him to be?"

The sailor drew a long breath, with the air of a man relieved of some intolerable burden, and then replied, in an assured tone:

"I have no way of telling—but he can't be more than four or five years old. Have you got him here?"

"Oh, no, we had no conveniences for keeping him here. He is at a livery stable in the Rue Dubourg, just by. You can get him in the morning. Of course you are prepared to identify the property?"

"To be sure I am, sir."

"I shall be sorry to part with him," said Dupin.

"I don't mean that you should be at all this trouble for nothing, sir," said the man. "Couldn't expect it. Am very

COUNTENANCE (<u>kown</u> tuh nuhns) *n.*
  appearance, facial expression
    Synonyms: face, features, visage

ATROCITY (uh <u>trah</u> sih tee) *n.*
  revolting wickedness, cruelty
    Synonyms: horror, barbarity, abomination, outrage

IMPLICATE (<u>ihm</u> pluh kayt) *v.* **-ing,-ed.**
  to involve in a crime, incriminate
    Synonyms: embroil, ensnare

CULPABLE (<u>kuhl</u> puh buhl) *adj.*
  guilty, responsible for wrong
    Synonyms: blameworthy, answerable

PERPETRATOR (<u>puhr</u> peh tray tuhr) *n.*
  one who commits a crime; one who carries out or does
    Synonyms: culprit; performer

willing to pay a reward for the finding of the animal—that is to say, any thing in reason."

"Well," replied my friend, "that is all very fair, to be sure. Let me think, what should I have? Oh! I will tell you. My reward shall be this. You shall give me all the information in your power about these murders in the Rue Morgue."

Dupin said the last words in a very low tone, and very quietly. Just as quietly, too, he walked toward the door, locked it, and put the key in his pocket. He then drew a pistol from his bosom and placed it, without the least flurry, upon the table.

The sailor's face flushed up as if he were struggling with suffocation. He started to his feet and grasped his cudgel; but the next moment he fell back into his seat, trembling violently, and with the **countenance** of death itself. He spoke not a word. I pitied him from the bottom of my heart.

"My friend," said Dupin, in a kind tone, "you are alarming yourself unnecessarily—you are indeed. We mean you no harm whatever. I pledge you the honor of a gentleman, and of a Frenchman, that we intend you no injury. I perfectly well know that you are innocent of the **atrocities** in the Rue Morgue. It will not do, however, to deny that you are in some measure **implicated** in them. From what I have already said, you must know that I have had means of information about this matter—means of which you could never have dreamed. Now the thing stands thus. You have done nothing which you could have avoided—nothing, certainly, which renders you **culpable**. You were not even guilty of robbery, when you might have robbed with <u>impunity</u>. You have nothing to conceal. You have no reason for concealment. On the other hand, you are bound by every principle of honor to confess all you know. An innocent man is now imprisoned, charged with that crime of which you can point out the **perpetrator**."

ARCHIPELAGO (ahr kuh <u>pehl</u> uh goh) *n.*
   large group of islands
      Synonyms: cluster, scattering

INTRACTABLE (ihn <u>traak</u> tuh buhl) *adj.*
   not easily managed
      Synonyms: unruly, stubborn, refractory,
      recalcitrant, headstrong

SECLUDED (sih <u>cloo</u> dihd) *adj.*
   isolated and remote
      Synonyms: solitary, sequestered, out-of-the-way

The sailor had recovered his presence of mind, in a great measure, while Dupin uttered these words; but his original boldness of bearing was all gone.

"So help me God!" said he, after a brief pause. "I *will* tell you all I know about this affair, but I do not expect you to believe one half of what I say—I would be a fool indeed if I did. Still, I *am* innocent, and I will make a clean breast if I die for it."

What he stated was, in substance, this. He had lately made a voyage to the Indian **Archipelago**. A party, of which he formed one, landed at Borneo, and passed into the interior on an excursion of pleasure. Himself and a companion had captured the Ourang-Outang. His companion dying, the animal fell into his own exclusive possession. After great trouble, occasioned by the **intractable** ferocity of his captive during the home voyage, he at length succeeded in lodging it safely at his own residence in Paris, where, not to attract toward himself the unpleasant curiosity of his neighbors, he kept it carefully **secluded**, until such time as it should recover from a wound in the foot, received from a splinter on board ship. His ultimate design was to sell it.

Returning home from some sailors' frolic on the night, or rather in the morning, of the murder, he found the beast occupying his own bedroom, into which it had broken from a closet adjoining, where it had been, as was thought, securely confined. Razor in hand, and fully lathered, it was sitting before a looking-glass, attempting the operation of shaving, in which it had no doubt previously watched its master through the keyhole of the closet. Terrified at the sight of so dangerous a weapon in the possession of an animal so ferocious, and so well able to use it, the man, for some moments, was at a loss what to do. He had been accustomed, however, to quiet the creature, even in its fiercest moods, by the use of a whip, and to this he now resorted. Upon sight of it, the Ourang-Outang sprang at once through the door of the chamber, down

GESTICULATE (jeh <u>stih</u> kyuh layt) *v.* **-ing,-ed.**
to make expressive gestures
Synonyms: motion, indicate, signal, wave, flag
PROFOUNDLY (pruh <u>fownd</u> lee) (proh <u>fownd</u> lee) *adv.*
deeply, extremely, infinitely
Synonyms: intensely, thoroughly, severely

AGILITY (uh <u>jihl</u> ih tee) *n.*
great coordination, nimbleness
Synonyms: spryness, dexterity, litheness

ASCEND (uh <u>sehnd</u>) *v.* **-ing,-ed.**
to move upward; to rise to another level or climb
Synonyms: hoist, lift; elevate, escalate, mount

the stairs, and thence, through a window, unfortunately open, into the street.

The Frenchman followed in despair; the ape, razor still in hand, occasionally stopping to look back and **gesticulate** at his pursuer, until the latter had nearly come up with it. It then again made off. In this manner the chase continued for a long time. The streets were **profoundly** quiet, as it was nearly three o'clock in the morning. In passing down an alley in the rear of the Rue Morgue, the fugitive's attention was arrested by a light gleaming from the open window of Madame L'Espanaye's chamber, in the fourth story of her house. Rushing to the building, it perceived the lightning-rod, clambered up with inconceivable **agility**, grasped the shutter, which was thrown fully back against the wall, and, by its means, swung itself directly upon the headboard of the bed. The whole feat did not occupy a minute. The shutter was kicked open again by the Ourang-Outang as it entered the room.

The sailor, in the meantime, was both rejoiced and perplexed. He had strong hopes of now recapturing the brute, as it could scarcely escape from the trap into which it had ventured, except by the rod, where it might be intercepted as it came down. On the other hand, there was much cause for anxiety as to what it might do in the house. This latter reflection urged the man still to follow the fugitive. A lightning-rod is **ascended** without difficulty, especially by a sailor; but, when he had arrived as high as the window, which lay far to his left, his career was stopped; the most that he could accomplish was to reach over so as to obtain a glimpse of the interior of the room. At this glimpse he nearly fell from his hold through excess of horror. Now it was that those hideous shrieks arose upon the night, which had startled from slumber the inmates of the Rue Morgue. Madame L'Espanaye and her daughter, habited in their night clothes, had apparently been occupied in arranging some papers in the iron

INGRESS (<u>ihn</u> grehs) *n.*
   the act of going in or the ability to enter; an entrance
      Synonyms: access, admittance, permission; entry,
      doorway
PROSTRATE (<u>prah</u> strayt) *adj.*
   face downward, flat on ground
      Synonyms: horizontal, submissive, overcome
PACIFIC (puh <u>sih</u> fihk) *adj.*
   calm, peaceful
      Synonyms: tranquil, appeasing, placating
WRATH (raath) *n.*
   anger, rage
      Synonyms: fury, ire, resentment, indignation
TALON (<u>taa</u> luhn) *n.*
   claw of an animal, especially a bird of prey
      Synonyms: nail, claw
RETAIN (rih <u>tayn</u>) *v.* **-ing,-ed.**
   to hold, keep possession of
      Synonyms: withhold, reserve, maintain, remember
EXPIRE (ehk <u>spier</u>) *v.* **-ing,-ed.**
   die; to come to an end; breathe out
      Synonyms: perish; terminate; exhale
DISCERNIBLE (dihs <u>uhrn</u> ih buhl) *adj.*
   able to be perceived or recognized
      Synonyms: observable, distinguishable, visible, evident
AGITATION (aa gih <u>tay</u> shuhn) *n.*
   uneasiness; commotion, excitement
      Synonyms: restlessness, anxiety; disturbance

chest already mentioned, which had been wheeled into the middle of the room. It was open, and its contents lay beside it on the floor. The victims must have been sitting with their backs toward the window; and, from the time elapsing between the ingress of the beast and the screams, it seems probable that it was not immediately perceived. The flapping-to of the shutter would naturally have been attributed to the wind.

As the sailor looked in, the gigantic animal had seized Madame L'Espanaye by the hair (which was loose, as she had been combing it), and was flourishing the razor about her face, in imitation of the motions of a barber. The daughter lay prostrate and motionless; she had swooned. The screams and struggles of the old lady (during which the hair was torn from her head) had the effect of changing the probably pacific purposes of the Ourang-Outang into those of wrath. With one determined sweep of its muscular arm it nearly severed her head from her body. The sight of blood inflamed its anger into frenzy. Gnashing its teeth, and flashing fire from its eyes, it flew upon the body of the girl, and imbedded its fearful talons in her throat, retaining its grasp until she expired. Its wandering and wild glances fell at this moment upon the head of the bed, over which the face of its master, rigid with horror, was just discernible. The fury of the beast, who no doubt bore still in mind the dreaded whip, was instantly converted into fear. Conscious of having deserved punishment, it seemed desirous of concealing its bloody deeds, and skipped about the chamber in an agony of nervous agitation; throwing down and breaking the furniture as it moved, and dragging the bed from the bedstead. In conclusion, it seized first the corpse of the daughter, and thrust it up the chimney, as it was found; then that of the old lady, which it immediately hurled through the window headlong.

As the ape approached the casement with its mutilated burden, the sailor shrank aghast to the rod, and, rather

SOLICITUDE (suh <u>lih</u> sih tood) *n.*
  concern, attentiveness; anxiety
    Synonyms: thoughtfulness, consideration;
    uneasiness

SUBSEQUENTLY (<u>suhb</u> suh kwehnt lee) *adv.*
  in time or order, in succession, behind
    Synonyms: next, afterward

CHAGRIN (shuh <u>grihn</u>) *n.*
  shame, embarrassment, humiliation
    Synonyms: mortification, discomfiture
INDULGE (ihn <u>duhlj</u>) *v.* **-ing,-ed.**
  to give in, as to a craving or desire
    Synonyms: humor, gratify, allow, pamper
DISCOURSE (<u>dihs</u> kohrs) *v.* **-ing,-ed.**
  to talk or converse
    Synonyms: speak, discuss, lecture

PROFOUND (pruh <u>fownd</u>) (proh <u>fownd</u>) *adj.*
  intelligent; deep, infinite; difficult to understand
    Synonyms: smart; bottomless, unending; thorough,
    weighty
INGENUITY (ihn jeh <u>noo</u> ih tee) *n.*
  cleverness
    Synonyms: inventiveness, imagination, creativity

252

gliding than clambering down it, hurried at once home—dreading the consequences of the butchery, and gladly abandoning, in his terror, all **solicitude** about the fate of the Ourang-Outang. The words heard by the party upon the staircase were the Frenchman's exclamations of horror and affright, <u>commingled</u> with the fiendish jabberings of the brute.

I have scarcely anything to add. The Ourang-Outang must have escaped from the chamber, by the rod, just before the breaking of the door. It must have closed the window as it passed through it. It was **subsequently** caught by the owner himself, who obtained for it a very large sum at the *Jardin des Plantes*. Le Bon was instantly released, upon our narration of the circumstances (with some comments from Dupin) at the *bureau* of the Prefect of Police. This functionary, however well-disposed to my friend, could not altogether conceal his **chagrin** at the turn which affairs had taken, and was <u>fain</u> to **indulge** in a sarcasm or two about the propriety of every person minding his own business.

"Let him talk," said Dupin, who had not thought it necessary to reply. "Let him **discourse**; it will ease his conscience. I am satisfied with having defeated him in his own castle. Nevertheless, that he failed in the solution of this mystery, is by no means that matter for wonder which he supposes it; for, in truth, our friend the Prefect is somewhat too cunning to be **profound**. In his wisdom is no stamen. It is all head and no body, like the pictures of the Goddess Laverna—or, at best, all head and shoulders, like a codfish. But he is a good creature after all. I like him especially for one master stroke of <u>cant,</u> by which he has attained his reputation for **ingenuity**. I mean the way he has '*de nier ce qui est, et d'exploquer ce qui n'est pas.*' "[44]

ESTRANGE (ih <u>straynj</u>) *v.* **-ing,-ed.**
  to alienate, keep at a distance
    Synonyms: disaffect, separate, divorce
DILIGENTLY (<u>dihl</u> uh guhnt lee) *adv.*
  steadily and earnestly
    Synonyms: doggedly, persistently, assiduously
GARNER (<u>gahr</u> nuhr) *v.* **-ing,-ed.**
  to gather and store
    Synonyms: reap, glean, harvest, amass, acquire
ELOQUENT (<u>eh</u> luh kwuhnt) *adj.*
  persuasive and effective, often with regards to speech
    Synonyms: clear, expressive, fluent
REPROACH (rih <u>prohch</u>) *v.* **-ing,-ed.**
  to express disappointment or displeasure; to disgrace
    Synonyms: blame, rebuke, admonish; discredit
ARIDITY (aar <u>ih</u> dih tee) *n.*
  lack of interest, dullness; extreme dryness
    Synonyms: boredom, lifelessness; thirst, desiccation
IMPUTE (ihm <u>pyoot</u>) *v.* **-ing,-ed.**
  to attribute
    Synonyms: ascribe, credit, assign, refer, charge
NOTORIOUS (noh <u>tohr</u> ee uhs) *adj.*
  unfavorably known for negative traits or actions
    Synonyms: infamous, disgraced
RELISH (<u>reh</u> lihsh) *n.*
  great enjoyment
    Synonyms: zest, fondness, love, fancy
SUSCEPTIBLE (suh <u>sehp</u> tuh buhl) *adj.*
  vulnerable, unprotected
    Synonyms: sensitive, impressionable, prone, subject
REVERY or REVERIE (<u>rehv</u> uh ree) *n.*
  a daydream
    Synonyms: dream, absorption, muse, meditation
NULLITY (<u>nuh</u> lih tee) *n.*
  a worthless or unimportant point of reasoning,
  something which has no legal validity
    Synonyms: untruth, negation, contradiction

Ms. Found in a Bottle

Qui n'a plus qu'um moment à vivre
N'a plus rien à dissimuler.
Quinault—Atys[45]

Of my country and of my family I have little to say. Ill usage and length of years have driven me from the one, and **estranged** me from the other. Hereditary wealth afforded me an education of no common order, and a contemplative turn of mind enabled me to methodise the stories which early study **diligently garnered** up. Beyond all things, the works of the German moralists gave me great delight; not from my ill-advised admiration of their **eloquent** madness, but from the ease with which my habits of rigid thoughts enabled me to detect their falsities. I have often been **reproached** with the **aridity** of my genius; a deficiency of imagination has been **imputed** to me as a crime; and the Pyrrhonism[46] of my opinions has at all times rendered me **notorious**. Indeed, a strong **relish** for physical philosophy has, I fear, <u>tinctured</u> my mind with a very common error of this age—I mean the habit of referring occurrences, even the least **susceptible** of such reference, to the principles of that science. Upon the whole, no person could be less liable than myself to be led away from the severe precincts of truth by the *ignes fatui*[47] of superstition. I have thought proper to premise thus much, lest the incredible tale I have to tell should be considered rather the raving of a crude imagination, than the positive experience of a mind to which the **reveries** of fancy have been a dead letter and a **nullity**.

After many years spent in foreign travel, I sailed in the year 18—, from the port of Batavia, in the rich and

MS. FOUND IN A BOTTLE

ARCHIPELAGO (ahr kuh <u>pehl</u> uh goh) *n.*
  large group of islands
    Synonyms: cluster, scattering
INDUCEMENT (ih <u>doos</u> mehnt) *n.*
  an incentive, something that persuades
    Synonyms: encouragement, motive, urging

BEGUILE (buh <u>giel</u>) *v.* **-ing,-ed.**
  to pass time; to charm; to deceive, mislead
    Synonyms: amuse, occupy; enchant, inveigle; lure,
    coax, cozen
MONOTONY (muh <u>naht</u> uh nee) *n.*
  repetition, lack of variation
    Synonyms: tedium, boredom, dullness

populous island of Java, on a voyage to the **Archipelago** Islands. I went as passenger—having no other **inducement** than a kind of nervous restlessness which haunted me as a fiend.

Our vessel was a beautiful ship of about four hundred tons, copper-fastened, and built at Bombay of Malabar teak. She was freighted with cotton-wool and oil, from the Lachadive Islands. We had also on board coir, jaggeree, ghee,[48] cocoanuts, and a few cases of opium. The stowage was clumsily done, and the vessel consequently <u>crank</u>.

We got under way with a mere breath of wind, and for many days stood along the eastern coast of Java, without any other incident to **beguile** the **monotony** of our course than the occasional meeting with some of the small grabs of the **archipelago** to which we were bound.

One evening, leaning over the taffrail, I observed a very singular isolated cloud, to the N.W. It was remarkable, as well from its color as from its being the first we had seen since our departure from Batavia. I watched it attentively until sunset, when it spread all at once to the eastward and westward, <u>girting</u> in the horizon with a narrow strip of vapor, and looking like a long line of low beach. My notice was soon afterward attracted by the dusky-red appearance of the moon, and the peculiar character of the sea. The latter was undergoing a rapid change, and the water seemed more than usually transparent. Although I could distinctly see the bottom, yet, heaving the lead, I found the ship in fifteen fathoms. The air now became intolerably hot, and was loaded with spiral exhalations similar to those arising from heated iron. As night came on, every breath of wind died away, and a more entire calm it is impossible to conceive. The flame of a candle burned upon the poop without the least perceptible motion, and a long hair, held between the finger and thumb, hung without the possibility of detecting a vibration. However, as the captain said he could perceive no

MS. FOUND IN A BOTTLE

PRESENTIMENT (prih <u>sehn</u> tih mehnt) *n.*
the anticipation or sense that something may happen
Synonyms: expectation, premonition
APPREHEND (aa pree <u>hehnd</u>) *v.* **-ing,-ed.**
1. to anticipate fearfully; to become aware of something through one's senses; to understand
Synonyms: dread; perceive; comprehend, grasp
2. to arrest
Synonyms: capture, seize, take, nab
DEIGN (dayn) *v.* **-ing,-ed.**
to do something beneath one's dignity; to stoop
Synonyms: condescend, patronize, deem worthy
ASCERTAIN (aa suhr <u>tayn</u>) *v.* **-ing,-ed.**
to determine, discover, make certain of
Synonyms: verify, calculate, detect

TEMPEST (<u>tehm</u> pehst) *n.*
a storm; rage or fury
Synonyms: inclemency; tumult, turbulence, torrent

indication of danger, and as we were drifting in bodily to shore, he ordered the sails to be furled, and the anchor let go. No watch was set, and the crew, consisting principally of Malays, stretched themselves deliberately upon deck. I went below—not without a full **presentiment** of evil. Indeed, every appearance warranted me in **apprehending** a simoon. I told the captain of my fears; but he paid no attention to what I said, and left me without **deigning** to give a reply. My uneasiness, however, prevented me from sleeping, and about midnight I went upon deck. As I placed my foot upon the upper step of the companion-ladder, I was startled by a loud, humming noise, like that occasioned by the rapid revolution of a mill-wheel, and before I could **ascertain** its meaning, I found the ship quivering to its centre. In the next instant a wilderness of foam hurled us upon our beam-ends, and, rushing over us fore and aft, swept the entire decks from stem to stern.

The extreme fury of the blast proved, in a great measure, the salvation of the ship. Although completely water-logged, yet, as her masts had gone by the board, she rose, after a minute, heavily from the sea, and, staggering awhile beneath the immense pressure of the **tempest**, finally righted.

By what miracle I escaped destruction, it is impossible to say. Stunned by the shock of the water, I found myself, upon recovery, jammed in between the stern-post and rudder. With great difficulty I regained my feet, and looking dizzily around, was at first struck with the idea of our being among breakers; so terrific, beyond the wildest imagination, was the whirlpool of mountainous and foaming ocean within which we were engulfed. After a while I heard the voice of an old Swede, who had shipped with us at the moment of leaving port. I hallooed to him with all my strength, and presently he came reeling aft. We soon discovered that we were the sole survivors of the accident. All on deck, with the exception of ourselves, had been swept overboard; the captain and mates must

MS. FOUND IN A BOTTLE

DELUGE (<u>dehl</u> yooj) (<u>dehl</u> yoozh) (<u>day</u> looj) (<u>day</u> loozh) (dih <u>looj</u>) (dih <u>loozh</u>) *v.* **-ing,-ed.**
    to submerge, overwhelm
        Synonyms: engulf, immerse, inundate, swamp

BREACH (breech) *n.*
    the crashing of a wave; a break or gap; a violation
        Synonyms: crest; lapse, rift; contravention, dereliction

APPREHEND (aa pree <u>hehnd</u>) *v.* **-ing,-ed.**
    1. to anticipate fearfully; to become aware of something through one's senses; to understand
        Synonyms: dread; perceive; comprehend, grasp
    2. to arrest
        Synonyms: capture, seize, take, nab

CESSATION (seh <u>say</u> shuhn) *n.*
    temporary or complete halt
        Synonyms: stoppage, arrest, termination, conclusion

INEVITABLY (ihn <u>ehv</u> ih tuh blee) *adv.*
    certainly, unavoidably
        Synonyms: inescapably, surely, predictably

APPREHENSION (aa prih <u>hehn</u> shuhn) *n.*
    suspicion or fear of future or unknown evil; the act of perceiving or comprehending; a legal seizure
        Synonyms: concern, worry; understanding; capture

SUBSISTENCE (suhb <u>sihs</u> tehnts) *n.*
    means for existence, the necessities of life
        Synonyms: nourishment, livelihood, sustenance

PROCURE (proh <u>kyoor</u>) *v.* **-ing,-ed.**
    to obtain
        Synonyms: acquire, secure, get, gain

TEMPEST (<u>tehm</u> pehst) *n.*
    a storm; rage or fury
        Synonyms: inclemency; tumult, turbulence, torrent

TRIFLING (<u>trie</u> fling) *adj.*
    of slight worth, trivial, insignificant
        Synonyms: paltry, petty, picayune, frivolous, idle

SULLEN (<u>suh</u> luhn) *adj.*
    brooding, gloomy
        Synonyms: morose, sulky, somber, glum

have perished while they slept, for the cabins were **deluged** with water. Without assistance we could expect to do little for the security of the ship, and our exertions were at first paralyzed by the momentary expectation of going down. Our cable had, of course, parted like pack-thread, at the first breath of the hurricane, or we should have been instantaneously overwhelmed. We scudded with frightful velocity before the sea, and the water made clear **breaches** over us. The framework of our stern was shattered excessively, and, in almost every respect, we had received considerable injury; but to our extreme joy we found the pumps unchoked, and that we had made no great shifting of our ballast. The main fury of the blast had already blown over, and we **apprehended** little danger from the violence of the wind; but we looked forward to its total **cessation** with dismay; well believing, that in our shattered condition, we should **inevitably** perish in the tremendous swell which would ensue. But this very just **apprehension** seemed by no means likely to be soon verified. For five entire days and nights—during which our only **subsistence** was a small quantity of jaggeree,[48] **procured** with great difficulty from the forecastle—the hulk flew at a rate defying computation, before rapidly succeeding flaws of wind, which, without equalling the first violence of the simoon, were still more terrific than any **tempest** I had before encountered. Our course for the first four days was, with **trifling** variations, S.E. and by S.; and we must have run down the coast of New Holland. On the fifth day the cold became extreme, although the wind had hauled round a point more to the northward. The sun arose with a sickly yellow lustre, and clambered a very few degrees above the horizon—emitting no decisive light. There were no clouds apparent, yet the wind was upon the increase, and blew with a fitful and unsteady fury. About noon, as nearly as we could guess, our attention was again arrested by the appearance of the sun. It gave out no light, properly so called, but a dull and **sullen**

MS. FOUND IN A BOTTLE

POLARIZE (<u>poh</u> luhr iez) *v.* **-ing,-ed.**
to tend towards opposite extremes
Synonyms: split, separate
TURGID (<u>tuhr</u> jihd) *adj.*
swollen, bloated; bombastic
Synonyms: orotund, distended; grandiloquent,
overwrought
UNFATHOMABLE (uhn <u>faath</u> uhm uh buhl) *adj.*
incapable of being measured; very difficult to
understand
Synonyms: infinite, unending; incomprehensible
ENSHROUDED or SHROUDED (ehn <u>shrowd</u> ihd) *adj.*
wrapped up, hidden from sight
Synonyms: blanketed, obscured, concealed,
cloaked, enveloped
TEMPEST (<u>tehm</u> pehst) *n.*
a storm; rage or fury
Synonyms: inclemency; tumult, turbulence, torrent
UNABATED (uhn uh <u>bayt</u> ihd) *adj.*
steady and unrelenting
Synonyms: nonstop, sustained, unflagging
WRAPT or RAPT (raapt) *adj.*
deeply absorbed
Synonyms: engrossed, immersed, moved, entranced,
smitten
IMPEDIMENT (ihm <u>pehd</u> uh muhnt) *n.*
barrier, obstacle; speech disorder
Synonyms: obstruction, hindrance, block, hurdle
BILLOW (<u>bih</u> loh) *n.*
a great wave of sea water
Synonyms: surge, flood
SURPASS (suhr <u>paas</u>) *v.* **-ing,-ed.**
to do better than, be superior to
Synonyms: transcend, exceed, excel, outdo
DEFER (dih <u>fuhr</u>) *v.* **-ring,-red.**
to delay; to delegate to another
Synonyms: extend, impede, postpone; submit, yield

glow without reflection, as if all its rays were **polarized**. Just before sinking within the **turgid** sea, its central fires suddenly went out, as if hurriedly extinguished by some unaccountable power. It was a dim, silver-like rim, alone, as it rushed down the **unfathomable** ocean.

We waited in vain for the arrival of the sixth day—that day to me has not yet arrived—to the Swede never did arrive. Thenceforward we were **enshrouded** in pitchy darkness, so that we could not have seen an object at twenty paces from the ship. Eternal night continued to envelop us, all unrelieved by the phosphoric sea-brilliancy to which we had been accustomed in the tropics. We observed, too, that, although the **tempest** continued to rage with **unabated** violence, there was no longer to be discovered the usual appearance of surf, or foam, which had hitherto attended us. All around were horror, and thick gloom, and a black sweltering desert of ebony. Superstitious terror crept by degrees into the spirit of the old Swede, and my own soul was **wrapt** in silent wonder. We neglected all care of the ship, as worse than useless, and securing ourselves as well as possible, to the stump of the mizen-mast, looked out bitterly into the world of ocean. We had no means of calculating time, nor could we form any guess of our situation. We were, however, well aware of having made farther to the southward than any previous navigators, and felt great amazement at not meeting with the usual **impediments** of ice. In the meantime every moment threatened to be our last—every mountainous **billow** hurried to overwhelm us. The swell **surpassed** anything I had imagined possible, and that we were not instantly buried is a miracle. My companion spoke of the lightness of our cargo, and reminded me of the excellent qualities of our ship; but I could not help feeling the utter hopelessness of hope itself, and prepared myself gloomily for that death which I thought nothing could **defer** beyond an hour, as, with every knot of way the ship made, the swelling of the black stupendous seas

APPALLING (uh <u>pahl</u> lihng) *adj.*
  shocking, dismaying
    Synonyms: horrifying, dreadful, astounding
DESCENT (dih <u>sehnt</u>) (dee <u>sehnt</u>) *n.*
  1. the passing from a higher place to a lower place;
  a decline
    Synonyms: lowering, dismount, gravitation; slope
  2. one's ancestry
    Synonyms: heredity, lineage
STAGNANT (<u>staag</u> nuhnt) *adj.*
  immobile, stale
    Synonyms: motionless, foul, inactive, sluggish, dull
SULLEN (<u>suh</u> luhn) *adj.*
  brooding, gloomy
    Synonyms: morose, sulky, somber, glum
PRECIPITOUS (pree <u>sih</u> puh tuhs) *adj.*
  extremely steep
    Synonyms: inclined, headlong, reckless, abrupt

INNUMERABLE (ih <u>noo</u> muhr uh buhl)
(ih <u>nyoo</u> muhr uh buhl) *adj.*
  too many to be counted, inestimable
    Synonyms: incalculable, immeasurable, infinite
PINNACLE (<u>pih</u> nuh kuhl) *n.*
  peak, highest point of development
    Synonyms: summit, acme, apex, zenith, climax
SUBLIMITY (suh <u>blih</u> mih tee) *n.*
  magnificence, grandeur
    Synonyms: nobility, supremacy, glory, excellence
TOTTER (<u>tah</u> tuhr) *v.* **-ing,-ed.**
  to stand with much unsteadiness
    Synonyms: wobble, sway, reel, stagger

became more dismally **appalling**. At times we gasped for breath at an elevation beyond the <u>albatross</u>—at times became dizzy with the velocity of our **descent** into some watery hell, where the air grew **stagnant**, and no sound disturbed the slumbers of the kraken.[49]

We were at the bottom of one of these abysses, when a quick scream from my companion broke fearfully upon the night. "See! See!" cried he, shrieking in my ears, "Almighty God! See! See!" As he spoke I became aware of a dull **sullen** glare of red light, which streamed down the sides of the vast chasm where we lay, and threw a fitful brilliancy upon our deck. Casting my eyes upwards, I beheld a spectacle, which froze the current of my blood. At a terrific height directly above us, and upon the very verge of the **precipitous descent**, hovered a gigantic ship of perhaps four thousand tons. Although <u>upreared</u> upon the summit of a wave more than a hundred times her own altitude, her apparent size still exceeded that of any ship of the line or East Indiaman in existence. Her huge hull was of a deep dingy black, unrelieved by any of the customary carvings of a ship. A single row of brass cannon protruded from her open ports, and dashed from the polished surfaces the fires of **innumerable** battle-lanterns which swung to and fro about her rigging. But what mainly inspired us with horror and astonishment, was that she bore up under a press of sail in the very teeth of that supernatural sea, and of that ungovernable hurricane. When we first discovered her, her bows were alone to be seen, as she rose slowly from the dim and horrible gulf beyond her. For a moment of intense terror she paused upon the giddy **pinnacle** as if in contemplation of her own **sublimity**, then trembled, and **tottered**, and came down.

At this instant, I know not what sudden self-possession came over my spirit. Staggering as far aft as I could, I awaited fearlessly the ruin that was to overwhelm. Our own vessel was at length ceasing from her struggles, and sinking with her head to the sea. The shock of the

MS. FOUND IN A BOTTLE

DESCENDING (dih <u>sehn</u> dihng) (dee <u>sehn</u> dihng) *adj.*
passing from a higher place to a lower place
Synonyms: falling, dismounting, gravitating

INEVITABLE (ihn <u>ehv</u> ih tuh buhl) *adj.*
certain, unavoidable
Synonyms: inescapable, sure, predictable

CURSORY (<u>kuhr</u> suh ree) *adj.*
hastily done, superficial
Synonyms: shallow, careless

NOVELTY (<u>nah</u> vuhl tee) *n.*
something new, original, and unfamiliar
Synonyms: surprise, change, innovation

APPREHENSION (aa prih <u>hehn</u> shuhn) *n.*
suspicion or fear of future or unknown evil; the act of
perceiving or comprehending; a legal seizure
Synonyms: concern, worry; understanding; capture

CONTRIVE (kuhn <u>triev</u>) *v.* **-ing,-ed.**
to devise, plan, or manage; to form in an artistic manner
Synonyms: concoct, scheme; create, design

GAIT (gayt) *n.*
the way one moves on foot, a manner of walking
Synonyms: tread, walk, march, pace

INFIRMITY (ihn <u>fuhr</u> mih tee) *n.*
disease, ailment
Synonyms: weakness, frailty, affliction, illness

TOTTER (<u>tah</u> tuhr) *v.* **-ing,-ed.**
to stand with much unsteadiness
Synonyms: wobble, sway, reel, stagger

SOLEMN (<u>sah</u> luhm) *adj.*
somberly impressive; quiet, deeply serious
Synonyms: dignified, ceremonial; earnest, brooding

descending mass struck her, consequently in that portion of her frame, which was nearly under water, and the **inevitable** result was to hurl me, with irresistible violence, upon the rigging of the stranger.

As I fell, the ship hove in stays,[50] and went about; and to the confusion <u>ensuing</u> I attributed my escape from the notice of the crew. With little difficulty I made my way, unperceived, to the main hatchway, which was partially open, and soon found an opportunity of secreting myself in the hold. Why I did so I can hardly tell. An indefinite sense of awe, which at first sight of the navigators of the ship had taken hold of my mind, was perhaps the principle of my concealment. I was unwilling to trust myself with a race of people who had offered, to the **cursory** glance I had taken, so many points of vague **novelty**, doubt, and **apprehension**. I therefore thought proper to **contrive** a hiding-place in the hold. This I did by removing a small portion of the shifting-boards, in such a manner as to afford me a convenient retreat between the huge timbers of the ship.

I had scarcely completed my work, when a footstep in the hold forced me to make use of it. A man passed by my place of concealment with a feeble and unsteady **gait**. I could not see his face, but had an opportunity of observing his general appearance. There was about it an evidence of great age and **infirmity**. His knees **tottered** beneath a load of years, and his entire frame quivered under the burden. He muttered to himself, in a low broken tone, some words of a language which I could not understand, and groped in a corner among a pile of instruments, and decayed charts of navigation. His manner was a wild mixture of the <u>peevishness</u> of second childhood, and the **solemn** dignity of a God. He at length went on deck, and I saw him no more.

———————◄———————

CONSTITUTE (kahn stih <u>toot</u>) *v.* **-ing,-ed.**
to compose or be made of, to be the parts or
components of something; to equal
   Synonyms: comprise, form, make up; amount to
NOVEL (<u>nah</u> vuhl) *adj.*
new, original
   Synonyms: fresh, newfangled, innovative, unusual,
different

DIVINE (dih <u>vien</u>) *v.* **-ing,-ed.**
to foretell or know by inspiration
   Synonyms: predict, intuit, auger, foresee, presage

SINGULARITY (sihn gyuh <u>laar</u> ih tee) *n.*
something which is uncommon or peculiar
   Synonyms: uniqueness, strangeness
UNWITTINGLY (uhn <u>wih</u> ting lee) *adv.*
unconsciously, unintentionally
   Synonyms: obliviously, inadvertently
DAUB (dawb) *v.* **-ing,-ed.**
to apply with short, quick strokes; to dab
   Synonyms: smudge, smear, blot, spot

A feeling, for which I have no name, has taken possession of my soul—a sensation which will admit of no analysis, to which the lessons of bygone time are inadequate, and for which I fear futurity itself will offer me no key. To a mind **constituted** like my own, the latter consideration is an evil. I shall never—I know that I shall never—be satisfied with regard to the nature of my conceptions. Yet it is not wonderful that these conceptions are indefinite, since they have their origin in sources so utterly **novel**. A new sense—a new entity is added to my soul.

***

It is long since I first trod the deck of this terrible ship, and the rays of my destiny are, I think, gathering to a focus. Incomprehensible men! Wrapped up in meditations of a kind, which I cannot **divine**, they pass me by unnoticed. Concealment is utter folly on my part, for the people *will not* see. It is but just now that I passed directly before the eyes of the mate; it was no long while ago that I ventured into the captain's own private cabin, and took thence the materials with which I write, and have written. I shall from time to time continue this journal. It is true that I may not find an opportunity of transmitting it to the world, but I will not fail to make the endeavor. At the last moment I will enclose the MS. in a bottle, and cast it within the sea.

***

An incident has occurred which has given me new room for meditation. Are such things the operation of ungoverned chance? I had ventured upon deck and thrown myself down, without attracting any notice, among a pile of ratlin-stuff [51] and old sails, in the bottom of the yawl. While musing upon the **singularity** of my fate, I **unwittingly daubed** with a tar-brush the edges of a neatly-folded studding-sail which lay near me on a barrel.

SCRUTINIZE (<u>skroot</u> niez) *v.* **-ing,-ed.**
to observe carefully
Synonyms: examine, study, survey

SINGULAR (<u>sihn</u> gyuh luhr) *adj.*
uncommon, peculiar
Synonyms: unusual, odd, rare, unique, individual

ANTIQUATED (<u>aan</u> tih kway tihd) *adj.*
outdated, obsolete
Synonyms: archaic, old-fashioned

POROUSNESS (<u>pohr</u> uhs nehs) *n.*
the quality of having many holes
Synonyms: sponginess, permeability

DISTEND (dih <u>stehnd</u>) *v.* **-ing,-ed.**
to swell, inflate, bloat
Synonyms: broaden, bulge

VERACITY (vuhr <u>aa</u> sih tee) *n.*
accuracy, truth
Synonyms: reliability, authenticity, correctness,
exactitude

The studding-sail is now bent upon the ship, and the thoughtless touches of the brush are spread out into the word DISCOVERY.

I have made my observations lately upon the structure of the vessel. Although well armed, she is not, I think, a ship of war. Her rigging, build, and general equipment, all negative a <u>supposition</u> of this kind. What she *is not*, I can easily perceive; what she *is*, I fear it is impossible to say. I know not how it is, but in **scrutinizing** her strange model and **singular** cast of span, her huge size and overgrown suits of canvas, her severely simple bow and **antiquated** stern, there will occasionally flash across my mind a sensation of familiar things, and there is always mixed up with such indistinct shadows of recollection, an unaccountable memory of old foreign chronicles and ages long ago. ———

I have been looking at the timbers of the ship. She is built of a material to which I am a stranger. There is a peculiar character about the wood which strikes me as rendering it unfit for the purpose to which it has been applied. I mean its extreme **porousness**, considered independently of the worm-eaten condition which is a consequence of navigation in these seas, and apart from the rottenness attendant upon age. It will appear perhaps an observation somewhat over-curious, but this would have every characteristic of Spanish oak, if Spanish oak were **distended** by any unnatural means.

In reading the above sentence, a curious <u>apothegm</u> of an old weather-beaten Dutch navigator comes full upon my recollection. "It is as sure," he was wont to say, when any doubt was entertained of his **veracity**, "as sure as there is a sea where the ship itself will grow in bulk like the living body of the seaman." ———

About an hour ago, I made bold to trust myself among a group of the crew. They paid me no manner of attention, and although I stood in the very midst of them all, seemed utterly unconscious of my presence. Like the one

HOARY (<u>hohr</u> ee) (<u>haw</u> ree) *adj.*
   very old; whitish or gray from age
      Synonyms: antediluvian, antique, vintage, ancient,
      venerable
INFIRMITY (ihn <u>fuhr</u> mih tee) *n.*
   disease, ailment
      Synonyms: weakness, frailty, affliction, illness
TREMULOUS (<u>treh</u> myoo luhs) *adj.*
   trembling, quivering; fearful, timid
      Synonyms: shaking, palsied; timorous, anxious
TEMPEST (<u>tehm</u> pehst) *n.*
   a storm; rage or fury
      Synonyms: inclemency; tumult, turbulence, torrent
OBSOLETE (ahb soh <u>leet</u>) *adj.*
   no longer in use
      Synonyms: outmoded, passé, old-fashioned,
      antiquated, dated
APPALLING (uh <u>pahl</u> lihng) *adj.*
   shocking, dismaying
      Synonyms: horrifying, dreadful, astounding
BILLOW (<u>bih</u> loh) *n.*
   a great wave of sea water
      Synonyms: surge, flood
FACILITY (faa <u>sihl</u> ih tee) *n.*
   ease, proficiency
      Synonyms: simplicity, dexterity, poise, assuredness

IMPETUOUS (ihm <u>peh</u> choo uhs) *adj.*
   forceful, rapid; quick to act without thinking
      Synonyms: fierce, raging; impulsive, passionate
REVERENCE (<u>rehv</u> uhr ehnts) *n.*
   a feeling of great awe and respect
      Synonyms: veneration, adoration, idolization,
      admiration

I had at first seen in the hold, they all bore about them the marks of a **hoary** old age. Their knees trembled with **infirmity**; their shoulders were bent double with <u>decrepitude</u>; their shrivelled skins rattled in the wind; their voices were low, **tremulous**, and broken; their eyes glistened with the <u>rheum</u> of years; and their gray hairs streamed terribly in the **tempest**. Around them, on every part of the deck, lay scattered mathematical instruments of the most quaint and **obsolete** construction. ——

I mentioned, some time ago, the bending of a studding-sail. From that period, the ship, being thrown dead off the wind, has continued her terrific course due south, with every rag of canvas packed upon her, from her truck to her lower studding-sail booms, and rolling every moment her top-gallant yard-arms into the most **appalling** hell of water which it can enter into the mind of man to imagine. I have just left the deck, where I find it impossible to maintain a footing, although the crew seem to experience little inconvenience. It appears to me a miracle of miracles that our enormous bulk is not swallowed up at once and forever. We are surely doomed to hover continually upon the brink of eternity, without taking a final plunge into the abyss. From **billows** a thousand times more stupendous than any I have ever seen, we glide away with the **facility** of the arrowy sea-gull; and the colossal waters rear their heads above us like demons of the deep, but like demons confined to simple threats, and forbidden to destroy. I am led to attribute these frequent escapes to the only natural cause which can account for such effect. I must suppose the ship to be within the influence of some strong current, or **impetuous** undertow. ——

I have seen the captain face to face, and in his own cabin—but, as I expected, he paid me no attention. Although in his appearance there is, to a casual observer, nothing which might bespeak him more or less than man, still, a feeling of irrepressible **reverence** and awe mingled with the sensation of wonder with which I regarded him. In

ROBUST (roh <u>buhst</u>) *adj.*
  strong and healthy; hardy
    Synonyms: vigorous, sturdy, sound, well, hale

SINGULARITY (sihn gyuh <u>laar</u> ih tee) *n.*
  something which is uncommon or peculiar
    Synonyms: uniqueness, strangeness

SENTIMENT (<u>sehn</u> tuh muhnt) *n.*
  an attitude, thought, or judgment prompted by
  feeling; a romantic or nostalgic feeling
    Synonyms: idea; emotion

MYRIAD (<u>mihr</u> ee uhd) *n.*
  immense number, multitude
    Synonyms: crowd, army, legion, mass

OBSOLETE (ahb soh <u>leet</u>) *adj.*
  no longer in use
    Synonyms: outmoded, passé, old-fashioned,
    antiquated, dated

PORE (pohr) *v.* **-ing,-ed.**
  to study closely or meditatively
    Synonyms: peruse, gaze, ponder

IMBUE (ihm <u>byoo</u>) *v.* **-ing,-ed.**
  to infuse; to dye, wet
    Synonyms: charge, freight, permeate; moisten

ATHWART (athwahrt) *adv.*
  across, from side to side,
    Synonyms: crosswise, obliquely, aslant, blocking

ANTIQUITY (aan <u>tih</u> kwih tee) *n.*
  an ancient item; ancient times; the quality of being
  very old
    Synonyms: relic; history; hoariness

APPREHENSION (aa prih <u>hehn</u> shuhn) *n.*
  suspicion or fear of future or unknown evil; the act of
  perceiving or comprehending; a legal seizure
    Synonyms: concern, worry; understanding; capture

CHAOS (<u>kay</u> ahs) *n.*
  extreme disorder
    Synonyms: incoherence, randomness, disorganization

stature, he is nearly my own height; that is, about five feet eight inches. He is of a well-knit and compact frame of body, neither **robust** nor remarkable otherwise. But it is the **singularity** of the expression which reigns upon the face—it is the intense, the wonderful, the thrilling evidence of old age so utter, so extreme, which excites within my spirit a sense—a **sentiment** <u>ineffable</u>. His forehead, although little wrinkled, seems to bear upon it the stamp of a **myriad** of years. His gray hairs are records of the past, and his grayer eyes are sibyls[52] of the future. The cabin floor was thickly strewn with strange, iron-clasped folios, and <u>mouldering</u> instruments of science, and **obsolete** long-forgotten charts. His head was bowed down upon his hands, and he **pored**, with a fiery, unquiet eye, over a paper which I took to be a commission, and which, at all events, bore the signature of a monarch. He murmured to himself—as did the first seaman whom I saw in the hold—some low <u>peevish</u> syllables of a foreign tongue; and although the speaker was close at my elbow, his voice seemed to reach my ears from the distance of a mile. ————

The ship and all in it are **imbued** with the spirit of Eld.[53] The crew glide to and fro like the ghosts of buried centuries; their eyes have an eager and uneasy meaning; and when their fingers fall **athwart** my path in the wild glare of the battle-lanterns, I feel as I have never felt before, although I have been all my life a dealer in **antiquities**, and have <u>imbibed</u> the shadows of fallen columns at Balbec, and Tadmor, and Persepolis,[54] until my very soul has become a ruin. ————

When I look around me, I feel ashamed of my former **apprehension**. If I trembled at the blast which has hitherto attended us, shall I not stand aghast at a warring of wind and ocean, to convey any idea of which, the words tornado and <u>simoon</u> are trivial and ineffective? All in the immediate vicinity of the ship, is the blackness of eternal night, and a **chaos** of foamless water; but, about a league on either side of us, may be seen, indistinctly and at intervals, stupendous

DESOLATE (<u>deh</u> soh liht) *adj.*
　devoid of warmth or comfort; showing the effects of
　abandonment or neglect
　　Synonyms: cheerless, somber, wretched; barren,
　　bleak, forsaken, vacant

APPELLATION (aa puhl <u>ay</u> shuhn) *n.*
　a title or name
　　Synonyms: denomination, designation, moniker, tag

PRESUME (prih <u>zoom</u>) *v.* **-ing,-ed.**
　to assume or believe something without proof; to dare
　　Synonyms: take for granted; venture

RECONCILE (<u>reh</u> kuhn siel) *v.* **-ing,-ed.**
　1. to bring to accept
　　Synonyms: resign, submit, placate, pacify, appease
　2. to resolve a dispute
　　Synonyms: agree, accommodate, rectify, reunite

IMPART (ihm <u>pahrt</u>) *v.* **-ing,-ed.**
　to give or share, to pass on
　　Synonyms: bestow, contribute, reveal, convey

TREMULOUS (<u>treh</u> myoo luhs) *adj.*
　trembling, quivering; fearful, timid
　　Synonyms: shaking, palsied; timorous, anxious

COUNTENANCE (<u>kown</u> tuh nuhns) *n.*
　appearance, facial expression
　　Synonyms: face, features, visage

APATHY (<u>aa</u> pah thee) *n.*
　lack of feeling or emotion
　　Synonyms: indifference, insouciance, disregard,
　　unconcern

PONDER (<u>pahn</u> duhr) *v.* **-ing,-ed.**
　to consider or think about something in depth
　　Synonyms: contemplate, reflect, ruminate

TEMPEST (<u>tehm</u> pehst) *n.*
　a storm; rage or fury
　　Synonyms: inclemency; tumult, turbulence, torrent

<u>ramparts</u> of ice, towering away into the **desolate** sky, and looking like the walls of the universe. ———

As I imagined, the ship proves to be in a current—if that **appellation** can properly be given to a tide which, howling and shrieking by the white ice, thunders on to the southward with a velocity like the headlong dashing of a <u>cataract</u>. ———

To conceive the horror of my sensations is, I **presume**, utterly impossible; yet a curiosity to penetrate the mysteries of these awful regions, predominates even over my despair, and will **reconcile** me to the most hideous aspect of death. It is evident that we are hurrying onward to some exciting knowledge—some never-to-be-**imparted** secret, whose attainment is destruction. Perhaps this current leads us to the southern pole itself. It must be confessed that a <u>supposition</u> apparently so wild has every probability in its favor.

The crew pace the deck with unquiet and **tremulous** step; but there is upon their **countenance** an expression more of the eagerness of hope than of the **apathy** of despair.

In the meantime the wind is still in our poop, and, as we carry a crowd of canvas, the ship is at times lifted bodily from out the sea! Oh, horror upon horror!—the ice opens suddenly to the right, and to the left, and we are whirling dizzily, in immense concentric circles, round and round the borders of a gigantic amphitheatre, the summit of whose walls is lost in the darkness and the distance. But little time will be left me to **ponder** upon my destiny! The circles rapidly grow small—we are plunging madly within the grasp of the whirlpool—and amid a roaring, and bellowing, and thundering of ocean and **tempest**, the ship is quivering—oh God!—and going down!

PROVIDENCE (<u>prah</u> vih dehnts) *adj.*
the control and guardianship exercised by a deity or
God, divine intervention
Synonyms: foresight, fate, destiny, luck
COMMENSURATE (kuh <u>mehn</u> suhr ayt) *adj.*
proportional
Synonyms: corresponding, comparable
PROFUNDITY (pruh <u>fuhn</u> dih tee) *n.*
depth, infinity; intelligence, insight
Synonyms: intensity, deepness; wisdom, knowledge

PRECIPICE (<u>prehs</u> ih pihs) *n.*
an edge, a steep overhang
Synonyms: crag, cliff, brink
PERILOUS (<u>pehr</u> uh luhs) *adj.*
full of danger
Synonyms: risky, hazardous, unsafe

A DESCENT INTO THE <u>MAELSTRÖM</u>

The ways of God in Nature, as in **Providence**, are not as our ways; nor are the models that we frame in any way **commensurate** to the vastness, **profundity**, and unsearchableness of His works, *which have a depth in them greater than the well of Democritus.*[55]

—*Joseph Glanvill*

We had now reached the summit of the loftiest crag. For some minutes the old man seemed too much exhausted to speak.

"Not long ago," said he at length, " I could have guided you on this route as well as the youngest of my sons; but, about three years past, there happened to me an event such as never happened before to mortal man—or at least such as no man ever survived to tell of—and the six hours of deadly terror which I then endured have broken me up body and soul. You suppose me a very old man—but I am not. It took less than a single day to change these hairs from a jetty black to white, to weaken my limbs, and to unstring my nerves, so that I tremble at the least exertion, and am frightened at a shadow. Do you know I can scarcely look over this little cliff without getting giddy?"

The "little cliff," upon whose edge he had so carelessly thrown himself down to rest that the weightier portion of his body hung over it, while he was only kept from falling by the <u>tenure</u> of his elbow on its extreme and slippery edge—this "little cliff" arose, a sheer unobstructed **precipice** of black shining rock, some fifteen or sixteen hundred feet from the world of crags beneath us. Nothing would have tempted me to be within half a dozen yards of its brink. In truth so deeply was I excited by the **perilous**

DIVEST (dih <u>vehst</u>) (die <u>vehst</u>) *v.* **-ing,-ed.**
to take away, as in one's possessions or character
Synonyms: deprive, strip, dispossess, remove

DEPLORABLY (dih <u>plohr</u> uh blee) *adv.*
woefully; in a regrettable or condemnable manner
Synonyms: unfortunately, lamentably, pitifully;
wretchedly

DESOLATE (<u>deh</u> soh liht) *adj.*
devoid of warmth or comfort; showing the effects of
abandonment or neglect
Synonyms: cheerless, somber, wretched; barren,
bleak, forsaken, vacant

APEX (<u>ay</u> pehks) *n.*
highest point, summit, zenith
Synonyms: acme, crown, peak, crest

DISCERNIBLE (dihs <u>uhrn</u> ih buhl) *adj.*
able to be perceived or recognized
Synonyms: observable, distinguishable, visible, evident

position of my companion, that I fell at full length upon the ground, clung to the shrubs around me, and dared not even glance upward at the sky—while I struggled in vain to **divest** myself of the idea that the very foundations of the mountain were in danger from the fury of the winds. It was long before I could reason myself into sufficient courage to sit up and look out into the distance.

"You must get over these fancies," said the guide, "for I have brought you here that you might have the best possible view of the scene of that event I mentioned—and to tell you the whole story with the spot just under your eyes.

"We are now," he continued, in that particularizing manner which distinguished him, "we are now close upon the Norwegian coast—in the sixty-eighth degree of latitude—in the great province of Nordland and in the dreary district of Lofoden. The mountain upon whose top we sit is Helseggen, the Cloudy. Now raise yourself up a little higher, hold on to the grass if you feel giddy, and look out, beyond the belt of vapor beneath us, into the sea."

I looked dizzily and beheld a wide expanse of ocean, whose waters wore so inky a hue as to bring at once to my mind the Nubian geographer's account of the *Mare Tenebrarum*.[56] A panorama more **deplorably desolate** no human imagination can conceive. To the right and left, as far as the eye could reach, there lay outstretched, like <u>ramparts</u> of the world, lines of horridly black and beetling cliff, whose character of gloom was but the more forcibly illustrated by the surf which reared high up against it its white and ghastly crest, howling and shrieking for ever. Just opposite the <u>promontory</u> upon whose **apex** we were placed, and at a distance of some five or six miles out at sea, there was visible a small, bleak-looking island; or, more properly, its position was **discernible** through the wilderness of surge in which it was enveloped. About two miles nearer the land, arose another of smaller size, hideously craggy and barren,

A DESCENT INTO THE MAELSTRÖM

ENCOMPASS (ehn <u>kuhm</u> puhs) *v.* **-ing,-ed.**
   to cover, surround; to include, take in
      Synonyms: enclose, envelop; constitute, involve

ASCEND (uh <u>sehnd</u>) *v.* **-ing,-ed.**
   to rise to another level or climb; to move upward
      Synonyms: elevate, escalate, mount; hoist, lift

IMPETUOSITY (ihm peh choo <u>ah</u> sih tee) *n.*
   rapid force, violence; quickness to act without thinking
      Synonyms: ferocity, rage; impulsiveness, passion
UPROAR (<u>uhp</u> rohr) *n.*
   noisy and forceful turbulence or commotion
      Synonyms: clamor, mayhem, turmoil

and **encompassed** at various intervals by a cluster of dark rocks.

The appearance of the ocean, in the space between the more distant island and the shore, had something very unusual about it. Although, at the time, so strong a gale was blowing landward that a brig in the remote offing lay to under a double-reefed trysail, and constantly plunged her whole hull out of sight, still there was here nothing like a regular swell, but only a short, quick, angry cross dashing of water in every direction—as well in the teeth of the wind as otherwise. Of foam there was little except in the immediate vicinity of the rocks.

"The island in the distance," resumed the old man, "is called by the Norwegians Vurrgh. The one midway is Moskoe. That a mile to the northward is Ambaaren. Yonder are Islesen, Hotholm, Keildhelm, Suarven, and Buckholm. Further off—between Moskoe and Vurrgh—are Otterholm, Flimen, Sandflesen, and Stockholm. These are the true names of the places, but why it has been thought necessary to name them at all, is more than either you or I can understand. Do you hear any thing? Do you see any change in the water?"

We had now been about ten minutes upon the top of Helseggen, to which we had **ascended** from the interior of Lofoden, so that we had caught no glimpse of the sea until it had burst upon us from the summit. As the old man spoke, I became aware of a loud and gradually increasing sound, like the moaning of a vast herd of buffaloes upon an American prairie; and at the same moment I perceived that what seamen term the chopping character of the ocean beneath us, was rapidly changing into a current which set to the eastward. Even while I gazed, this current acquired a monstrous velocity. Each moment added to its speed—to its headlong **impetuosity**. In five minutes the whole sea, as far as Vurrgh, was lashed into ungovernable fury; but it was between Moskoe and the coast that the main **uproar** held its sway. Here the vast

INNUMERABLE (ih <u>noo</u> muhr uh buhl)
(ih <u>nyoo</u> muhr uh buhl) *adj.*
  too many to be counted, inestimable
    Synonyms: incalculable, immeasurable, infinite

PRECIPITOUS (pree <u>sih</u> puh tuhs) *adj.*
  very steep; hasty, quickly, with too little caution
    Synonyms: high, craggy, sharp; impetuous,
    reckless, abrupt, rash

DESCENT (dih <u>sehnt</u>) (dee <u>sehnt</u>) *n.*
  1. the passing from a higher place to a lower place;
  a decline
    Synonyms: lowering, dismount, gravitation; slope
  2. one's ancestry
    Synonyms: heredity, lineage

PRODIGIOUS (pruh <u>dih</u> juhs) *adj.*
  vast, enormous, extraordinary
    Synonyms: huge, gigantic, impressive, marvelous

FATHOM (<u>faath</u> uhm) *v.* **-ing,-ed.**
  to measure the depth of; to understand fully, to gauge
    Synonyms: sound; comprehend

INCLINE (ihn <u>klien</u>) *v.* **-ing,-ed.**
  1. to bend or tilt upward
    Synonyms: slope, slant, lean, deviate, point
  2. to have a specific tendency, to be predisposed
    Synonyms: lean to, influence, impel, prefer

APPALLING (uh <u>pahl</u> lihng) *adj.*
  shocking, dismaying
    Synonyms: horrifying, dreadful, ghastly, awful

AGITATION (aa gih <u>tay</u> shuhn) *n.*
  uneasiness; commotion, excitement
    Synonyms: restlessness, anxiety; disturbance

bed of the waters, seamed and scarred into a thousand conflicting channels, burst suddenly into frenzied convulsion—heaving, boiling, tossing—gyrating in gigantic and **innumerable** vortices, and all whirling and plunging on to the eastward with a rapidity which water never elsewhere assumes, except in **precipitous descents**.

In a few minutes more, there came over the scene another radical alteration. The general surface grew somewhat more smooth, and the whirlpools, one by one, disappeared, while **prodigious** streaks of foam became apparent where none had been seen before. These streaks, at length, spreading out to a great distance, and entering into combination, took unto themselves the gyratory motion of the subsided vortices, and seemed to form the germ of another more vast. Suddenly—very suddenly—this assumed a distinct and definite existence, in a circle of more than a mile in diameter. The edge of the whirl was represented by a broad belt of gleaming spray; but no particle of this slipped into the mouth of the terrific funnel, whose interior, as far as the eye could **fathom** it, was a smooth, shining, and jet-black wall of water, **inclined** to the horizon at an angle of some forty-five degrees, speeding dizzily round and round with a swaying and sweltering motion, and sending forth to the winds an **appalling** voice, half shriek, half roar, such as not even the mighty cataract of Niagara ever lifts up in its agony to Heaven.

The mountain trembled to its very base, and the rock rocked. I threw myself upon my face, and clung to the scant herbage in an excess of nervous **agitation**.

"This," said I at length, to the old man, "this can be nothing else than the great whirlpool of the Maelström."

"So it is sometimes termed," said he. "We Norwegians call it the Moskoe-ström, from the island of Moskoe in the midway."

The ordinary account of this vortex had by no means prepared me for what I saw. That of Jonas Ramus, which

A DESCENT INTO THE MAELSTRÖM

IMPART (ihm <u>pahrt</u>) *v.* **-ing,-ed.**
  to give or share, to pass on
    Synonyms: bestow, contribute, reveal, convey
NOVEL (<u>nah</u> vuhl) *n.*
  newness, originality
    Synonyms: freshness, innovation, unusual,
    difference
CONFOUND (kuhn <u>fownd</u>) *v.* **-ing,-ed.**
  to baffle, perplex; to mistake something for another
    Synonyms: overwhelm, disconcert, entangle,
    muddle; confuse, misidentify

BOISTEROUS (<u>boy</u> stuhr uhs) (<u>boy</u> struhs) *adj.*
  rowdy, loud, unrestrained
    Synonyms: clamorous, uproarious
IMPETUOUS (ihm <u>peh</u> choo uhs) *adj.*
  forceful, rapid; quick to act without thinking
    Synonyms: fierce, raging; impulsive, passionate
EBB (ehb) *n.*
  the reflux of the tide
    Synonyms: retreat, abatement, waning, withdrawal
INEVITABLY (ihn <u>ehv</u> ih tuh blee) *adv.*
  certainly, unavoidably
    Synonyms: inescapably, surely, predictably

is perhaps the most circumstantial of any, cannot **impart** the faintest conception either of the magnificence, or of the horror of the scene—or of the wild bewildering sense of the **novel** which **confounds** the beholder. I am not sure from what point of view the writer in question surveyed it, nor at what time; but it could neither have been from the summit of Helseggen, nor during a storm. There are some passages of his description, nevertheless, which may be quoted for their details, although their effect is exceedingly feeble in conveying an impression of the spectacle.

"Between Lofoden and Moskoe," he says, "the depth of the water is between thirty-six and forty fathoms; but on the other side, toward Ver (Vurrgh) this depth decreases so as not to afford a convenient passage for a vessel, without the risk of splitting on the rocks, which happens even in the calmest weather. When it is flood, the stream runs up the country between Lofoden and Moskoe with a **boisterous** rapidity; but the roar of its **impetuous ebb** to the sea is scarce equalled by the loudest and most dreadful <u>cataracts</u>; the noise being heard several leagues off, and the <u>vortices</u> or pits are of such an extent and depth, that if a ship comes within its attraction, it is **inevitably** absorbed and carried down to the bottom, and there beat to pieces against the rocks; and when the water relaxes, the fragments thereof are thrown up again. But these intervals of tranquillity are only at the turn of the **ebb** and flood, and in calm weather, and last but a quarter of an hour, its violence gradually returning. When the stream is most **boisterous**, and its fury heightened by a storm, it is dangerous to come within a Norway mile of it. Boats, yachts, and ships have been carried away by not guarding against it before they were carried within its reach. It likewise happens frequently, that whales come too near the stream and are overpowered by its violence, and then it is impossible to describe their howling and bellowings in their fruitless struggles to disengage themselves. A bear once, attempting to swim from Lofoden to

IMPETUOSITY (ihm peh choo <u>ah</u> sih tee) *n.*
  rapid force, violence; quickness to act without thinking
    Synonyms: ferocity, rage; impulsiveness, passion
ASCERTAIN (aa suhr <u>tayn</u>) *v.* **-ing,-ed.**
  to determine, discover, make certain of
    Synonyms: verify, calculate, detect

PINNACLE (<u>pih</u> nuh kuhl) *n.*
  peak, highest point of development
    Synonyms: summit, acme, apex, zenith, climax
ANECDOTE (<u>aa</u> nihk doht) *n.*
  a short, usually funny account of an event
    Synonyms: story, joke

PLAUSIBLE (<u>plaw</u> zih buhl) *adj.*
  believable and valid
    Synonyms: probable, likely, credible
PERUSAL (puh <u>roo</u> zuhl) *n.*
  a close examination
    Synonyms: scrutiny, inspection

Moskoe, was caught by the stream and borne down, while he roared terribly, so as to be heard on shore. Large stocks of firs and pine trees, after being absorbed by the current, rise again broken and torn to such a degree as if bristles grew upon them. This plainly shows the bottom to consist of craggy rocks, among which they are whirled to and fro. This stream is regulated by the flux and reflux of the sea—it being constantly high and low water every six hours. In the year 1645, early in the morning of Sexagesima Sunday,[57] it raged with such noise and **impetuosity** that the very stones of the houses on the coast fell to the ground."

In regard to the depth of the water, I could not see how this could have been **ascertained** at all in the immediate vicinity of the <u>vortex</u>. The "forty fathoms" must have reference only to portions of the channel close upon the shore either of Moskoe or Lofoden. The depth in the center of the Moskoe-ström must be unmeasurably greater; and no better proof of this fact is necessary than can be obtained from even the sidelong glance into the abyss of the whirl which may be had from the highest crag of Helseggen. Looking down from this **pinnacle** upon the howling Phlegethon[58] below, I could not help smiling at the simplicity with which the honest Jonas Ramus records, as a matter difficult of belief, the **anecdotes** of the whales and the bears. For it appeared to me, in fact, a self-evident thing, that the largest ships of the line in existence, coming within the influence of that deadly attraction, could resist it as little as a feather the hurricane, and must disappear bodily and at once.

The attempts to account for the phenomenon—some of which I remember, seemed to me sufficiently **plausible** in **perusal**—now wore a very different and unsatisfactory aspect. The idea generally received is that this, as well as three smaller <u>vortices</u> among the Ferroe Islands, "have no other cause than the collision of waves rising and falling, at flux and reflux, against a ridge of rocks and shelves,

A DESCENT INTO THE MAELSTRÖM

PRECIPITATE (preh <u>sih</u> puh tayt) *v.* **-ing,-ed.**
    to move rapidly, to bring about abruptly; to throw
        Synonyms: speed, launch, accelerate; cast, hurl
PRODIGIOUS (pruh <u>dih</u> juhs) *adj.*
    vast, enormous, extraordinary
        Synonyms: huge, gigantic, impressive, marvelous

ASSENT (uh <u>sehnt</u>) *v.* **-ing,-ed.**
    to agree
        Synonyms: accede, concur, acquiesce

which confines the water so that it **precipitates** itself like a cataract; and thus the higher the flood rises, the deeper must the fall be, and the natural result of all is a whirlpool or vortex, the **prodigious** suction of which is sufficiently known by lesser experiments." These are the words of the Encyclopeadia Britannica. Kircher and others imagine that in the centre of the channel of the maelström is an abyss penetrating the globe, and issuing in some very remote part—the Gulf of Bothnia being somewhat decidedly named in one instance. This opinion, idle in itself, was the one to which, as I gazed, my imagination most readily **assented**; and, mentioning it to the guide, I was rather surprised to hear him say that, although it was the view almost universally entertained of the subject by the Norwegians, it nevertheless was not his own. As to the former notion he confessed his inability to comprehend it; and here I agreed with him—for however conclusive on paper, it becomes altogether unintelligible, even absurd, amid the thunder of the abyss.

"You have had a good look at the whirl now," said the man, "and if you will creep 'round this crag, so as to get in its lee, and deaden the roar of the water, I will tell you a story that will convince you I ought to know something the Moskoe-ström."

I placed myself as desired, and he proceeded.

"Myself and my two brothers once owned a schooner-rigged smack of about seventy tons burden, with which we were in the habit of fishing among the islands beyond Moskoe, nearly to Vurrgh. In all violent eddies at sea there is good fishing, and proper opportunities if one has only the courage to attempt it. But among the whole of the Lofoden coastmen, we three were the only ones who made regular business of going out to the islands, as I tell you. The usual grounds are a great way lower down to the southward. There fish can be got at all hours without much risk, and therefore these places are prefered. The choice spots over here among the rocks, however, not only yield

BOISTEROUS (<u>boy</u> stuhr uhs) (<u>boy</u> struhs) *adj.*
  rowdy, loud, unrestrained
    Synonyms: clamorous, uproarious

INNUMERABLE (ih <u>noo</u> muhr uh buhl)
(ih <u>nyoo</u> muhr uh buhl) *adj.*
  too many to be counted, inestimable
    Synonyms: incalculable, immeasurable, infinite

the finest variety, but in far greater abundance; so that we often got in a single day, what the more timid of the craft could not scrape together in a week. In fact, we made it a matter of desperate speculation—the risk of life standing instead of labor, and courage answering for capital.

"We kept the smack in a cove about five miles higher up the coast than this; and it was our practice, in fine weather, to take advantage of the fifteen minutes slack to push across the main channel of the Moskoe-ström, far above the pool, and then drop down upon anchorage somewhere near Otterholm, or Sandflesen, where the eddies are not so violent as elsewhere. Here we used to remain until nearly time for slack-water again, when we weighed and made for home. We never set out upon this expedition without a steady side wind for going and coming—one that we felt sure would not fail us before our return—and we seldom made a miscalculation upon this point. Twice, during six years, we were forced to stay all night at anchor on account of a dead calm, which is a rare thing indeed just about here; and once we had to remain on the grounds nearly a week, starving to death, owing to a gale which blew up shortly after our arrival, and made the channel too boisterous to be thought of. Upon this occasion we should have been driven out to sea in spite of every thing (for the whirlpools threw us round and round so violently, that, at length, we fouled our anchor and dragged it), if it had not been that we drifted into one of the innumerable cross currents—here to-day and gone to-morrow—which drove us under the lee of Flimen, where, by good luck, we brought up.

"I could not tell you the twentieth part of the difficulties we encountered 'on the ground'—it is a bad spot to be in, even in good weather—but we make shift always to run the gauntlet of the Moskoe-ström itself without accident; although at times my heart has been in my mouth when we happened to be a minute or so behind or before the slack. The wind sometimes was not as strong as we thought it at

APPREHEND (aa pree <u>hehnd</u>) *v.* **-ing,-ed.**
1. to anticipate fearfully; to become aware of something through one's senses; to understand
   Synonyms: dread; perceive; comprehend, grasp
2. to arrest
   Synonyms: capture, seize, take, nab

starting, and then we made rather less way than we could wish, while the current rendered the <u>smack</u> unmanageable. My eldest brother had a son eighteen years old, and I had two stout boys of my own. These would have been of great assistance at such times, in using the sweeps as well as afterward in fishing—but, somehow, although we ran the risk ourselves, we had not the heart to let the young ones get into the danger—for, after all said and done, it was a horrible danger, and that is the truth.

"It is now within a few days of three years since what I am going to tell you occurred. It was on the tenth of July, 18—, a day which the people of this part of the world will never forget—for it was one in which blew the most terrible hurricane that ever came out of the heavens. And yet all the morning, and indeed until late in the afternoon, there was a gentle and steady breeze from the southwest, while the sun shone brightly, so that the oldest seaman among us could not have foreseen what was to follow.

"The three of us—my two brothers and myself—had crossed over to the islands about two o'clock P.M., and soon nearly loaded the <u>smack</u> with fine fish, which, we all remarked, were more plenty that day than we had ever known them. It was just seven, by my watch, when we weighed and started for home, so as to make the worst of the Ström at slack water, which we knew would be at eight.

"We set out with a fresh wind on our starboard quarter, and for some time spanked along at a great rate, never dreaming of danger, for indeed we saw not the slightest reason to **apprehend** it. All at once we were taken aback by a breeze from over Helseggen. This was most unusual—something that had never happened to us before—and I began to feel a little uneasy, without exactly knowing why. We put the boat on the wind, but could make no headway at all for the eddies, and I was upon the point of proposing to return to the anchorage, when, looking astern, we saw the whole horizon covered

SINGULAR (<u>sihn</u> gyuh luhr) *adj.*
   uncommon, peculiar
      Synonyms: unusual, odd, rare, unique, individual

FOUNDER (<u>fown</u> duhr) *v.* **-ing,-ed.**
   to fall helplessly, to sink
      Synonyms: miscarry, immerse, plunge
ASCERTAIN (aa suhr <u>tayn</u>) *v.* **-ing,-ed.**
   to determine, discover, make certain of
      Synonyms: verify, calculate, detect

DELUGE (<u>dehl</u> yooj) (<u>dehl</u> yoozh) (<u>day</u> looj) (<u>day</u> loozh)
(dih <u>looj</u>) (dih <u>loozh</u>) *v.* **-ing,-ed.**
   to submerge, overwhelm
      Synonyms: engulf, immerse, inundate, swamp

with a **singular** copper-colored cloud that rose with the most amazing velocity.

"In the meantime the breeze that had headed us off fell away and we were dead becalmed, drifting about in every direction. This state of things, however, did not last long enough to give us time to think about it. In less than a minute the storm was upon us—in less than two the sky was entirely overcast—and what with this and the driving spray, it became suddenly so dark that we could not see each other in the <u>smack</u>.

"Such a hurricane as then blew it is folly to attempt describing. The oldest seaman in Norway never experienced any thing like it. We had let our sails go by the run before it cleverly took us; but, at the first puff, both our masts went by the board as if they had been sawed off—the mainmast taking with it my youngest brother, who had lashed himself to it for safety.

"Our boat was the lightest feather of a thing that ever sat upon water. It had a complete flush deck, with only a small hatch near the bow, and this hatch it had always been our custom to batten down when about to cross the Ström, by way of precaution against the chopping seas. But for this circumstance we should have **foundered** at once—for we lay entirely buried for some moments. How my elder brother escaped destruction I cannot say, for I never had an opportunity of **ascertaining**. For my part, as soon as I had let the foresail run, I threw myself flat on deck, with my feet against the narrow gunwale of the bow, and with my hands grasping a ring-bolt near the foot of the foremast. It was there instinct that prompted me to do this—which was undoubtedly the very best thing I could have done—for I was too much flurried to think.

"For some moments we were completely **deluged**, as I say, and all this time I held my breath, and clung to the bolt. When I could stand it no longer I raised myself upon my knees, still keeping hold with my hands, and thus got my head clear. Presently our little boat gave

STUPOR (<u>stoo</u> puhr) *n.*
    a state of having numbed senses; astonishment
        Synonyms: daze, trance; bewilderment, amazement

TEMPEST (<u>tehm</u> pehst) *n.*
    a storm; rage or fury
        Synonyms: inclemency; tumult, turbulence, torrent

SINGULAR (<u>sihn</u> gyuh luhr) *adj.*
    uncommon, peculiar
        Synonyms: unusual, odd, rare, unique, individual

herself a shake, just as a dog does in coming out of the water, and thus rid herself, in some measure, of the seas. I was now trying to get the better of the **stupor** that had come over me, and to collect my senses so as to see what was to be done, when I felt somebody grasp my arm. It was my elder brother, and my heart leaped for joy, for I had made sure that he was overboard—but the next moment all this joy was turned into horror—for he put his mouth close to my ear, and screamed out the word '*Moskoe-ström!*'

"No one ever will know what my feelings were at that moment. I shook from head to foot as if I had had the most violent fit of the ague. I knew what he meant by that one word well enough—I knew what he wished to make me understand. With the wind that now drove us on, we were bound for the whirl of the Ström, and nothing could save us!

"You perceive that in crossing the Ström channel, we always went a long way up above the whirl, even in the calmest weather, and then had to wait and watch carefully for slack—but now we were driving right upon the pool itself, and in such a hurricane as this! 'To be sure,' I thought, 'we shall get there just about the slack—there is some little hope in that'—but in the next moment I cursed myself for being so great a fool as to dream of hope at all. I knew very well that we were doomed, had we been ten times a ninety-gun ship.

"By this time the first fury of the **tempest** had spent itself, or perhaps we did not feel it so much, as we scudded before it, but at all events the seas, which at first had been kept down by the wind, and lay flat and frothing, now got up into absolute mountains. A **singular** change, too, had come over the heavens. Around in every direction it was still as black as pitch, but nearly overhead there burst out, all at once, a circular rift of clear sky—as clear as I ever saw—and of a deep bright blue—and through it there blazed forth the full moon with a lustre that I never before

A DESCENT INTO THE MAELSTRÖM

DIN (dihn) *n.*
   blaring noise
      Synonyms: loudness, clamor, cacophony, commotion

knew her to wear. She lit up every thing about us with the greatest distinctness—but, oh God, what a scene it was to light up!

"I now made one or two attempts to speak to my brother—but in some manner which I could not understand, the din had so increased that I could not make him hear a single word, although I screamed at the top of my voice in his ear. Presently he shook his head, looking as pale as death, and held up one of his fingers, as if to say '*listen!*'

"At first I could not make out what he meant—but soon a hideous thought flashed upon me. I dragged my watch from its <u>fob</u>. It was not going. I glanced at its face by the moonlight, and then burst into tears as I flung it far away into the ocean. It had run down at seven o'clock! We were behind the time of the slack, and the whirl of the Ström was in full fury!

"When a boat is well built, properly trimmed, and not deep laden, the waves in a strong gale, when she is going large, seem always to slip from beneath her—which appears strange to a landsman—and this is what is called *riding*, in sea phrase.

"Well, so far we had ridden the swells very cleverly; but presently a gigantic sea happened to take us right under the counter, and bore us with it as it rose—up—up—as if into the sky. I would not have believed that any wave could rise so high. And then down we came with a sweep, a slide, and a plunge that made me feel sick and dizzy, as if I was falling from some lofty mountain-top in a dream. But while we were up I had thrown a quick glance around—and that one glance was all-sufficient. I saw our exact position in an instant. The Moskoe-ström whirlpool was about a quarter of a mile dead ahead—but no more like the every-day Moskoe-ström than the whirl, as you now see it, is like a mill-race. If I had not known where we were, and what we had to expect, I should not have recognized the place at all. As it was, I involuntarily closed my

PALTRY (<u>pahl</u> tree) *adj.*
   pitifully small or worthless
      Synonyms: trivial, trifling, petty, picayune, meager
MANIFESTATION (maan uh fehs <u>tay</u> shuhn) *n.*
   a clear appearance or certain display
      Synonyms: expression, exhibition, indication
KEEN *adj.*
   intellectually sharp, perceptive; having a sharp edge
      Synonyms: acute, quick, canny; pointed, razorlike

eyes in horror. The lids clenched themselves together as if in a spasm.

"It could not have been more than two minutes afterwards until we suddenly felt the waves subside, and were enveloped in foam. The boat made a sharp half turn to larboard, and then shot off in its new direction like a thunderbolt. At the same moment the roaring noise of the water was completely drowned in a kind of shrill shriek—such a sound as you might imagine given out by the water-pipes of many thousand steam-vessels letting off their steam all together. We were now in the belt of surf that always surrounds the whirl; and I thought, of course, that another moment would plunge us into the abyss, down which we could only see indistinctly on account of the amazing velocity with which we were borne along. The boat did not seem to sink into the water at all, but to skim like an air-bubble upon the surface of the surge. Her starboard side was next to the whirl, and on the larboard arose the world of ocean we had left. It stood like a huge writhing wall between us and the horizon.

"It may appear strange, but now, when we were in the very jaws of the gulf, I felt more composed than when we were only approaching it. Having made up my mind to hope no more, I got rid of a great deal of that terror which unmanned me at first. I supposed it was despair that strung my nerves.

"It may look like boasting—but what I tell you is truth—I began to reflect how magnificent a thing it was to die in such a manner, and how foolish it was in me to think of so **paltry** a consideration as my own individual life, in view of so wonderful a **manifestation** of God's power. I do believe that I blushed with shame when this idea crossed my mind. After a little while I became possessed with the **keenest** curiosity about the whirl itself. I positively felt a wish to explore its depths, even at the sacrifice I was going to make; and my principal grief was

A DESCENT INTO THE MAELSTRÖM

SINGULAR (<u>sihn</u> gyuh luhr) *adj.*
uncommon, peculiar
Synonyms: unusual, odd, rare, unique, individual

CESSATION (seh <u>say</u> shuhn) *n.*
temporary or complete halt
Synonyms: stoppage, arrest, termination, conclusion

INDULGENCE (ihn <u>duhl</u> jehns) *n.*
lenience, the act of giving into desires
Synonyms: gratification, tolerance, pampering

that I should never be able to tell my old companions on shore about the mysteries I should see. These, no doubt, were **singular** fancies to occupy a man's mind in such extremity—and I have often thought since that the revolutions of the boat around the pool might have rendered me a little light-headed.

"There was another circumstance which tended to restore my self-possession; and this was the **cessation** of the wind, which could not reach us in our present situation—for, as you saw for yourself, the belt of the surf is considerably lower than the general bed of the ocean, and this latter now towered above us, a high, black, mountainous ridge. If you have never been at sea in a heavy gale, you can form no idea of the confusion of mind occasioned by the wind and spray together. They blind, deafen, and strangle you, and take away all power of action or reflection. But we were now, in a great measure, rid of these annoyances—just as death-condemned felons in prison are allowed petty **indulgences**, forbidden them while their doom is yet uncertain.

"How often we made the circuit of the belt it is impossible to say. We careered round and round for perhaps an hour, flying rather than floating, getting gradually more and more into the middle of the surge, and then nearer and nearer to its horrible inner edge. All this time I had never let go of the ring-bolt. My brother was at the stern, holding on to a small empty water-cask which had been securely lashed under the coop of the counter, and was the only thing on deck that had not been swept overboard when the gale first took us. As we approached the brink of the pit he let go his hold upon this, and made for the ring, from which, in the agony of his terror, he endeavored to force my hands, as it was not large enough to afford us both a secure grasp. I never felt deeper grief than when I saw him attempt this act—although I knew he was a madman when he did it—a raving maniac through sheer fright. I did not care, however, to contest the point with him. I

DESCENT (dih <u>sehnt</u>) (dee <u>sehnt</u>) *n.*
  1. the passing from a higher place to a lower place;
  a decline
    Synonyms: lowering, dismount, gravitation; slope
  2. one's ancestry
    Synonyms: heredity, lineage

PRODIGIOUS (pruh <u>dih</u> juhs) *adj.*
  vast, enormous, extraordinary
    Synonyms: huge, gigantic, impressive, marvelous

INCLINED (ihn <u>kliend</u>) *adj.*
  bent or tilted upward
    Synonyms: sloped, slanted, leaning, deviating

knew it could make no difference whether either of us held on at all; so I let him have the bolt, and went astern to the cask. This there was no great difficulty in doing; for the smack flew round steadily enough, and upon an even keel—only swaying to and fro with the immense sweeps and swelters of the whirl. Scarcely had I secured myself in my new position, when we gave a wild lurch to starboard, and rushed headlong into the abyss. I muttered a hurried prayer to God, and thought all was over.

"As I felt the sickening sweep of the **descent**, I had instinctively tightened my hold upon the barrel, and closed my eyes. For some seconds I dared not open them—while I expected instant destruction, and wondered that I was not already in my death-struggles with the water. But moment after moment elapsed. I still lived. The sense of falling had ceased; and the motion of the vessel seemed much as it had been before, while in the belt of foam, with the exception that she now lay more along. I took courage and looked once again upon the scene.

"Never shall I forget the sensation of awe, horror, and admiration with which I gazed about me. The boat appeared to be hanging, as if by magic, midway down, upon the interior surface of a funnel vast in circumference, **prodigious** in depth, and whose perfectly smooth sides might have been mistaken for ebony, but for the bewildering rapidity with which they spun around, and for the gleaming and ghastly radiance they shot forth, as the rays of the full moon, from that circular rift amid the clouds which I have already described, streamed in a flood of golden glory along the black walls, and far away down into the inmost recesses of the abyss.

"At first I was too much confused to observe any thing accurately. The general burst of terrific grandeur was all that I beheld. When I recovered myself a little, however, my gaze fell instinctively downward. In the direction I was able to obtain an unobstructed view, from the manner in which the smack hung on the **inclined** surface of the

PROFOUND (pruh <u>fownd</u>) (proh <u>fownd</u>) *adj.*
  deep, infinite; intelligent; difficult to understand
    Synonyms: bottomless, unending; smart; thorough,
    weighty

TOTTERING (<u>tah</u> tuhr ihng) *adj.*
  barely standing
    Synonyms: unsteady, wobbly, swaying, reeling,
    staggering

DESCENT (dih <u>sehnt</u>) (dee <u>sehnt</u>) *n.*
  1. the passing from a higher place to a lower place;
  a decline
    Synonyms: lowering, dismount, gravitation; slope
  2. one's ancestry
    Synonyms: heredity, lineage
UNIFORM (<u>yoo</u> nuh fohrm) *adj.*
  consistent and unchanging; identical
    Synonyms: unvarying, steady, even, homogeneous;
    indistinguishable

pool. She was quite upon an even keel—that is to say, her deck lay in a plane parallel with that of the water—but this latter sloped at an angle of more than forty-five degrees, so that we seemed to be lying upon our beam-ends. I could not help observing, nevertheless, that I had scarcely more difficulty maintaining my hold and footing in this situation, than if we had been upon a dead level; and this, I suppose, was owing to the speed at which we revolved.

"The rays of the moon seemed to search the very bottom of the **profound** gulf; but still I could make out nothing distinctly on account of a thick mist in which every thing there was enveloped, and over which there hung a magnificent rainbow, like that narrow and **tottering** bridge which Mussulmen say is the only pathway between Time and Eternity. This mist, or spray, was no doubt occasioned by the clashing of the great walls of the funnel, as they all met together at the bottom—but the yell that went up to the Heavens from out of that mist I dare not attempt to describe.

"Our first slide into the abyss itself, from the belt of foam above, had carried us to a great distance down the slope; but our farther **descent** was by no means proportionate. Round and round we swept—not with any **uniform** movement—but in dizzying swings and jerks, that sent us sometimes only a few hundred yards—sometimes nearly the complete circuit of the whirl. Our progress downward, at each revolution, was slow, but very perceptible.

"Looking about me upon the wide waste of liquid ebony on which we were thus borne, I perceived that our boat was not the only object in the embrace of the whirl. Both above and below us were visible fragments of vessels, large masses of building-timber and trunks of trees, with many smaller articles, such as pieces of house furniture, broken boxes, barrels and staves. I have already described the unnatural curiosity, which had taken the

DESCENT (dih <u>sehnt</u>) (dee <u>sehnt</u>) *n.*
1. the passing from a higher place to a lower place;
a decline
   Synonyms: lowering, dismount, gravitation; slope
2. one's ancestry
   Synonyms: heredity, lineage

BUOYANT (<u>boy</u> ehnt) *adj.*
   having the tendency to float or rise; lively and cheerful
   Synonyms: light, airy, floatable, bouncy; carefree,
   jovial

DESCEND (dih <u>sehnd</u>) (dee <u>sehnd</u>) *v.* **-ing,-ed.**
   to pass from a higher place to a lower place
   Synonyms: fall, dismount, gravitate
EBB (ehb) *n.*
   the reflux of the tide
   Synonyms: retreat, abatement, waning, withdrawal
DRAW *v.* **-ing, drew, drawn**
   to pull, drag; to lead, to bring about on purpose; to
   attract or be attracted to
   Synonyms: haul, tow, yank; provoke, elicit; lure, entice

place of my original terrors. It appeared to grow upon me as I drew nearer and nearer to my dreadful doom. I now began to watch, with a strange interest, the numerous things that floated in our company. I *must* have been delirious, for I even sought *amusement* in speculating upon the relative velocities of their several **descents** toward the foam below. 'This fir-tree,' I found myself at one time saying, 'will certainly be the next thing that takes the awful plunge and disappears,' and then I was disappointed to find that the wreck of a Dutch merchant ship overtook it and went down before. At length, after making several guesses of this nature, and being deceived in all—this fact—the fact of my invariable miscalculation, set me upon a train of reflection that made my limbs again tremble, and my heart beat heavily once more.

"It was not a new terror that thus affected me, but the dawn of a more exciting hope. This hope arose partly from memory and partly from present observation. I called to mind the great variety of **buoyant** matter that strewed the coast of Lofoden, having been absorbed and then thrown forth by the Moskoe-ström. By far the greater number of the articles were shattered in the most extraordinary way—so chafed and roughened as to have the appearance of being stuck full of splinters—but then I distinctly recollected that there were some of them which were not disfigured at all. Now I could not account for this difference except by supposing that the roughened fragments were the only ones which had been *completely absorbed*—that the others had entered the whirl at so late a period of the tide, or, from some reason, had **descended** so slowly after entering, that they did not reach the bottom before the turn of the flood came, or of the **ebb**, as the case might be. I conceived it possible, in either instance that they might thus be whirled up again to the level of the ocean, without undergoing the fate of those, which had been **drawn** in more early or absorbed more rapidly. I made, also, three important observations. The

A DESCENT INTO THE MAELSTRÖM

DESCENT (dih <u>sehnt</u>) (dee <u>sehnt</u>) *n.*
  1. the passing from a higher place to a lower place;
  a decline
    Synonyms: lowering, dismount, gravitation; slope
  2. one's ancestry
    Synonyms: heredity, lineage

DRAW *v.* **-ing, drew, drawn**
  to pull, drag; to lead, to bring about on purpose; to
  attract or be attracted to
    Synonyms: haul, tow, yank; provoke, elicit; lure, entice

RESOLVE (rih <u>sahlv</u>) *v.* **-ing,-ed.**
  to determine or to make a firm decision about
    Synonyms: solve, decide

first was that as a general rule, the larger the bodies were, the more rapid their **descent**—the second, that between two masses of equal extent, the one spherical, and the other of any other shape, the superiority in speed of **descent** was with the sphere—the third, that, between two masses of equal size, the one cylindrical, and the other of any other shape, the cylinder was absorbed the more slowly. Since my escape, I have had several conversations on this subject with an old school-master of the district; and it was from him that I learned the use of the words 'cylinder' and 'sphere.' He explained to me—although I have forgotten the explanation—how what I observed was, in fact, the natural consequence of the forms of the floating fragments—and showed me how it happened that a cylinder, swimming in a <u>vortex</u>, offered more resistance to its suction, and was **drawn** in with greater difficulty than an equally bulky body, of any form whatever.

"There was one startling circumstance which went a great way in enforcing these observations, and rendering me anxious to turn them to account, and this was that, at every revolution, we passed something like a barrel, or else the yard or the mast of a vessel, while many of these things, which had been on our level when I first opened my eyes upon the wonders of the whirlpool, were now high up above us, and seemed to have moved but little from their original station.

"I no longer hesitated what to do. I **resolved** to lash myself securely to the water-cask upon which I now held, to cut it loose from the counter, and to throw myself with it into the water. I attracted my brother's attention by signs, pointed to the floating barrels that came near us, and did every thing in my power to make him understand what I was about to do. I thought at length that he comprehended my design—but, whether this was the case or not, he shook his head despairingly, and refused to move from his station by the ring-bolt. It was impossible to reach him; the emergency admitted of no delay; and so,

PRECIPITATE (preh <u>sih</u> puh tayt) *v.* **-ing,-ed.**
  to throw; to move rapidly, to bring about abruptly
    Synonyms: cast, hurl; speed, launch, accelerate

DESCEND (dih <u>sehnd</u>) (dee <u>sehnd</u>) *v.* **-ing,-ed.**
  to pass from a higher place to a lower place
    Synonyms: fall, dismount, gravitate
CHAOS (<u>kay</u> ahs) *n.*
  extreme disorder
    Synonyms: incoherence, randomness, disorganization

with a bitter struggle, I resigned him to his fate, fastened myself to the cask by means of the lashings which secured it to the counter, and **precipitated** myself with it into the sea, without another moment's hesitation.

"The result was precisely what I had hoped it might be. As it is myself who now tell you this tale—as you see that I did escape—and as you are already in possession of the mode in which this escape was effected, and must therefore anticipate all that I have farther to say—I will bring my story quickly to conclusion. It might have been an hour, or thereabout, after my quitting the <u>smack</u>, when, having **descended** to a vast distance beneath me, it made three or four wild gyrations in rapid succession, and, bearing my loved brother with it, plunged headlong, at once and forever, into the **chaos** of foam below. The barrel to which I was attached sunk very little farther than half the distance between the bottom of the gulf and the spot at which I leaped overboard, before a great change took place in the character of the whirlpool. The slope of the sides of the vast funnel became momently less and less steep. The gyrations of the whirl grew gradually less and less violent. By degrees, the froth and the rainbow disappeared, and the bottom of the gulf seemed slowly to uprise. The sky was clear, the winds had gone down, and the full moon was setting radiantly in the west, when I found myself on the surface of the ocean, in full view of the shores of Lofoden, and above the spot where the pool of the Moskoe-ström had been. It was the hour of the slack—but the sea still heaved in mountainous waves from the effects of the hurricane. I was borne violently into the channel of the Ström, and in a few minutes, was hurried down the coast into the 'grounds' of the fishermen. A boat picked me up—exhausted from fatigue—and (now that the danger was removed) speechless from the memory of its horror. Those who drew me on board were my old mates and daily companions—but they knew me no more than they would have known a traveller from the

A DESCENT INTO THE MAELSTRÖM

COUNTENANCE (<u>kown</u> tuh nuhns) *n.*
appearance, facial expression
    Synonyms: face, features, visage

spirit-land. My hair, which had been raven black the day before, was as white as you see it now. They say too that the whole expression of my **countenance** had changed. I told them my story—they did not believe it. I now tell it to you—and I can scarcely expect you to put more faith in it than did the merry fishermen of Lofoden."

RESOLUTION (reh suh <u>loo</u> shuhn) *n.*
a firm decision
Synonyms: determination, will, explanation
CONTEMPT (kuhn <u>tehmpt</u>) *n.*
disrespect, scorn
Synonyms: derision, disdain

THE PIT AND THE PENDULUM

Impia tortorum longas hic turba furores
sanguinis innocui, non satiata, aluit.
Sospite nunc patria, fracto nunc funeris antro,
Mors ubi dira fuit vita salusque patent.
[*Quatrain composed for the gates of a market to be erected
upon the site of the Jacobin Club House at Paris.*][59]

I was sick—sick unto death with that long agony; and
when they at length unbound me, and I was permitted to
sit, I felt that my senses were leaving me. The sentence—
the dread sentence of death—was the last of distinct
accentuation which reached my ears. After that, the
sound of the inquisitorial voices[60] seemed merged in one
dreamy indeterminate hum. It conveyed to my soul the
idea of revolution—perhaps from its association in fancy
with the burr of a mill-wheel. This only for a brief period,
for presently I heard no more. Yet, for a while, I saw—but
with how terrible an exaggeration! I saw the lips of the
black-robed judges. They appeared to me white—whiter
than the sheet upon which I trace these words—and thin
even to grotesqueness; thin with the intensity of their
expression of firmness—of immovable resolution—of
stern contempt of human torture. I saw that the decrees of
what to me was Fate were still issuing from those lips. I
saw them writhe with a deadly locution. I saw them fashion the syllables of my name; and I shuddered because no
sound succeeded. I saw, too, for a few moments of delirious horror, the soft and nearly imperceptible waving of
the sable draperies which enwrapped the walls of the
apartment. And then my vision fell upon the seven tall
candles upon the table. At first they wore the aspect of

STEALTHILY (<u>stehl</u> thuh lee) *adv.*
quietly and cautiously
Synonyms: furtively, secretly, surreptitiously,
covertly

DESCENT (dih <u>sehnt</u>) (dee <u>sehnt</u>) *n.*
1. the passing from a higher place to a lower place;
a decline
Synonyms: lowering, dismount, gravitation; slope
2. one's ancestry
Synonyms: heredity, lineage

PROFOUND (pruh <u>fownd</u>) (proh <u>fownd</u>) *adj.*
deep, infinite; intelligent; difficult to understand
Synonyms: bottomless, unending; smart; thorough,
weighty

ELOQUENT (<u>eh</u> luh kwuhnt) *adj.*
persuasive and effective, often with regards to speech
Synonyms: clear, expressive, fluent

charity, and seemed white slender angels who would save me; but then, all at once, there came a most deadly nausea over my spirit, and I felt every fibre in my frame thrill as if I had touched the wire of a <u>galvanic</u> battery, while the angel forms became meaningless spectres, with heads of flame, and I saw that from them there would be no help. And then there stole into my fancy, like a rich musical note, the thought of what sweet rest there must be in the grave. The thought came gently and **stealthily**, and it seemed long before it attained full appreciation; but just as my spirit came at length properly to feel and entertain it, the figures of the judges vanished, as if magically, from before me; the tall candles sank into nothingness; their flames went out utterly; the blackness of darkness <u>supervened</u>; all sensations appeared swallowed up in a mad rushing **descent** as of the soul into Hades.[61] Then silence, and stillness, and night were the universe.

I had swooned; but still will not say that all of consciousness was lost. What of it there remained I will not attempt to define, or even to describe; yet all was not lost. In the deepest slumber—no! In delirium—no! In a swoon—no! In death—no! Even in the grave all is not lost. Else there is no immortality for man. Arousing from the most **profound** of slumbers, we break the gossamer web of some dream. Yet in a second afterward (so frail may that web have been) we remember not that we have dreamed. In the return to life from the swoon there are two stages: first, that of the sense of mental or spiritual; secondly, that of the sense of physical existence. It seems probable that if, upon reaching the second stage, we could recall the impressions of the first, we should find these impressions **eloquent** in memories of the gulf beyond. And that gulf is—what? How at least shall we distinguish its shadows from those of the tomb? But if the impressions of what I have termed the first stage are not, at will, recalled, yet, after long interval, do they not come unbidden, while we marvel whence they come? He who has

PONDER (<u>pahn</u> duhr) *v.* **-ing,-ed.**
to consider or think about something in depth
Synonyms: contemplate, reflect, ruminate
NOVEL (<u>nah</u> vuhl) *adj.*
new, original
Synonyms: fresh, newfangled, innovative, unusual, different

CONJURE (<u>kahn</u> juhr) *v.* **-ing,-ed.**
to bring to mind; to summon a devil or spirit by invocation; to affect or effect as if by magic
Synonyms: recollect; materialize; invoke, arouse
LUCID (<u>loo</u> sihd) *adj.*
clear and easily understood
Synonyms: intelligible, translucent, transparent, sane, rational
DESCENT (dih <u>sehnt</u>) (dee <u>sehnt</u>) *n.*
1. the passing from a higher place to a lower place; a decline
Synonyms: lowering, dismount, gravitation; slope
2. one's ancestry
Synonyms: heredity, lineage

TUMULTUOUS (tuh <u>muhl</u> choo uhs) *adj.*
confusing or disorderly, agitated
Synonyms: disturbed, turbulent, chaotic, hectic
PERVADE (puhr <u>vayd</u>) *v.* **-ing,-ed.**
to become diffused throughout every part of
Synonyms: permeate, spread, fill, transfuse

never swooned, is not he who finds strange palaces and wildly familiar faces in coals that glow; is not he who beholds floating in mid-air the sad visions that the many may not view; is not he who **ponders** over the perfume of some **novel** flower; is not he whose brain grows bewildered with the meaning of some musical <u>cadence</u> which has never before arrested his attention.

Amid frequent and thoughtful endeavors to remember, amid earnest struggles to regather some token of the state of seeming nothingness into which my soul had lapsed, there have been moments when I have dreamed of success; there have been brief, very brief periods when I have **conjured** up remembrances which the **lucid** reason of a later <u>epoch</u> assures me could have had reference only to that condition of seeming unconsciousness. These shadows of memory tell, indistinctly, of tall figures that lifted and bore me in silence down—down—still down—till a hideous dizziness oppressed me at the mere idea of the <u>interminableness</u> of the **descent**. They tell also of a vague horror at my heart, on account of that heart's unnatural stillness. Then comes a sense of sudden motionlessness throughout all things; as if those who bore me (a ghastly train!) had outrun, in their **descent**, the limits of the limitless, and paused from the wearisomeness of their toil. After this I call to mind flatness and dampness; and then all is madness—the madness of a memory which busies itself among forbidden things.

Very suddenly there came back to my soul motion and sound—the **tumultuous** motion of the heart, and in my ears, the sound of its beating. Then a pause in which all is blank. Then again sound and motion and touch—a tingling sensation **pervading** my frame. Then the mere consciousness of existence, without thought—a condition which lasted long. Then, very suddenly, thought, and shuddering terror, and earnest endeavor to comprehend my true state. Then a strong desire to lapse into insensibility. Then a rushing revival of soul and a successful

ENCOMPASS (ehn <u>kuhm</u> puhs) *v.* **-ing,-ed.**
to cover, surround; to include, take in
Synonyms: enclose, envelop; constitute, involve
STIFLE (<u>stie</u> fuhl) *v.* **-ing,-ed.**
to smother or suffocate; suppress, hold back
Synonyms: strangle, throttle; repress, restrain

effort to move. And now a full memory of the trial, of the judges, of the sable draperies, of the sentence, of the sickness, of the swoon. Then entire forgetfulness of all that followed; of all that a later day and much earnestness of endeavor have enabled me vaguely to recall.

So far, I had not opened my eyes. I felt that I lay upon my back, unbound. I reached out my hand, and it fell heavily upon something damp and hard. There I suffered it to remain for many minutes, while I strove to imagine where and *what* I could be. I longed, yet dared not, to employ my vision. I dreaded the first glance at objects around me. It was not that I feared to look upon things horrible, but that I grew aghast lest there should be *nothing* to see. At length, with a wild desperation at heart, I quickly unclosed my eyes. My worst thoughts, then, were confirmed. The blackness of eternal night encompassed me. I struggled for breath. The intensity of the darkness seemed to oppress and stifle me. The atmosphere was intolerably close. I still lay quietly, and made effort to exercise my reason. I brought to mind the inquisitorial proceedings, and attempted from that point to deduce my real condition. The sentence had passed, and it appeared to me that a very long interval of time had since elapsed. Yet not for a moment did I suppose myself actually dead. Such a supposition, notwithstanding what we read in fiction, is altogether inconsistent with real existence; but where and in what state was I? The condemned to death, I knew, perished usually at the *auto-da-fés*,[62] and one of these had been held on the very night of the day of my trial. Had I been remanded to my dungeon, to await the next sacrifice, which would not take place for many months? This I at once saw could not be. Victims had been in immediate demand. Moreover, my dungeon, as well as all the condemned cells at Toledo, had stone floors, and light was not altogether excluded.

A fearful idea now suddenly drove the blood in torrents upon my heart, and for a brief period I once more

IMPEDE (ihm <u>peed</u>) *v.* **-ing,-ed.**
   to prevent progress, to act as a barrier or obstacle
      Synonyms: obstruct, hinder, block
SUSPENSE (suh <u>spents</u>) *n.*
   a period of anxiety caused by a mysterious situation
      Synonyms: apprehension, anticipation, waiting

SUBTERRANEAN (suhb tuh <u>ray</u> nee uhn) *adj.*
   hidden, secret; underground
      Synonyms: concealed; sunken, covered, buried

ASCERTAIN (aa suhr <u>tayn</u>) *v.* **-ing,-ed.**
   to determine, discover, make certain of
      Synonyms: verify, calculate, detect
UNIFORM (<u>yoo</u> nuh fohrm) *adj.*
   consistent and unchanging; identical
      Synonyms: unvarying, steady, even, homogeneous;
      indistinguishable

relapsed into insensibility. Upon recovering, I at once started to my feet, trembling convulsively in every fibre. I thrust my arms wildly above and around me in all directions. I felt nothing; yet dreaded to move a step, lest I should be **impeded** by the walls of a tomb. Perspiration burst from every pore, and stood in cold big beads upon my forehead. The agony of **suspense** grew at length intolerable, and I cautiously moved forward, with my arms extended, and my eyes straining from their sockets in the hope of catching some faint ray of light. I proceeded for many paces; but still all was blackness and vacancy. I breathed more freely. It seemed evident that mine was not, at least, the most hideous of fates.

And now, as I still continued to step cautiously onward, there came <u>thronging</u> upon my recollection a thousand vague rumors of the horrors of Toledo. Of the dungeons there had been strange things narrated—fables I had always deemed them—but yet strange, and too ghastly to repeat, save in a whisper. Was I left to perish of starvation in this **subterranean** world of darkness; or what fate, perhaps even more fearful, awaited me? That the result would be death, and a death of more than customary bitterness, I knew too well the character of my judges to doubt. The mode and the hour were all that occupied or distracted me.

My outstretched hands at length encountered some solid obstruction. It was a wall, seemingly of stone masonry—very smooth, slimy, and cold. I followed it up; stepping with all the careful distrust with which certain antique narratives had inspired me. This process, however, afforded me no means of **ascertaining** the dimensions of my dungeon, as I might make its circuit and return to the point whence I set out without being aware of the fact, so perfectly **uniform** seemed the wall. I therefore sought the knife, which had been in my pocket when led into the inquisitorial chamber; but it was gone; my clothes had been exchanged for a wrapper of coarse

MINUTE (mie <u>noot</u>) (mih <u>noot</u>) *adj.*
precise, detailed; very small
Synonyms: attentive, critical; tiny, diminutive,
infinitesimal

INSUPERABLE (ihn <u>soo</u> puhr uh buhl) *adj.*
insurmountable, unconquerable
Synonyms: unbeatable, undefeatable, invincible

INDUCE (ih <u>doos</u>) (ihn <u>dyoos</u>) *v.* **-ing,-ed.**
to persuade, to bring about
Synonyms: prevail, convince, lead, effect, occasion

PROSTRATE (<u>prah</u> strayt) *adj.*
face downward, flat on ground
Synonyms: horizontal, submissive, overcome

AVIDITY (aa <u>vihd</u> ih tee) *n.*
greedy desire; enthusiasm
Synonyms: craving, ardor; interest

PRESUME (prih <u>zoom</u>) *v.* **-ing,-ed.**
to assume or believe something without proof; to dare
Synonyms: take for granted; venture

RESOLVE (rih <u>sahlv</u>) *v.* **-ing,-ed.**
to determine or to make a firm decision about
Synonyms: solve, decide

TREACHEROUS (<u>treh</u> chuhr uhs) *adj.*
dangerous, deceptive; untrustworthy, deceitful
Synonyms: hazardous; perfidious, treasonous,
disloyal, false

serge. I had thought of forcing the blade in some **minute** crevice of the masonry, so as to identify my point of departure. The difficulty, nevertheless, was but trivial; although, in the disorder of my fancy, it seemed at first **insuperable**. I tore a part of the hem from the robe and placed the fragment at full length, and at right angles to the wall. In groping my way around the prison, I could not fail to encounter this rag upon completing the circuit. So, at least, I thought; but I had not counted upon the extent of the dungeon, or upon my own weakness. The ground was moist and slippery. I staggered onward for some time, when I stumbled and fell. My excessive fatigue **induced** me to remain **prostrate**; and sleep soon overtook me as I lay.

Upon awaking, and stretching forth an arm, I found beside me a loaf and a pitcher with water. I was too much exhausted to reflect upon this circumstance, but ate and drank with **avidity**. Shortly afterward, I resumed my tour around the prison, and with much toil, came at last upon the fragment of the serge. Up to the period when I fell, I had counted fifty-two paces, and, upon resuming my walk, I had counted forty-eight more—when I arrived at the rag. There were in all, then, a hundred paces; and, admitting two paces to the yard, I **presumed** the dungeon to be fifty yards in circuit. I had met, however, with many angles in the wall, and thus I could form no guess at the shape of the vault, for vault I could not help supposing it to be.

I had little object—certainly no hope—in these researches; but a vague curiosity prompted me to continue them. Quitting the wall, I **resolved** to cross the area of the enclosure. At first, I proceeded with extreme caution, for the floor, although seemingly of solid material, was **treacherous** with slime. At length, however, I took courage, and did not hesitate to step firmly—endeavoring to cross in as direct a line as possible. I had advanced some ten or twelve paces in this manner, when the remnant of the torn

THE PIT AND THE PENDULUM

APPREHEND (aa pree <u>hehnd</u>) *v.* **-ing,-ed.**
1. to anticipate fearfully; to become aware of something through one's senses; to understand
    Synonyms: dread; perceive; comprehend, grasp
2. to arrest
    Synonyms: capture, seize, take, nab

PROSTRATE (<u>prah</u> strayt) *adj.*
face downward, flat on ground
    Synonyms: horizontal, submissive, overcome

ASCERTAIN (aa suhr <u>tayn</u>) *v.* **-ing,-ed.**
to determine, discover, make certain of
    Synonyms: verify, calculate, detect

DESCENT (dih <u>sehnt</u>) (dee <u>sehnt</u>) *n.*
1. the passing from a higher place to a lower place; a decline
    Synonyms: lowering, dismount, gravitation; slope
2. one's ancestry
    Synonyms: heredity, lineage

SULLEN (<u>suh</u> luhn) *adj.*
brooding, gloomy
    Synonyms: morose, sulky, somber, glum

FRIVOLOUS (<u>frihv</u> uh luhs) *adj.*
silly, petty, trivial, flippant
    Synonyms: frothy, light, vapid

hem of my robe became entangled between my legs. I stepped on it, and fell violently on my face.

In the confusion attending my fall, I did not immediately **apprehend** a somewhat startling circumstance, which yet, in a few seconds afterward, and while I still lay **prostrate**, arrested my attention. It was this: my chin rested upon the floor of the prison, but my lips, and the upper portion of my head, although seemingly at a less elevation than the chin, touched nothing. At the same time, my forehead seemed bathed in a clammy vapor, and the peculiar smell of decayed fungus arose to my nostrils. I put forward my arm, and shuddered to find that I had fallen at the very brink of a circular pit, whose extent, of course, I had no means of **ascertaining** at the moment. Groping about the masonry just below the margin, I succeeded in dislodging a small fragment, and let it fall into the abyss. For many seconds I <u>hearkened</u> to its reverberations as it dashed against the sides of the chasm in its **descent**; at length, there was a **sullen** plunge into water, succeeded by loud echoes. At the same moment, there came a sound resembling the quick opening and as rapid closing of a door overhead, while a faint gleam of light flashed suddenly through the gloom, and as suddenly faded away.

I saw clearly the doom, which had been prepared for me, and congratulated myself upon the timely accident by which I had escaped. Another step before my fall, and the world had seen me no more. And the death just avoided was of that very character which I had regarded as fabulous and **frivolous** in the tales respecting the Inquisition. To the victims of its tyranny, there was the choice of death with its direst physical agonies, or death with its most hideous moral horrors. I had been reserved for the latter. By long suffering my nerves had been unstrung, until I trembled at the sound of my own voice, and had become in every respect a fitting subject for the species of torture, which awaited me.

Shaking in every limb, I groped my way back to the

RESOLVE (rih <u>sahlv</u>) *v.* **-ing,-ed.**
    to determine or to make a firm decision about
        Synonyms: solve, decide

EXTINCTION (ihk <u>stingk</u> shuhn) *n.*
    end of a living thing or species
        Synonyms: extermination, eradication,
        annihilation, elimination, destruction

AGITATION (aa gih <u>tay</u> shuhn) *n.*
    uneasiness; commotion, excitement
        Synonyms: restlessness, anxiety; disturbance

TRIFLE (<u>trie</u> fuhl) *n.*
    something of slight worth or little importance
        Synonyms: triviality, novelty, trinket

wall—**resolving** there to perish rather than risk the terrors of the wells, of which my imagination now pictured many in various positions about the dungeon. In other conditions of mind, I might have had courage to end my misery at once, by a plunge into one of these abysses; but now I was the veriest of cowards. Neither could I forget what I had read of these pits—that the sudden **extinction** of life formed no part of their most horrible plan.

Agitation of spirit kept me awake for many long hours, but at length I again slumbered. Upon arousing, I found by my side, as before, a loaf and a pitcher of water. A burning thirst consumed me, and I emptied the vessel at a <u>draught</u>. It must have been drugged—for scarcely had I drunk, before I became irresistibly drowsy. A deep sleep fell upon me—a sleep like that of death. How long it lasted, of course I know not; but when, once again, I unclosed my eyes, the objects around me were visible. By a wild, <u>sulphurous</u> lustre, the origin of which I could not at first determine, I was enabled to see the extent and aspect of the prison.

In its size I had been greatly mistaken. The whole circuit of its walls did not exceed twenty-five yards. For some minutes this fact occasioned me a world of vain trouble; vain indeed—for what could be of less importance, under the terrible circumstances which environed me, than the mere dimensions of my dungeon? But my soul took a wild interest in **trifles**, and I busied myself in endeavors to account for the error I had committed in my measurement. The truth at length flashed upon me. In my first attempt at exploration I had counted fifty-two paces, up to the period when I fell: I must then have been within a pace or two of the fragment of serge; in fact, I had nearly performed the circuit of the vault. I then slept—and, upon awaking, I must have returned upon my steps—thus supposing the circuit nearly double what it actually was. My confusion of mind prevented me from

LETHARGY (<u>lehth</u> uhr jee) *n.*
  sluggishness
    Synonyms: lassitude, torpor, stupor, languor
NICHE (nihch) *n.*
  recess in a wall; best position for something
    Synonyms: alcove, cranny, crevice; place, station
DAUB (dawb) *v.* **-ing,-ed.**
  to apply with short, quick strokes; to dab
    Synonyms: smudge, smear, blot, spot
REPULSIVE (rih <u>puhl</u> sihv) *adj.*
  sickening, disgusting; repellant
    Synonyms: nauseating; offensive

CONVOLUTION (kahn vuh <u>loo</u> shuhn) *n.*
  a state in which something is rolled or folded on itself,
  a complex twist
    Synonyms: intricacy, whirl, coil

PUNGENTLY (<u>puhn</u> juhnt lee) *adv.*
  in a strong or sharp manner, often with regards to
  taste or smell
    Synonyms: acridly, penetratingly, caustically

334

observing that I began my tour with the wall to the left, and ended it with the wall to the right.

I had been deceived, too, in respect to the shape of the enclosure. In feeling my way I had found many angles, and thus deduced an idea of great irregularity; so potent is the effect of total darkness upon one arousing from **lethargy** or sleep! The angles were simply those of a few slight depressions, or **niches**, at odd intervals. The general shape of the prison was square. What I had taken for masonry seemed now to be iron, or some other metal, in huge plates, whose sutures or joints occasioned the depression. The entire surface of this metallic enclosure was rudely **daubed** in all the hideous and **repulsive** devices to which the <u>charnel</u> superstition of the monks has given rise. The figures of fiends in aspects of menace, with skeleton forms, and other more really fearful images, overspread and disfigured the walls. I observed that the outlines of these monstrosities were sufficiently distinct, but that the colors seemed faded and blurred, as if from the effects of a damp atmosphere. I now noticed the floor, too, which was of stone. In the centre yawned the circular pit from whose jaws I had escaped; but it was the only one in the dungeon.

All this I saw indistinctly and by much effort—for my personal condition had been greatly changed during slumber. I now lay upon my back, and at full length, on a species of low framework of wood. To this I was securely bound by a long strap resembling a surcingle. It passed in many **convolutions** about my limbs and body, leaving at liberty only my head, and my left arm to such extent, that I could, by <u>dint</u> of much exertion, supply myself with food from an earthen dish which lay by my side on the floor. I saw, to my horror, that the pitcher had been removed. I say to my horror—for I was consumed with intolerable thirst. This thirst it appeared to be the design of my persecutors to stimulate—for the food in the dish was meat **pungently** seasoned.

Looking upward, I surveyed the ceiling of my prison. It

SINGULAR (<u>sihn</u> gyuh luhr) *adj.*
  uncommon, peculiar
    Synonyms: unusual, odd, rare, unique, individual

TRAVERSE (truh <u>vuhrs</u>) (<u>traa</u> vuhrs) *v.* **-ing,-ed.**
  to travel or move across; to turn or move laterally
    Synonyms: cross, intersect, pass through; swivel,
    zigzag
RAVENOUS (<u>raa</u> vehn uhs) *adj.*
  extremely hungry
    Synonyms: voracious, gluttonous, rapacious,
    predatory, famished
ALLURE (uh <u>lohr</u>) *v.* **-ing,-ed.**
  to attract; to entice by charm
    Synonyms: lure, draw; captivate
CONFOUND (kuhn <u>fownd</u>) *v.* **-ing,-ed.**
  to baffle, perplex; to mistake something for another
    Synonyms: overwhelm, disconcert, entangle,
    muddle; confuse, misidentify
DESCEND (dih <u>sehnd</u>) (dee <u>sehnd</u>) *v.* **-ing,-ed.**
  to pass from a higher place to a lower place
    Synonyms: fall, dismount, gravitate
KEEN *adj.*
  having a sharp edge; intellectually sharp, perceptive
    Synonyms: pointed, razorlike; acute, quick, canny

was some thirty or forty feet overhead, and constructed much as the side walls. In one of its panels a very **singular** figure riveted my whole attention. It was the painted figure of Time as he is commonly represented, save that, in lieu of a scythe,[63] he held what, at a casual glance, I supposed to be the pictured image of a huge pendulum, such as we see on antique clocks. There was something, however, in the appearance of this which caused me to regard it more attentively. While I gazed directly upward at it (for its position was immediately over my own) I fancied that I saw it in motion. In an instant afterward the fancy was confirmed. Its sweep was brief, and of course slow. I watched it for some minutes somewhat in fear, but more in wonder. Wearied at length with observing its dull movement, I turned my eyes upon the other objects in the cell.

A slight noise attracted my notice, and, looking to the floor, I saw several enormous rats **traversing** it. They had issued from the well which lay just within view to my right. Even then, while I gazed, they came up in troops, hurriedly, with **ravenous** eyes, **allured** by the scent of the meat. From this it required much effort and attention to scare them away.

It might have been half an hour, perhaps even an hour (for I could take but imperfect note of time), before I again cast my eyes upward. What I then saw **confounded** and amazed me. The sweep of the pendulum had increased in extent by nearly a yard. As a natural consequence its velocity was also much greater. But what mainly disturbed me was the idea that it had perceptibly *descended.* I now observed—with what horror it is needless to say—that its nether extremity was formed of a crescent of glittering steel, about a foot in length from horn to horn; the horns upward, and the under edge evidently as **keen** as that of a razor. Like a razor also, it seemed massy and heavy, tapering from the edge into a solid and broad structure above. It was appended to a

INGENUITY (ihn jeh <u>noo</u> ih tee) *n.*
    cleverness
        Synonyms: inventiveness, imagination, creativity
COGNIZANCE (<u>kahg</u> nih zehnce) *n.*
    knowledge or awareness
        Synonyms: consciousness, familiarity, experience

OSCILLATION (ah sihl <u>ay</u> shuhn) *n.*
    a back and forth motion
        Synonyms: swinging, swaying, fluctuation,
        vacillation, undulation
DESCENT (dih <u>sehnt</u>) (dee <u>sehnt</u>) *n.*
    1. the passing from a higher place to a lower place;
    a decline
        Synonyms: lowering, dismount, gravitation; slope
    2. one's ancestry
        Synonyms: heredity, lineage
ACRID (<u>aak</u> rihd) *adj.*
    harsh, bitter
        Synonyms: sharp, pungent, caustic

weighty rod of brass, and the whole *hissed* as it swung through the air.

I could no longer doubt the doom prepared for me by monkish ingenuity in torture. My cognizance of the pit had become known to the inquisitorial agents—*the pit*, whose horrors had been destined for so bold a recusant as myself—*the pit*, typical of hell and regarded by rumor as the Ultima Thule[64] of all their punishments. The plunge into this pit I had avoided by the merest of accidents, and I knew that surprise, or entrapment into torment, formed an important portion of all the grotesquerie[42] of these dungeon deaths. Having failed to fall, it was no part of the demon plan to hurl me into the abyss, and thus (there being no alternative) a different and a milder destruction awaited me. Milder! I half smiled in my agony as I thought of such application of such a term.

What boots it to tell of the long, long hours of horror more than mortal, during which I counted the rushing oscillations of the steel! Inch by inch—line by line—with a descent only appreciable at intervals that seemed ages—down and still down it came! Days passed—it might have been that many days passed—ere it swept so closely over me as to fan me with its acrid breath. The odor of the sharp steel forced itself into my nostrils. I prayed—I wearied heaven with my prayer for its more speedy descent. I grew frantically mad, and struggled to force myself upward against the sweep of the fearful scimitar.[65] And then I fell suddenly calm, and lay smiling at the glittering death, as a child at some rare bauble.

There was another interval of utter insensibility; it was brief; for, upon again lapsing into life, there had been no perceptible descent in the pendulum. But it might have been long—for I knew there were demons who took note of my swoon, and who could have arrested the vibration at pleasure. Upon my recovery, too, I felt very—oh, inexpressibly—sick and weak, as if through long inanition. Even amid the agonies of that period, the

DESCENT (dih <u>sehnt</u>) (dee <u>sehnt</u>) *n.*
  1. the passing from a higher place to a lower place;
  a decline
    Synonyms: lowering, dismount, gravitation; slope
  2. one's ancestry
    Synonyms: heredity, lineage
PERTINACITY (puhr tih <u>naa</u> sih tee) *n.*
  stubborn persistence
    Synonyms: obstinacy, diligence
PONDER (<u>pahn</u> duhr) *v.* **-ing,-ed.**
  to consider or think about something in depth
    Synonyms: contemplate, reflect, ruminate
FRIVOLITY (frih <u>vahl</u> ih tee) *n.*
  triviality, silliness
    Synonyms: lightness, childishness, nonsense
STEALTHY (<u>stehl</u> thee) *adj.*
  sly and cautious, sneaky
    Synonyms: furtive, secretive, unperceived

human nature craved food. With painful effort I out-stretched my left arm as far as my bonds permitted, and took possession of the small remnant which had been spared me by the rats. As I put a portion of it within my lips, there rushed to my mind a half-formed thought of joy—of hope. Yet what business had I with hope? It was, as I say, a half-formed thought—man has many such, which are never completed. I felt that it was of joy—of hope; but I felt also that it had perished in its formation. In vain I struggled to perfect—to regain it. Long suffering had nearly annihilated all my ordinary powers of mind. I was an imbecile—an idiot.

The vibration of the pendulum was at right angles to my length. I saw that the crescent was designed to cross the region of the heart. It would fray the serge of my robe—it would return and repeat its operations—again—and again. Notwithstanding its terrifically wide sweep (some thirty feet or more), and the hissing vigor of its descent, sufficient to <u>sunder</u> these very walls of iron, still the fray-ing of my robe would be all that, for several minutes, it would accomplish. And at this thought I paused. I dared not go further than this reflection. I dwelt upon it with a **pertinacity** of attention—as if, in so dwelling, I could arrest *here* the **descent** of the steel. I forced myself to **ponder** upon the sound of the crescent as it should pass across the garment—upon the peculiar thrilling sensation, which the friction of cloth produces on the nerves. I **pondered** upon all this **frivolity** until my teeth were on edge.

Down—steadily down it crept. I took a frenzied pleas-ure in contrasting its downward with its lateral velocity. To the right—to the left—far and wide—with the shriek of a damned spirit! To my heart, with the **stealthy** pace of the tiger! I alternately laughed and howled, as the one or the other idea grew predominant.

Down—certainly, relentlessly down! It vibrated within three inches of my bosom! I struggled violently—furi-ously—to free my left arm. This was free only from the

INEVITABLY (ihn <u>ehv</u> ih tuh blee) *adv.*
certainly, unavoidably
Synonyms: inescapably, surely, predictably
DESCENT (dih <u>sehnt</u>) (dee <u>sehnt</u>) *n.*
1. the passing from a higher place to a lower place;
a decline
Synonyms: lowering, dismount, gravitation; slope
2. one's ancestry
Synonyms: heredity, lineage
PRECIPITATE (preh <u>sih</u> puh tayt) *v.* **-ing,-ed.**
to throw; to move rapidly, to bring about abruptly
Synonyms: cast, hurl; speed, launch, accelerate
KEEN *adj.*
having a sharp edge; intellectually sharp, perceptive
Synonyms: pointed, razorlike; acute, quick, canny

ATHWART (athwahrt) *adv.*
across, from side to side
Synonyms: crosswise, obliquely, aslant, blocking

elbow to the hand. I could reach the latter, from the platter beside me, to my mouth, with great effort, but no farther. Could I have broken the fastenings above the elbow, I would have seized and attempted to arrest the pendulum. I might as well have attempted to arrest an avalanche!

Down—still unceasingly—still **inevitably** down! I gasped and struggled at each vibration. I shrunk convulsively at its every sweep. My eyes followed its outward or upward whirls with the eagerness of the most unmeaning despair; they closed themselves spasmodically at the **descent**, although death would have been a relief, oh, how unspeakable! Still I quivered in every nerve to think how slight a sinking of the machinery would **precipitate** that **keen**, glistening axe upon my bosom. It was *hope* that prompted the nerve to quiver—the frame to shrink. It was hope—the *hope* that triumphs on the rack—that whispers to the death-condemned even in the dungeons of the Inquisition.

I saw that some ten or twelve vibrations would bring the steel in actual contact with my robe—and with this observation there suddenly came over my spirit all the **keen**, collected calmness of despair. For the first time during many hours—or perhaps days—I *thought*. It now occurred to me, that the bandage, or surcingle, which enveloped me, was unique. I was tied by no separate cord. The first stroke of the razor-like crescent **athwart** any portion of the band would so detach it that it might be unwound from my person by means of my left hand. But how fearful, in that case, the proximity of the steel! The result of the slightest struggle, how deadly! Was it likely, moreover, that the minions of the torturer had not foreseen and provided for this possibility? Was it probable that the bandage crossed my bosom in the track of the pendulum? Dreading to find my faint and, as it seemed, my last hope frustrated, I so far elevated my head as to obtain a distinct view of my breast. The surcingle enveloped my limbs and body close in all directions—save in the path of the destroying crescent.

ALLUDE (uh <u>lood</u>) *v.* **-ing,-ed.**
to make an indirect reference
    Synonyms: intimate, suggest, hint

EXECUTION (ehk sih <u>kyoo</u> shuhn) *n.*
1. the act of performing or carrying out a task
    Synonyms: operation, enactment, accomplishment,
    achievement
2. the act of putting to death
    Synonyms: killing, suicide, murder

RAVENOUS (<u>raa</u> vehn uhs) *adj.*
extremely hungry
    Synonyms: voracious, gluttonous, rapacious,
    predatory, famished

UNIFORMITY (yoo nuh <u>fohr</u> mih tee) *n.*
consistency; lack of variation or diversity, sameness
    Synonyms: steadiness, evenness, homogeneity;
      similarity, likeness

VORACITY (vohr <u>aas</u> ih tee) *n.*
a great appetite, desire for food
    Synonyms: ravenousness, greed, gluttony, rapacity

CESSATION (seh <u>say</u> shuhn) *n.*
temporary or complete halt
    Synonyms: stoppage, arrest, termination, conclusion

Scarcely had I dropped my head back into its original position, when there flashed upon my mind what I cannot better describe than as the unformed half of that idea of deliverance to which I have previously **alluded**, and of which a <u>moiety</u> only floated indeterminately through my brain when I raised food to my burning lips. The whole thought was now present—feeble, scarcely sane, scarcely definite—but still entire. I proceeded at once, with the nervous energy of despair, to attempt its **execution**.

For many hours the immediate vicinity of the low framework upon which I lay had been literally swarming with rats. They were wild, bold, **ravenous**—their red eyes glaring upon me as if they waited but for motionlessness on my part to make me their prey. "To what food," I thought, "have they been accustomed in the well?"

They had devoured, in spite of all my efforts to prevent them, all but a small remnant of the contents of the dish. I had fallen into an habitual see-saw or wave of the hand about the platter; and, at length, the unconscious **uniformity** of the movement deprived it of effect. In their **voracity**, the vermin frequently fastened their sharp fangs in my fingers. With the particles of the oily and spicy <u>viand</u> which now remained, I thoroughly rubbed the bandage wherever I could reach it; then, raising my hand from the floor, I lay breathlessly still.

At first, the **ravenous** animals were startled and terrified at the change—at the **cessation** of movement. They shrank alarmedly back; many sought the well. But this was only for a moment. I had not counted in vain upon their **voracity**. Observing that I remained without motion, one or two of the boldest leaped upon the framework, and smelt at the surcingle. This seemed the signal for a general rush. Forth from the well they hurried in fresh troops. They clung to the wood—they overran it, and leaped in hundreds upon my person. The measured movement of the pendulum disturbed them not at all. Avoiding its strokes, they busied themselves with the anointed bandage. They

THE PIT AND THE PENDULUM

ACCUMULATING (uh <u>kyoom</u> yuh lay tihng) *adj.*
increasing, collective
Synonyms: intensifying, additive, gradual, accruing

STIFLE (<u>stie</u> fuhl) *v.* **-ing,-ed.**
to smother or suffocate; suppress, hold back
Synonyms: strangle, throttle; repress, restrain

RESOLUTION (reh suh <u>loo</u> shuhn) *n.*
a firm decision
Synonyms: determination, will, explanation

TUMULTUOUSLY (tuh <u>muhl</u> choo uhs lee) *adv.*
with much noise; in a confused and disorderly manner
Synonyms: boisterously; turbulently, excitedly

DRAW *v.* **-ing, drew, drawn**
to pull, drag; to lead, to bring about on purpose; to
attract or be attracted to
Synonyms: haul, tow, yank; provoke, elicit; lure, entice

CONJECTURE (kuhn <u>jehk</u> shuhr) *n.*
speculation, prediction
Synonyms: postulation, hypothesis, supposition, guess

346

pressed—they swarmed upon me in ever **accumulating** heaps. They writhed upon my throat; their cold lips sought my own; I was half **stifled** by their <u>thronging</u> pressure; disgust, for which the world has no name, swelled my bosom, and chilled, with a heavy clamminess, my heart. Yet one minute, and I felt that the struggle would be over. Plainly I perceived the loosening of the bandage. I knew that in more than one place it must be already severed. With a more than human **resolution,** I lay still.

Nor had I erred in my calculations—nor had I endured in vain. I at length felt that I was *free*. The surcingle hung in ribands from my body. But the stroke of the pendulum already pressed upon my bosom. It had divided the serge of the robe. It had cut through the linen beneath. Twice again it swung, and a sharp sense of pain shot through every nerve. But the moment of escape had arrived. At a wave of my hand my deliverers hurried **tumultuously** away. With a steady movement—cautious, sidelong, shrinking, and slow—I slid from the embrace of the bandage and beyond the reach of the scimitar.[65] For the moment, at least, I was *free*.

Free! And in the grasp of the Inquisition! I had scarcely stepped from my wooden bed of horror upon the stone floor of the prison, when the motion of the hellish machine ceased, and I beheld it **drawn** up, by some invisible force, through the ceiling. This was a lesson which I took desperately to heart. My every motion was undoubtedly watched. Free! I had but escaped death in one form of agony, to be delivered unto worse than death in some other. With that thought I rolled my eyes nervously around on the barriers of iron that hemmed me in. Something unusual—some change, which, at first, I could not appreciate distinctly—it was obvious, had taken place in the apartment. For many minutes of a dreamy and trembling abstraction, I busied myself in vain, unconnected **conjecture**. During this period, I became aware, for the first time, of the origin of the <u>sulphurous</u>

VIVACITY (vih <u>vahs</u> ih tee) *n.*
  liveliness, spiritedness
    Synonyms: vibrance, zest
LURID (<u>loor</u> ihd) *adj.*
  harshly shocking, revolting; glowing
    Synonyms: ghastly, garish, gruesome, grisly,
    macabre
PERVADE (puhr <u>vayd</u>) *v.* **-ing,-ed.**
  to become diffused throughout every part of
    Synonyms: permeate, spread, fill, transfuse
DIFFUSE (dih <u>fyooz</u>) *v.* **-ing,-ed.**
  to spread out widely
    Synonyms: scatter, disperse
IMPEND (ihm <u>pehnd</u>) *v.* **-ing,-ed.**
  to hover threateningly, to be about to occur
    Synonyms: loom, near, progress, meet
BALM (bahm) *n.*
  a soothing, healing influence
    Synonyms: succor, comfort, palliative, anodyne, salve
ENKINDLED (ehn <u>kihn</u> duhld) *adj.*
  on fire, in flames; excited, inspired
      Synonyms: lit, burning; aroused, awakened

light which illumined the cell. It proceeded from a <u>fissure</u>, about half an inch in width, extending entirely around the prison at the base of the walls, which thus appeared, and were completely separated from the floor. I endeavored, but of course in vain, to look through the aperture.

As I arose from the attempt, the mystery of the alteration in the chamber broke at once upon my understanding. I have observed that, although the outlines of the figures upon the walls were sufficiently distinct, yet the colors seemed blurred and indefinite. These colors had now assumed, and were momentarily assuming, a startling and most intense brilliancy, that gave to the spectral and fiendish portraitures an aspect that might have thrilled even firmer nerves than my own. Demon eyes, of a wild and ghastly **vivacity**, glared upon me in a thousand directions, where none had been visible before, and gleamed with the **lurid** lustre of a fire that I could not force my imagination to regard as unreal.

Unreal! Even while I breathed there came to my nostrils the breath of the vapor of heated iron. A suffocating odor **pervaded** the prison. A deeper glow settled each moment in the eyes that glared at my agonies. A richer tint of crimson **diffused** itself over the pictured horrors of blood. I panted. I gasped for breath. There could be no doubt of the design of my tormentors—oh, most unrelenting! Oh, most demoniac of men! I shrank from the glowing metal to the centre of the cell. Amid the thought of the fiery destruction that **impended**, the idea of the coolness of the well came over my soul like **balm**. I rushed to its deadly brink. I threw my straining vision below. The glare from the **enkindled** roof illuminated its inmost recesses. Yet, for a wild moment, did my spirit refuse to comprehend the meaning of what I saw. At length it forced—it wrestled its way into my soul—it burned itself in upon my shuddering reason. Oh, for a voice to speak! Oh, horror! Oh, any horror but this! With a shriek, I rushed from the margin, and buried my face in my hands, weeping bitterly.

VENGEANCE (<u>vehn</u> juhns) *n.*
punishment inflicted in retaliation; vehemence
Synonyms: revenge, repayment; wrath

ACUTE (uh <u>kyoot</u>) *adj.*
1. less than 90°, used to describe angles in geometry
2. sensitive, heightened; sharp, pointed; severe
Synonyms: perceptive; piercing; intense, fierce

OBTUSE (uhb <u>toos</u>) *adj.*
1. more than 90°, used to describe angles in geometry
2. dull; insensitive, stupid, lacking interest
Synonyms: blunt; slow, dense, dim

TOTTER (<u>tah</u> tuhr) *v.* **-ing,-ed.**
to stand with much unsteadiness
Synonyms: wobble, sway, reel, stagger
AVERT (uh <u>vuhrt</u>) *v.* **-ing,-ed.**
to turn away; avoid
Synonyms: deflect, parry; deter, forestall, preclude
DISCORDANT (dihs <u>kohr</u> duhnt) *adj.*
inharmonious; disagreeing
Synonyms: cacophonous; dissonant

The heat rapidly increased, and once again I looked up, shuddering as with a fit of ague. There had been a second change in the cell—and now the change was obviously in the form. As before, it was in vain that I at first endeavored to appreciate or understand what was taking place. But not long was I left in doubt. The inquisitorial vengeance had been hurried by my two-fold escape, and there was to be no more dallying with the King of Terrors. The room had been square. I saw that two of its iron angles were now acute—two, consequently, obtuse. The fearful difference quickly increased with a low rumbling or moaning sound. In an instant the apartment had shifted its form into that of a lozenge. But the alteration stopped not here—I neither hoped nor desired it to stop. I could have clasped the red walls to my bosom as a garment of eternal peace. "Death," I said, "any death but that of the pit!" Fool! Might I not have known that *into the pit* was the object of the burning iron to urge me? Could I resist its glow? Or if even that, could I withstand its pressure? And now, flatter and flatter grew the lozenge, with a rapidity that left me no time for contemplation. Its centre, and of course its greatest width, came just over the yawning gulf. I shrank back—but the closing walls pressed me resistlessly onward. At length for my seared and writhing body there was no longer an inch of foothold on the firm floor of the prison. I struggled no more, but the agony of my soul found vent in one loud, long, and final scream of despair. I felt that I tottered upon the brink—I averted my eyes—

There was a discordant hum of human voices! There was a loud blast as of many trumpets! There was a harsh grating as of a thousand thunders! The fiery walls rushed back! An outstretched arm caught my own as I fell, fainting, into the abyss. It was that of General Lasalle. The French army had entered Toledo. The Inquisition was in the hands of its enemies.

TEMPERAMENT (<u>tehm</u> puhr uh mehnt) *n.*
an attitude, a manner of behaving
Synonyms: disposition, mood, mentality

SUSTAIN (suh <u>stayn</u>) *v.* **-ing,-ed.**
to support, uphold; endure, undergo
Synonyms: maintain, prop, confirm, encourage;
withstand

APPREHENSION (aa prih <u>hehn</u> shuhn) *n.*
suspicion or fear of future or unknown evil; the act of
perceiving or comprehending; a legal seizure
Synonyms: concern, worry; understanding; capture

GERMINATION (juhr muh <u>nay</u> shuhn) *n.*
the beginning of growth (as with a seed or idea)
Synonyms: sprouting, emergence, materialization

LATENT (<u>lay</u> tnt) *adj.*
present but hidden; potential
Synonyms: dormant, quiescent; capable

THE SPHINX

During the dread reign of cholera in New York, I had accepted the invitation of a relative to spend a <u>fortnight</u> with him in the retirement of his *cottage orné*[66] on the banks of the Hudson. We had here around us all the ordinary means of summer amusement; and what with rambling in the woods, boating, fishing, bathing, music, and books, we should have passed the time pleasantly enough, but for the fearful intelligence which reached us every morning from the populous city. Not a day elapsed which did not bring us news of the decease of some acquaintance. Then, as the fatality increased, we learned to expect daily the loss of some friend. At length we trembled at the approach of every messenger. The very air from the South seemed to us <u>redolent</u> with death. That palsying thought, indeed, took entire possession of my soul. I could neither speak, think, nor dream of any thing else. My host was of a less excitable **temperament**, and, although greatly depressed in spirits, exerted himself to **sustain** my own. His richly philosophical intellect was not at any time affected by unrealities. To the substances of terror he was sufficiently alive, but of its shadows he had no **apprehension**.

His endeavors to arouse me from the condition of abnormal gloom into which I had fallen were frustrated, in great measure, by certain volumes which I had found in his library. These were of a character to force into **germination** whatever seeds of hereditary superstition lay **latent** in my bosom. I had been reading these books without his knowledge, and thus he was often at a loss to account for the forcible impressions which had been made upon my fancy.

DISPOSE (dih spohz) *v.* **-ing,-ed.**
to incline or give a tendency to; to get rid of; to put in
place, to settle
Synonyms: determine, motivate; discard;
organize, position
ANIMATED (aa nih may tihd) *adj.*
lively, excited, filled with spirit
Synonyms: elated, vivacious, inspired
SENTIMENT (sehn tuh muhnt) *n.*
an attitude, thought, or judgment prompted by
feeling, a romantic or nostalgic feeling
Synonyms: idea, emotion
PORTENTOUS (pohr tehnt uhs) *adj.*
ominous, fateful
Synonyms: foreboding, heralding, foreshadowing
APPALL (uh pahl) *v.* **-ing,-ed.**
to overcome with shock or dismay
Synonyms: horrify, astound, petrify
CONFOUND (kuhn fownd) *v.* **-ing,-ed.**
to baffle, perplex; to mistake something for another
Synonyms: overwhelm, disconcert, entangle,
muddle; confuse, misidentify
DESOLATION (deh suh lay shuhn) *n.*
barren wasteland; sadness, loneliness
Synonyms: bleakness, devastation, ruin; despair
CONFORMATION (kahn fohr may shun) *n.*
1. the arrangment or structure of the parts of a thing
Synonyms: formation, shape, anatomy, configuration
2. compliance with accepted rules and customs
Synonyms: abidance, conformity, agreement

A favorite topic with me was the popular belief in omens—a belief which, at this one <u>epoch</u> of my life, I was almost seriously **disposed** to defend. On this subject we had long and **animated** discussions; he maintaining the utter groundlessness of faith in such matters, I contending that a popular **sentiment** arising with absolute spontaneity—that is to say, without apparent traces of suggestion—had in itself the unmistakable elements of truth, and was entitled to much respect.

The fact is that soon after my arrival at the cottage there had occurred to myself an incident so entirely inexplicable and which had in it so much of the **portentous** character, that I might well have been excused for regarding it as an omen. It **appalled**, and at the same time so **confounded** and bewildered me, that many days elapsed before I could make up my mind to communicate the circumstance to my friend.

Near the close of an exceedingly warm day, I was sitting, book in hand, at an open window, commanding through long vista of the river banks, a view of a distant hill, the face of which nearest my position had been denuded by what is termed a land-slide, of the principal portion of its trees. My thoughts had been long wandering from the volume before me to the gloom and **desolation** of the neighboring city. Uplifting my eyes from the page, they fell upon the naked face of the hill, and upon an object—upon some living monster of hideous **conformation**, which very rapidly made its way from the summit to the bottom, disappearing finally in the dense forest below. As this creature first came in sight, I doubted my own sanity—or at least the evidence of my own eyes—and many minutes passed before I succeeded in convincing myself that I was neither mad nor in a dream. Yet when I describe the monster (which I distinctly saw, and calmly surveyed through the whole period of its progress), my readers, I fear, will feel more difficulty in being convinced of these points than even I did myself.

APEX (<u>ay</u> pehks) *n.*
pointed end; highest point, summit, zenith
Synonyms: tip; acme, crown, peak, crest

SENTIMENT (<u>sehn</u> tuh muhnt) *n.*
an attitude, thought, or judgment prompted by
feeling, a romantic or nostalgic feeling
Synonyms: idea, emotion

QUELL (kwehl) *v.* **-ing,-ed.**
to crush or subdue
Synonyms: suppress, pacify, quiet, quash, stifle

Estimating the size of the creature by comparison with the diameter of the large trees near which it passed—the few giants of the forests, which had escaped the fury of the land-slide—I concluded it to be far larger than any ship of the line in existence. I say ship of the line, because the shape of the monster suggested the idea—the hull of one of our seventy-fours might convey a very tolerable conception of the general outline. The mouth of the animal was situated at the extremity of a <u>proboscis</u> some sixty or seventy feet in length, and about as thick as the body of an ordinary elephant. Near the root of this trunk was an immense quantity of black shaggy hair—more than could have been supplied by the coats of a score of buffaloes; and projecting from this hair downwardly and laterally, sprang two gleaming tusks not unlike those of the wild boar, but of infinitely greater dimension. Extending forward, parallel with the <u>proboscis</u>, and on each side of it, was a gigantic staff, thirty or forty feet in length, formed seemingly of pure crystal, and in shape a perfect prism—it reflected in the most gorgeous manner the rays of the declining sun. The trunk was fashioned like a wedge with the apex to the earth. From it there were outspread two pairs of wings—each wing nearly one hundred yards in length—one pair being placed above the other, and all thickly covered with metal scales; each scale apparently some ten or twelve feet in diameter. I observed that the upper and lower tiers of wings were connected by a strong chain. But the chief peculiarity of this horrible thing was the representation of a *Death's Head*, which covered nearly the whole surface of its breast, and which was as accurately traced in glaring white, upon the dark ground of the body, as if it had been there carefully designed by an artist. While I regarded this terrific animal, and more especially the appearance on its breast, with a feeling of horror and awe—with a sentiment of forthcoming evil, which I found it impossible to quell by any effort of the reason, I perceived the huge jaws at the

KNELL (nehl) *n.*
sound of a funeral bell; omen of death or failure
Synonyms: toll, chime, peal; warning
IMPULSE (<u>ihm</u> puhls) *n.*
sudden tendency, inclination
Synonyms: urge, whim
REPUGNANCE (rih <u>puhg</u> nehnts) *n.*
strong dislike, distaste, or antagonism; an instance of
contradiction or inconsistency
Synonyms: repulsion, aversion; incompatibility
APPARITION (aa puh <u>rih</u> shuhn) *n.*
an unexpected or unusual sight; a ghostly figure
Synonyms: illusion; spirit, specter
IMPEL (ihm <u>pehl</u>) *v.* **-ling,-led.**
to urge forward as if driven by a strong moral pressure
Synonyms: push, prompt, drive, incite, instigate
DEMEANOR (dih <u>meen</u> uhr) *n.*
one's behavior or conduct
Synonyms: attitude, disposition, manner, presence
MINUTELY (mie <u>noot</u> lee) (mih <u>noot</u> lee) *adv.*
precisely, in a detailed manner
Synonyms: attentively, critically

CONFORMATION (kahn fohr <u>may</u> shun) *n.*
1. the arrangement or structure of the parts of a thing
Synonyms: formation, shape, anatomy, configuration
2. compliance with accepted rules and customs
Synonyms: abidance, conformity, agreement

extremity of the <u>proboscis</u> suddenly expand themselves, and from them there proceeded a sound so loud and so expressive of woe, that it struck upon my nerves like a **knell**, and as the monster disappeared at the foot of the hill, I fell at once, fainting, to the floor.

Upon recovering, my first **impulse**, of course, was to inform my friend of what I had seen and heard—and I can scarcely explain what feeling of **repugnance** it was which in the end, operated to prevent me.

At length, one evening, some three or four days after the occurrence, we were sitting together in the room in which I had seen the **apparition**—I occupying the same seat at the same window, and he lounging on a sofa near at hand. The association of the place and time **impelled** me to give him an account of the phenomenon. He heard me to the end—at first laughed heartily—and then lapsed into an excessively grave **demeanor**, as if my insanity was a thing beyond suspicion. At this instant I again had a distinct view of the monster—to which, with a shout of absolute terror, I now directed his attention. He looked eagerly—but maintained that he saw nothing—although I designated **minutely** the course of the creature, as it made its way down the naked face of the hill.

I was now immeasurably alarmed, for I considered the vision either as an omen of my death, or worse, as the forerunner of an attack of mania. I threw myself passionately back in my chair, and for some moments buried my face in my hands. When I uncovered my eyes, the **apparition** was no longer visible.

My host, however, had in some degree resumed the calmness of his **demeanor**, and questioned me very rigorously in respect to the **conformation** of the visionary creature. When I had fully satisfied him on this head, he sighed deeply, as if relieved of some intolerable burden, and went on to talk with what I thought a cruel calmness, of various points of speculative philosophy, which had heretofore formed subject of discussion between us. I

DIFFUSION (dih <u>fyoo</u> zhuhn) *n.*
the act of spreading
Synonyms: scattering, dispersion, dissipation

SYNOPSIS (sih <u>nahp</u> sihs) *n.*
a summary
Synonyms: outline, abstract, compendium, digest,
epitome

DISCOURSE (<u>dihs</u> kohrs) *n.*
a formal, orderly, and extended expression of thought;
the verbal interchange of ideas
Synonyms: oration, lecture; dialogue, discussion

MINUTENESS (mie <u>noot</u> nehs) (mih <u>noot</u> nehs) *n.*
precision, attention to detail; the state of being tiny
Synonyms: accuracy, exactness, carefulness; smallness

RETAIN (rih <u>tayn</u>) *v.* **-ing,-ed.**
to hold, keep possession of
Synonyms: withhold, reserve, maintain, remember

MELANCHOLY (mehl uhn <u>kahl</u> ee) *adj.*
sad, depressing
Synonyms: dejected, despondent, woeful, sorrowful

remember his insisting very especially (among other things) upon the idea that the principal source of error in all human investigations lay in the liability of the understanding to underrate or to overvalue the importance of an object, through mere misadmeasurement of its propinquity. "To estimate properly, for example," he said, "the influence to be exercised on mankind at large by the thorough **diffusion** of Democracy, the distance of the epoch at which such **diffusion** may possibly be accomplished should not fail to form an item in the estimate. Yet can you tell me one writer on the subject of government who has ever thought this particular branch of the subject worthy of discussion at all?"

He here paused for a moment, stepped to a bookcase, and brought forth one of the ordinary **synopses** of Natural History. Requesting me then to exchange seats with him, that he might the better distinguish the fine print of the volume, he took my arm-chair at the window, and, opening the book, resumed his **discourse** very much in the same tone as before.

"But for your exceeding **minuteness**," he said, "in describing the monster, I might never have had it in my power to demonstrate to you what it was. In the first place, let me read to you a school-boy account of the genus Sphinx, of the family Crepuscularia,[67] of the order Lepidoptera,[68] of the class of Insecta—or insects. The account runs thus:

" 'Four membranous wings covered with little colored scales of metallic appearance; mouth forming a rolled proboscis, produced by an elongation of the jaws, upon the sides of which are found the rudiments of mandibles and downy palpi; the inferior wings **retained** to the superior by a stiff hair, antennae in the form of an elongated club, prismatic; abdomen pointed. The Death's-headed Sphinx has occasioned much terror among the vulgar at times, by the **melancholy** kind of cry which it utters, and the insignia of death which it wears upon its corslet.'"

THE SPHINX

REASCEND (ree uh <u>sehnd</u>) *v.* **-ing,-ed.**
to rise to another level or climb again; to move
upward more than once
    Synonyms: elevate, escalate, mount; hoist, lift

He here closed the book and leaned forward in the chair, placing himself accurately in the position which I had occupied at the moment of beholding "the monster."

"Ah, here it is," he presently exclaimed. "It is **reascending** the face of the hill, and a very remarkable looking creature I admit it to be. Still, it is by no means so large or so distant as you imagined it; for the fact is that, as it wriggles its way up this thread, which some spider has wrought along the window-sash, I find it to be about the sixteenth of an inch in its extreme length, and also about the sixteenth of an inch distant from the pupil of my eye."

SULLY (<u>suh</u> lee) *v.* **-ing,-ied.**
 to soil, stain, tarnish, taint
  Synonyms: mar, defile, besmirch
APPELLATION (aa puhl <u>ay</u> shuhn) *n.*
 a title or name
  Synonyms: denomination, designation, moniker, tag
DETESTATION (dee tehs <u>tay</u> shuhn) *n.*
 intense and violent hatred
  Synonyms: disgust, loathing, abhorrence
INDIGNANT (ihn <u>dihg</u> nuhnt) *adj.*
 angry, incensed, offended
  Synonyms: furious, irate, mad, wrathful, ireful
INFAMY (<u>ihn</u> fuh mee) *n.*
 reputation for bad deeds
  Synonyms: disgrace, dishonor, shame, ignominy
ASPIRATION (aa spuhr <u>ay</u> shuhn) *n.*
 a great hope or goal
  Synonyms: intention, purpose, expectation
TURPITUDE (<u>tuhr</u> pih tood) *n.*
 inherent vileness, foulness, depravity
  Synonyms: baseness, immorality, wickedness
BASE (bays) *adj.*
 lacking qualities of higher mind or spirit
  Synonyms: vulgar, corrupt, immoral, menial
ENORMITY (ih <u>nohr</u> muh tee) *n.*
 state of being gigantic or terrible
  Synonyms: outrageousness, atrociousness

WILLIAM WILSON

What say of it? What say CONSCIENCE grim,
That spectre in my path?
—Chamberlain's *Pharonnida*[69]

Let me call myself, for the present, William Wilson. The fair page now lying before me need not be sullied with my real appellation. This has been already too much an object for the scorn—for the horror—for the detestation of my race. To the uttermost regions of the globe have not the indignant winds bruited its unparalleled infamy? Oh, outcast of all outcasts most abandoned! To the earth art thou not for ever dead? To its honors, to its flowers, to its golden aspirations? And a cloud, dense, dismal, and limitless, does it not hang eternally between thy hopes and heaven?

I would not, if I could, here or to-day, embody a record of my later years of unspeakable misery, and unpardonable crime. This epoch—these later years—took unto themselves a sudden elevation in turpitude, whose origin alone it is my present purpose to assign. Men usually grow base by degrees. From me, in an instant, all virtue dropped bodily as a mantle. From comparatively trivial wickedness I passed, with the stride of a giant, into more than the enormities of an Elagabalus.[70] What chance—what one event brought this evil thing to pass, bear with me while I relate. Death approaches and the shadow which foreruns him has thrown a softening influence over my spirit. I long, in passing through the dim valley, for the sympathy—I had nearly said for the pity—of my fellow men. I would fain have them believe that I have been, in some measure, the slave of circumstances beyond human

DESCENDANT (dih <u>sehn</u> dehnt) *n.*
  an offspring or heir
    Synonyms: child, kin, progeny
TEMPERAMENT (<u>tehm</u> puhr uh mehnt) *n.*
  a manner of behaving, an attitude
    Synonyms: disposition, mood, mentality
DISQUIETUDE (dihs <u>kwie</u> eh tood) *n.*
  anxiety; lack of peace or tranquility
    Synonyms: edginess; uneasiness
CAPRICE (kuh <u>prees</u>) *n.*
  an impulsive change of mind, fickleness
    Synonym: whim
CONSTITUTIONAL (kahn stih <u>too</u> shuh nuhl) *adj.*
  having to do with the physical structure or health of
  something or someone
    Synonyms: natural, inherent, innate
INFIRMITY (ihn <u>fuhr</u> mih tee) *n.*
  disease, ailment
    Synonyms: weakness, frailty, affliction, illness
PROPENSITY (pruh <u>pehn</u> suh tee) *n.*
  inclination, tendency
    Synonyms: predilection, bias, leaning, penchant,
    proclivity
GNARLED (nahrld) *adj.*
  knotted, deformed
    Synonyms: twisted, contorted
VENERABLE (<u>veh</u> nehr uh buhl) *adj.*
  respected because of age
    Synonyms: respectable, distinguished, elderly

control. I would wish them to seek out for me, in the details I am about to give, some little oasis of fatality amid a wilderness of error. I would have them allow— what they cannot refrain from allowing—that, although temptation may have erewhile existed as great, man was never thus, at least, tempted before—certainly, never thus fell. And is it therefore that he has never thus suffered? Have I not indeed been living in a dream? And am I not now dying a victim to the horror and the mystery of the wildest of all <u>sublunary</u> visions?

I am the **descendant** of a race whose imaginative and easily excitable **temperament** has at all times rendered them remarkable; and, in my earliest infancy I gave evidence of having fully inherited the family character. As I advanced in years it was more strongly developed; becoming for many reasons, a cause of serious **disquietude** to my friends, and of positive injury to myself. I grew self-willed, addicted to the wildest **caprices**, and a prey to the most ungovernable passions. Weak-minded, and beset with **constitutional infirmities** akin to my own, my parents could do but little to check the evil **propensities** which distinguished me. Some feeble and ill-directed efforts resulted in complete failure on their part, and, of course, in total triumph on mine. Thenceforward my voice was a household law; and at an age when few children have abandoned their leading-strings, I was left to the guidance of my own will, and became, in all but name, the master of my own actions.

My earliest recollections of a school-life are connected with a large, rambling, Elizabethan house, in a misty-looking village of England, where were a vast number of gigantic and **gnarled** trees, and where all the houses were excessively ancient. In truth, it was a dream-like and spirit-soothing place, that **venerable** old town. At this moment, in fancy, I feel the refreshing chilliness of its deeply-shadowed avenues, inhale the fragrance of its thousand shrubberies, and thrill anew with indefinable delight, at the deep hollow note of the church-bell, break-

SULLEN (<u>suh</u> luhn) *adj.*
  brooding, gloomy
    Synonyms: morose, sulky, somber, glum
MINUTE (mie <u>noot</u>) (mih <u>noot</u>) *adj. (See page 328.)*
AMBIGUOUS (aam <u>bihg</u> yoo uhs) *adj.*
  uncertain, subject to multiple interpretations
    Synonyms: equivocal, dubious, unclear
MONITION (muh <u>nih</u> shuhn) *n.*
  a warning of danger; cautionary advice
    Synonyms: sign; reprimand, rebuke, counsel
ENCOMPASS (ehn <u>kuhm</u> puhs) *v.* **-ing,-ed.**
  to cover, surround; to include, take in
    Synonyms: enclose, envelop; constitute, involve
SOLEMN (<u>sah</u> luhm) *adj.*
  somberly impressive; quiet, deeply serious
    Synonyms: dignified, ceremonial; earnest, brooding
ASCEND (uh <u>sehnd</u>) *v.* **-ing,-ed.**
  to rise to another level or climb; to move upward
    Synonyms: elevate, escalate, mount; hoist, lift
COUNTENANCE (<u>kown</u> tuh nuhns) *n. (See page 316.)*
DEMURELY (dih <u>myoor</u> lee) *adv.*
  in a reserved manner; modestly, sometimes also
  flirtatiously
    Synonyms: seriously, reticently; shyly, bashfully, coyly
BENIGN (bih <u>nien</u>) *adj.*
  kindly, gentle, or harmless
    Synonyms: innocuous, mild, safe
MINUTELY (mie <u>noot</u> lee) *adv. (See page 358.)*
VISAGE (<u>vih</u> sihj) *n.*
  the appearance of a person or place
    Synonyms: expression, look, style, manner
PARADOX (<u>paar</u> uh dahks) *n.*
  contradiction, incongruity; dilemma, puzzle
    Synonyms: irony; conundrum, riddle
PONDEROUS (<u>pahn</u> duhr uhs) *adj.*
  weighty, heavy, large
    Synonyms: hefty, massive, cumbersome, unwieldy

ing, each hour, with **sullen** and sudden roar, upon the stillness of the dusky atmosphere in which the <u>fretted</u> Gothic steeple lay imbedded and asleep.

It gives me, perhaps, as much of pleasure as I can now in any manner experience, to dwell upon **minute** recollections of the school and its concerns. Steeped in misery as I am—misery, alas, only too real—I shall be pardoned for seeking relief, however slight and temporary, in the weakness of a few rambling details. These, moreover, utterly trivial, and even ridiculous in themselves, assume, to my fancy, <u>adventitious</u> importance, as connected with a period and a locality when and where I recognize the first **ambiguous monitions** of the destiny which afterward so fully overshadowed me. Let me then remember.

The house, I have said, was old and irregular. The grounds were extensive, and a high and solid brick wall, topped with a bed of mortar and broken glass, **encompassed** the whole. This prison-like <u>rampart</u> formed the limit of our domain; beyond it we saw but thrice a week—once every Saturday afternoon when, attended by two ushers, we were permitted to take brief walks in a body through some of the neighboring fields—and twice during Sunday, when we were paraded in the same formal manner to the morning and evening service in the one church of the village. Of this church the principal of our school was pastor. With how deep a spirit of wonder and perplexity was I wont to regard him from our remote pew in the gallery, as, with step **solemn** and slow, he **ascended** the pulpit! This reverend man, with **countenance** so **demurely benign**, with robes so glossy and so clerically flowing, with wig so **minutely** powdered, so rigid and so vast—could this be he who, of late, with sour **visage**, and in snuffy <u>habiliments</u>, administered, ferule in hand, the Draconian Laws[71] of the academy? Oh, gigantic **paradox**, too utterly monstrous for solution!

At an angle of the **ponderous** wall frowned a more **ponderous** gate. It was riveted and studded with iron bolts,

SURMOUNT (suhr <u>mownt</u>) *v.* **-ing,-ed.**
  1. to have something on top; to be on top of something
    Synonyms: cap, crown, cover
  2. to conquer, overcome
    Synonyms: clear, hurdle, leap, surpass, exceed

EGRESSION (ih <u>greh</u> shuhn) *n.*
  the act of leaving or the ability to leave; an exit
    Synonyms: emergence, departure; escape, doorway

INGRESSION (ihn <u>greh</u> shuhn) *n.*
  the act of going in or the ability to enter; an entrance
    Synonyms: access, admittance, permission; entry,
    doorway

PLENITUDE (<u>plehn</u> uh tood) *n.*
  abundance, plenty
    Synonyms: profusion, bounteousness, copiousness

SOLEMN (<u>sah</u> luhm) *adj.*
  somberly impressive; quiet, deeply serious
    Synonyms: dignified, ceremonial; earnest, brooding

CAPACIOUS (kuh <u>pay</u> shuhs) *adj.*
  large, roomy, extensive
    Synonyms: ample, commodious

CONSTITUTE (kahn stih <u>toot</u>) *v.* **-ing,-ed.**
  to be the parts or components of something,
  to compose; to equal
    Synonyms: comprise, form, make up; amount to

ASCENT (uh <u>sehnt</u>) *n.*
  movement upward; an upward slope; a climb or rising
  to another level
    Synonyms: scaling, escalation; incline, upgrade;
    mounting

DESCENT (dih <u>sehnt</u>) (dee <u>sehnt</u>) *n. (See page 342.)*

INNUMERABLE (ih <u>noo</u> muhr uh buhl)
(ih <u>nyoo</u> muhr uh buhl) *adj.*
  too many to be counted, inestimable
    Synonyms: incalculable, immeasurable, infinite

PONDER (<u>pahn</u> duhr) *v.* **-ing,-ed.** *(See page 340.)*

ASCERTAIN (aa suhr <u>tayn</u>) *v.* **-ing,-ed.** *(See page 330.)*

and **surmounted** with jagged iron spikes. What impressions of deep awe did it inspire! It was never opened save for the three periodical **egressions** and **ingressions** already mentioned; then, in every creak of its mighty hinges, we found a **plenitude** of mystery—a world of matter for **solemn** remark, or for more **solemn** meditation.

The extensive enclosure was irregular in form, having many **capacious** recesses. Of these, three or four of the largest **constituted** the play-ground. It was level, and covered with fine hard gravel. I well remember it had no trees, nor benches, nor any thing similar within it. Of course it was in the rear of the house. In front lay a small parterre planted with box and other shrubs, but through this sacred division we passed only upon rare occasions indeed—such as a first <u>advent</u> to school or final departure thence, or perhaps, when a parent or friend having called for us, we joyfully took our way home for the Christmas or Midsummer holidays.

But the house—how quaint an old building was this! How <u>veritably</u> a palace of enchantment! There was really no end to its windings—to its incomprehensible subdivisions. It was difficult, at any given time, to say with certainty upon which of its two stories one happened to be. From each room to every other there were sure to be found three or four steps either in **ascent** or **descent**. Then the lateral branches were **innumerable**—inconceivable—and so returning in upon themselves, that our most exact ideas in regard to the whole mansion were not very far different from those with which we **pondered** upon infinity. During the five years of my residence here, I was never able to **ascertain** with precision, in what remote locality lay the little sleeping apartment assigned to myself and some eighteen or twenty other scholars.

The school-room was the largest in the house—I could not help thinking, in the world. It was very long, narrow, and dismally low, with pointed Gothic windows and a ceiling of oak. In a remote and terror-inspiring angle was

SANCTUM (<u>saank</u> tuhm) *n.*
a sacred or holy place; a private place
Synonyms: altar, temple; refuge, asylum, shelter, retreat

REVERENCE (<u>reh</u> vuhr ehnts) *v.* **-ing,-ed.**
to worship, regard with awe
Synonyms: venerate, adore, idolize, admire

INTERSPERSE (ihn tuhr <u>spuhrs</u>) *v.* **-ing,-ed.**
to distribute among, mix with
Synonyms: commingle, scatter, infuse

INNUMERABLE (ih <u>noo</u> muhr uh buhl)
(ih <u>nyoo</u> muhr uh buhl) *adj.*
too many to be counted, inestimable
Synonyms: incalculable, immeasurable, infinite

ENCOMPASS (ehn <u>kuhm</u> puhs) *v.* **-ing,-ed.**
to cover, surround; to include, take in
Synonyms: enclose, envelop; constitute, involve

VENERABLE (<u>veh</u> nehr uh buhl) *adj.*
respected because of age
Synonyms: respectable, distinguished, elderly

TEDIUM (<u>tee</u> dee uhm) *n.*
boredom because of length or dullness
Synonyms: wearisomeness, fatigue, banality, routine

MONOTONY (muh <u>naht</u> nee) *n.*
tedium, dull sameness
Synonyms: repetitiousness, boredom, ennui

REPLETE (rih <u>pleet</u>) *adj.*
abundantly supplied
Synonyms: abounding, satiated, gorged, stuffed, full

DERIVE (dih <u>riev</u>) *v.* **-ing,-ed.**
to receive from a source, to originate
Synonyms: infer, descend, deduce, come (from)

LUXURY (<u>luhg</u> zhoor ee) *n.*
something done or had purely for enjoyment
Synonyms: comfort, indulgence, splendor, frill

a square enclosure of eight or ten feet, comprising the **sanctum**, "during hours," of our principal, the Reverend Dr. Bransby. It was a solid structure, with massy door, sooner than open which in the absence of the "dominie," we would all have willingly perished by the *peine forte et dure*.[72] In other angles were two other similar boxes, far less **reverenced** indeed, but still greatly matters of awe. One of these was the pulpit of the "classical" usher, one of the "English and mathematical." **Interspersed** about the room, crossing and recrossing in endless irregularity, were **innumerable** benches and desks, black, ancient, and time-worn, piled desperately with much bethumbed books, and so beseamed with initial letters, names at full length, grotesque figures, and other multiplied efforts of the knife, as to have entirely lost what little of original form might have been their portion in days long departed. A huge bucket with water stood at one extremity of the room, and a clock of stupendous dimensions at the other.

Encompassed by the massy walls of this **venerable** academy, I passed, yet not in **tedium** or disgust, the years of the third lustrum of my life. The teeming brain of childhood requires no external world of incident to occupy or amuse it; and the apparently dismal **monotony** of a school was **replete** with more intense excitement than my riper youth has **derived** from **luxury**, or my full manhood from crime. Yet I must believe that my first mental development had in it much of the uncommon—even much of the *outré*.[73] Upon mankind at large the events of very early existence rarely leave in mature age any definite impression. All is gray shadow—a weak and irregular remembrance— an indistinct regathering of feeble pleasures and phantasmagoric pains. With me this is not so. In childhood I must have felt with the energy of a man what I now find stamped upon memory in lines as vivid, as deep, and as durable as the exergues of the *Carthaginian medals*.[74]

Yet in fact—in the fact of the world's view—how little was there to remember! The morning's awakening, the

ARDOR (<u>ahr</u> duhr) *n.* *(See page 128.)*

IMPERIOUSNESS (ihm <u>pihr</u> ee uhs nehs) *n.*
 self-assured arrogance, pomposity, vanity
  Synonyms: ego, despotism, conceitedness

DISPOSITION (dihs puh <u>zih</u> shuhn) *n.* *(See page 46.)*

GRADATION (gray <u>day</u> shuhn) *n.*
 process occurring by regular degrees or stages;
 variation in color
  Synonyms: step, subtlety, nuance; shade

ASCENDENCY (uh <u>sehn</u> dehn see) *n.*
 a superior advantage, an influence
  Synonyms: power, control, sway, dominance

DESCENT (dih <u>sehnt</u>) (dee <u>sehnt</u>) *n.*
 1. one's ancestry
  Synonyms: heredity, lineage
 2. the passing from a high to a low place; a decline
  Synonyms: lowering, dismount, gravitation; slope

APPELLATION (aa puhl <u>ay</u> shuhn) *n.* *(See page 364.)*

PRESCRIPTIVE (prih <u>skrihp</u> tihv) *adj.*
 authorized according to customs, laws, or rules
  Synonyms: dictated, usual, accepted, standard

CONSTITUTE (kahn stih <u>toot</u>) *v.* **-ing,-ed.** *(See page 370.)*

PRESUME (prih <u>zoom</u>) *v.* **-ing,-ed.**
 to dare; to assume or believe something without proof
  Synonyms: venture; take for granted

IMPLICIT (ihm <u>plih</u> siht) *adj.*
 having no doubt; implied, not directly expressed
  Synonyms: unquestioning; tacit, inferred, understood

ARBITRARY (<u>ahr</u> bih trayr ee) *adj.*
 depending solely on individual will; inconsistent
  Synonyms: discretional; whimsical, impulsive

UNQUALIFIED (uhn <u>kwah</u> luh fied) *adj.*
 absolute and unconditional
  Synonyms: outright, clear, total, unfaltering

DESPOTISM (dehs <u>puh</u> tihz uhm) *n.*
 tyranny, oppression
  Synonyms: dictatorship, totalitarianism, autocracy

PRETENSION (prih <u>tehn</u> shuhn) *n.*
 a quality of being arrogant, snobbishness
  Synonyms: ostentation, conceit, phoniness

nightly summons to bed; the connings, the recitations; the periodical half-holidays and perambulations; the play-ground, with its broils, its pastimes, its intrigues—these, by a mental sorcery long forgotten, were made to involve a wilderness of sensation, a world of rich incident, a universe of varied emotion, of excitement the most passionate and spirit-stirring. *"Oh, le bon temps, que ce siècle de fer!"*[75]

In truth, the **ardor**, the enthusiasm, and the **imperiousness** of my **disposition**, soon rendered me a marked character among my schoolmates, and by slow, but natural **gradations**, gave me an **ascendency** over all not greatly older than myself—over all with a single exception. This exception was found in the person of a scholar, who, although no relation, bore the same Christian and surname as myself—a circumstance, in fact, little remarkable; for, notwithstanding a noble **descent**, mine was one of those everyday **appellations** which seem, by **prescriptive** right to have been, time out of mind, the common property of the mob. In this narrative I have therefore designated myself as William Wilson—a fictitious title not very dissimilar to the real. My namesake alone, of those who in school phraseology **constituted** "our set," **presumed** to compete with me in the studies of the class—in the sports and broils of the play-ground—to refuse **implicit** belief in my assertions, and submission to my will—indeed, to interfere with my **arbitrary** dictation in any respect whatsoever. If there is on earth a supreme and **unqualified despotism**, it is the **despotism** of a mastermind in boyhood over the less energetic spirits of its companions.

Wilson's rebellion was to me a source of the greatest embarrassment; the more so as, in spite of the bravado with which in public I made a point of treating him and his **pretensions**, I secretly felt that I feared him, and could not help thinking the equality which he maintained so easily with myself, a proof of his true superiority; since

PERPETUAL (puhr <u>peht</u> chyoo uhl) *adj.*
  endless, lasting
    Synonyms: continuous, constant, ceaseless, eternal,
    perennial
IMPERTINENT (ihm <u>puhr</u> tuh nuhnt) *adj.*
  rude, audacious; improper
    Synonyms: forward, bold; impolite, discourteous
DOGGED (<u>daw</u> gihd) *adj.*
  stubborn or persistent
    Synonyms: tenacious, obstinate, pertinacious
DESTITUTE (<u>dehs</u> tih toot) (<u>dehs</u> tih tyoot) *adj.*
  lacking; very poor, poverty-stricken
    Synonyms: without, wanting, deprived; insolvent,
    impecunious, penurious, needy, broke
ACTUATE (<u>aak</u> chuh wayt) (<u>aak</u> shuh wayt) *v.* **-ing,-ed.**
  to move into action; to put into mechanical action
    Synonyms: stimulate, motivate, inspire; activate
WHIMSICAL (<u>wihm</u> sih kuhl) *adj.*
  playful or fanciful
    Synonyms: capricious, erratic, chameleonic, fickle,
    mutable
THWART (thwahrt) *v.* **-ing,-ed.**
  to frustrate; to block or prevent from happening
    Synonyms: hinder, baffle; oppose, defeat, foil, balk
ABASEMENT (uh <u>bays</u> mehnt) *n.*
  shame, disgrace
    Synonyms: corruption, humiliation, downfall
PIQUE (peek) *n.*
  a fleeting feeling of hurt pride
    Synonyms: vexation, resentment, indignation,
    dudgeon, umbrage
SINGULAR (<u>sihn</u> gyuh luhr) *adj.*
  uncommon, peculiar
    Synonyms: unusual, odd, rare, unique, individual
CONSUMMATE (<u>kahn</u> suh muht) (<u>kahn</u> soo miht) *adj.*
  accomplished, complete, perfect
    Synonyms: thorough, exhaustive, ideal, flawless

not to be overcome, cost me a **perpetual** struggle. Yet this superiority—even this equality—was in truth acknowledged by no one but myself; our associates, by some unaccountable blindness, seemed not even to suspect it. Indeed, his competition, his resistance and especially his **impertinent** and **dogged** interference with my purposes, were not more pointed than private. He appeared to be **destitute** alike of the ambition, which urged, and of the passionate energy of mind which enabled me to excel. In his rivalry he might have been supposed **actuated** solely by a **whimsical** desire to **thwart**, astonish, or mortify myself; although there were times when I could not help observing, with a feeling made up of wonder, **abasement**, and **pique**, that he mingled with his injuries, his insults, or his contradictions, a certain most inappropriate, and assuredly most unwelcome affectionateness of manner. I could only conceive this **singular** behavior to arise from a **consummate** self-conceit assuming the vulgar airs of patronage and protection.

Perhaps it was this latter trait in Wilson's conduct, conjoined with our identity of name, and the mere accident of our having entered the school upon the same day, which set afloat the notion that we were brothers, among the senior classes in the academy. These do not usually inquire with much strictness into the affairs of their juniors. I have before said, or should have said, that Wilson was not, in a most remote degree, connected with my family. But assuredly if we *had* been brothers we must have been twins; for, after leaving Dr. Bransby's, I casually learned that my namesake was born on the nineteenth of January, 1813—and this is a somewhat remarkable coincidence; for the day is precisely that of my own nativity.

It may seem strange that in spite of the continual anxiety occasioned me by the rivalry of Wilson, and his intolerable spirit of contradiction, I could not bring myself to hate him altogether. We had, to be sure, nearly every day a quarrel in which, yielding me publicly the

CONTRIVE (kuhn <u>triev</u>) *v.* **-ing,-ed.** *(See page 266.)*

CONGENIALITY (kuhn jee nee <u>aal</u> ih tee) *n.*
  similarity in tastes and habits; a pleasant disposition
    Synonyms: compatibility, harmony; amiability,
    warmth, friendliness

SENTIMENT (<u>sehn</u> tuh muhnt) *n.* *(See page 356.)*

MOTLEY (<u>maht</u> lee) *adj.* *(See page 72.)*

HETEROGENEOUS (heh tuh ruh <u>jee</u> nee uhs) *adj.*
  composed of unlike parts, different, diverse
    Synonyms: miscellaneous, mixed, varied, motley

PETULANT (<u>peh</u> chuh luhnt) *adj.* *(See page 190.)*

ANIMOSITY (aa nih <u>mah</u> sih tee) *n.*
  hatred, hostility
    Synonyms: antipathy, enmity, malice, rancor

ANOMALOUS (uh <u>nah</u> moh luhs) *adj.* *(See page 142.)*

COVERT (<u>koh</u> vuhrt) (koh <u>vuhrt</u>) *adj.*
  not openly shown, shielded
    Synonyms: underground, clandestine

BANTER (<u>baan</u> tuhr) *n.*
  playful, teasing conversation
    Synonyms: chatter, palaver, prattle

UNIFORMLY (<u>yoo</u> nih fohrm lee) *adv.*
  consistently and without change; identically
    Synonyms: steadily, evenly; indistinguishably

AUSTERITY (aw <u>stayr</u> ih tee) *n.*
  strictness or severity of manner; lack of adornment
    Synonyms: discipline; bareness, simplicity

POIGNANCY (<u>poy</u> nyaan see) *n.*
  sharpness; the state of being emotionally moving
    Synonyms: affect; passion, piquancy

VULNERABLE (<u>vuhl</u> nuhr uh buhl) *adj.*
  defenseless, unprotected; innocent, naive
    Synonyms: susceptible, assailable; young

CONSTITUTIONAL (kahn stih <u>too</u> shuh nuhl) *adj.*
(See page 366.)

ANTAGONIST (aan <u>taag</u> uh nihst) *n.*
  foe, opponent, adversary
    Synonyms: enemy, rival

PRECLUDE (prih <u>clood</u>) *v.* **-ing,-ed.** *(See page 216.)*

SAGACITY (suh <u>gaa</u> sih tee) *n.* *(See page 4.)*

VEX (vehks) *v.* **-ing,-ed.** *(See page 42.)*

palm of victory, he, in some manner, **contrived** to make me feel that it was he who had deserved it; yet a sense of pride on my part, and a <u>veritable</u> dignity on his own, kept us always upon what are called "speaking terms," while there were many points of strong **congeniality** in our tempers, operating to awake in me a **sentiment** our position alone, perhaps, prevented from ripening into friendship. It is difficult indeed, to define, or even to describe, my real feelings toward him. They formed a **motley** and **heterogeneous** admixture—some **petulant animosity**, which was not yet hatred, some esteem, more respect, much fear, with a world of uneasy curiosity. To the moralist it will be necessary to say, in addition, that Wilson and myself were the most inseparable of companions.

It was no doubt the **anomalous** state of affairs existing between us, which turned all my attacks upon him (and there were many, either open or **covert**) into the channel of **banter** or practical joke (giving pain while assuming the aspect of mere fun) rather than into a more serious and determined hostility. But my endeavors on this head were by no means **uniformly** successful, even when my plans were the most wittily concocted; for my namesake had much about him, in character, of that unassuming and quiet **austerity** which, while enjoying the **poignancy** of its own jokes, has no heel of Achilles[25] in itself, and absolutely refuses to be laughed at. I could find, indeed, but one **vulnerable** point, and that, lying in a personal peculiarity, arising, perhaps, from **constitutional** disease, would have been spared by any **antagonist** less at his wit's end than myself—my rival had a weakness in the faucial or guttural organs, which **precluded** him from raising his voice at any time above a very low whisper. Of this defect I did not fail to take what poor advantage lay in my power.

Wilson's retaliations in kind were many; and there was one form of his practical wit that disturbed me beyond measure. How his **sagacity** first discovered at all that so petty a thing would **vex** me, is a question I never could

AVERSION (uh <u>vuhr</u> zhuhn) *n.*
   intense dislike
      Synonyms: antagonism, antipathy, abhorrence,
      repulsion, repugnance

PLEBEIAN (<u>plee</u> bee uhn) *adj.*
   crude, vulgar, low-class
      Synonyms: unrefined, coarse, common

VENOM (<u>vehn</u> uhm) *n.*
   poison; malice or spite
      Synonyms: toxin; harm, hatred

INEVITABLY (ihn <u>ehv</u> ih tuh blee) *adv.*
   certainly, unavoidably
      Synonyms: inescapably, surely, predictably

DETESTABLE (dee <u>tehst</u> uh buhl) *adj.*
   deserving of intense and violent hated
      Synonyms: disgusting, despicable, loathsome

CONFOUND (kuhn <u>fownd</u>) *v.* **-ing,-ed.**
   to mistake something for another; to baffle, perplex
      Synonyms: confuse, misidentify; overwhelm,
      disconcert, entangle, muddle

VEXATION (vehk <u>say</u> shuhn) *n.*
   irritation, annoyance; confusion, puzzlement
      Synonyms: aggravation, affliction; trouble, anxiety

ENGENDER (ehn <u>gehn</u> duhr) *v.* **-ing,-ed.**
   to produce, cause, bring about
      Synonyms: procreate, propagate, originate, generate

GALL (gahl) *v.* **-ing,-ed.**
   to exasperate and irritate
      Synonyms: vex, fret, harass, irk

SCRUPULOUSLY (<u>skroop</u> yuh luhs lee) *adv.*
   carefully and precisely, meticulously
      Synonyms: conscientiously, painstakingly

ALLUSION (uh <u>loo</u> zhuhn) *n.*
   indirect reference
      Synonyms: intimation, suggestion

GAIT (gayt) *n.*
   the way one moves on foot, a manner of walking
      Synonyms: tread, walk, march, pace

solve; but having discovered, he habitually practised the annoyance. I had always felt **aversion** to my uncourtly <u>patronymic</u>, and its very common, if not **plebeian** praenomen.[76] The words were **venom** in my ears; and when, upon the day of my arrival, a second William Wilson came also to the academy, I felt angry with him for bearing the name, and doubly disgusted with the name because a stranger bore it, who would be the cause of its twofold repetition, who would be constantly in my presence, and whose concerns, in the ordinary routine of the school business, must **inevitably**, on account of the **detestable** coincidence, be often **confounded** with my own.

The feeling of **vexation** thus **engendered** grew stronger with every circumstance tending to show resemblance, moral or physical, between my rival and myself. I had not then discovered the remarkable fact that we were of the same age; but I saw that we were of the same height, and I perceived that we were even singularly alike in general contour of person and outline of feature. I was **galled**, too, by the rumor touching a relationship, which had grown current in the upper forms. In a word, nothing could more seriously disturb me (although I **scrupulously** concealed such disturbance) than any **allusion** to a similarity of mind, person, or condition existing between us. But, in truth, I had no reason to believe that (with the exception of the matter of relationship, and in the case of Wilson himself) this similarity had ever been made a subject of comment, or even observed at all by our schoolfellows. That *he* observed it in all its bearings, and as fixedly as I, was apparent; but that he could discover in such circumstances so fruitful a field of annoyance, can only be attributed, as I said before, to his more than ordinary penetration.

His cue, which was to perfect an imitation of myself, lay both in words and in actions; and most admirably did he play his part. My dress it was an easy matter to copy; my **gait** and general manner were without difficulty

APPROPRIATE (uh <u>proh</u> pree ayt) *v.* **-ing,-ed.**
  to take possession of; to set aside for a purpose
      Synonyms: usurp, arrogate, commandeer; allocate, designate

CONSTITUTIONAL (kahn stih <u>too</u> shuh nuhl) *adj.*
(See page 366.)

SINGULAR (<u>sihn</u> gyuh luhr) *adj.* *(See page 376.)*

CARICATURE (<u>kaa</u> rih kah chuhr) *n.*
  exaggerated portrait, cartoon
      Synonyms: burlesque, travesty, lampoon

CONSOLATION (kahn suh <u>lay</u> shuhn) *n.*
  something providing comfort or solace for a loss or hardship
      Synonym: condolence

ELICIT (ih <u>lih</u> siht) *v.* **-ing,-ed.**
  to draw out, provoke
      Synonyms: evoke, educe, wring, extract, tap

RESOLVE (rih <u>sahlv</u>) *v.* **-ing,-ed.** *(See page 328.)*

GRADATION (gray <u>day</u> shuhn) *n.* *(See page 374.)*

DISDAIN (dihs <u>dayn</u>) *v.* **-ing,-ed.**
  to regard with scorn and contempt
      Synonyms: despise, scout, snub, spurn

OBTUSE (uhb <u>toos</u>) *adj.*
  insensitive, stupid, dull
      Synonyms: slow, dense, blunt

CHAGRIN (shuh <u>grihn</u>) *n.*
  shame, embarrassment, humiliation
      Synonyms: mortification, discomfiture

OFFICIOUS (uh <u>fihsh</u> uhs) *adj.*
  too helpful, meddlesome
      Synonyms: eager, unwanted, intrusive

INSINUATE (ihn <u>sihn</u> yoo ayt) *v.* **-ing,-ed.**
  to suggest, say indirectly, imply
      Synonyms: hint, intimate

REPUGNANCE (rih <u>puhg</u> nehnts) *n.* *(See page 358.)*

KEEN *adj.*
  intellectually sharp, perceptive; having a sharp edge
      Synonyms: acute, quick, canny; pointed, razorlike

appropriated; in spite of his **constitutional** defect, even my voice did not escape him. My louder tones were, of course, unattempted, but then the key—it was identical; *and his singular whisper, it grew the very echo of my own.*

How greatly this most exquisite portraiture harassed me (for it could not justly be termed a **caricature**), I will not now venture to describe. I had but one **consolation**— in the fact that the imitation, apparently, was noticed by myself alone, and that I had to endure only the knowing and strangely sarcastic smiles of my namesake himself. Satisfied with having produced in my bosom the intended effect, he seemed to chuckle in secret over the sting he had inflicted and was characteristically disregardful of the public applause which the success of his witty endeavors might have so easily **elicited**. That the school, indeed, did not feel his design, perceive its accomplishment, and participate in his sneer, was, for many anxious months, a riddle I could not **resolve**. Perhaps the **gradation** of his copy rendered it not readily perceptible; or, more possibly, I owed my security to the masterly air of the copyist, who, **disdaining** the letter (which in a painting is all the **obtuse** can see), gave but the full spirit of his original for my individual contemplation and **chagrin**.

I have already more than once spoken of the disgusting air of patronage which he assumed toward me, and of his frequent **officious** interference with my will. This interference often took the ungracious character of advice; advice not openly given, but hinted or **insinuated**. I received it with a **repugnance** which gained strength as I grew in years. Yet, at this distant day, let me do him the simple justice to acknowledge that I can recall no occasion when the suggestions of my rival were on the side of those errors or follies so usual to his immature age and seeming inexperience; that his moral sense, at least, if not his general talents and worldly wisdom, was far **keener** than my own; and that I might, to-day, have been a better and thus a happier man, had I less frequently rejected the

RESTIVE (<u>reh</u> stihv) *adj.*
impatient, uneasy, restless
Synonyms: anxious, agitated, fretful

ABATE (uh <u>bayt</u>) *v.* **-ing,-ed.**
to decrease, reduce
Synonyms: dwindle, ebb, recede, flag, wane

SENTIMENT (<u>sehn</u> tuh muhnt) *n.*
an attitude, thought, or judgment prompted by
feeling, a romantic or nostalgic feeling
Synonyms: idea, emotion

ALTERCATION (<u>awl</u> tehr <u>kay</u> shuhn) *n.*
noisy dispute
Synonyms: argument, clash, fight, quarrel

DEMEANOR (dih <u>meen</u> uhr) *n.*
one's behavior or conduct
Synonyms: attitude, disposition, manner, presence

SINGULAR (<u>sihn</u> gyuh luhr) *adj.*
uncommon, peculiar
Synonyms: unusual, odd, rare, unique, individual

counsels embodied in those meaning whispers which I then but too cordially hated and too bitterly despised.

As it was I at length grew **restive** in the extreme under his supervision, and daily resented more and more openly, what I considered his intolerable arrogance. I have said that, in the first years of our connection as school-mates, my feelings in regard to him might have been easily ripened into friendship; but, in the latter months of my residence at the academy, although the intrusion of his ordinary manner had, beyond doubt, in some measure, **abated**, my **sentiments**, in nearly similar proportion, par-took very much of positive hatred. Upon one occasion he saw this, I think, and afterward avoided, or made a show of avoiding me.

It was about the same period, if I remember aright, that, in an **altercation** of violence with him, in which he was more than usually thrown off his guard, and spoke and acted with an openness of **demeanor** rather foreign to his nature, I discovered, or fancied I discovered in his accent, in his air and general appearance, a something which first startled, and then deeply interested me, by bringing to mind dim visions of my earliest infancy—wild, confused, and <u>thronging</u> memories of a time when memory herself was yet unborn. I cannot better describe the sensation which oppressed me, than by saying that I could with difficulty shake off the belief of my having been acquainted with the being who stood before me, at some <u>epoch</u> very long ago—some point of the past even infinitely remote. The delusion, however, faded rapidly as it came; and I mention it at all but to define the day of the last conversation I there held with my **singular** namesake.

The huge old house, with its countless subdivisions, had several large chambers communicating with each other, where slept the greater number of the students. There were, however (as must necessarily happen in a building so awkwardly planned), many little nooks or recesses, the odds and ends of the structure; and these the

INGENUITY (ihn jeh <u>noo</u> ih tee) *n.*
  cleverness
    Synonyms: inventiveness, imagination, creativity
ALTERCATION (awl tehr <u>kay</u> shuhn) *n.*
  noisy dispute
    Synonyms: argument, clash, fight, quarrel
UNIFORMLY (<u>yoo</u> nih fohrm lee) *adv. (See page 378.)*
RESOLVE (rih <u>sahlv</u>) *v.* -ing,-ed.
  to determine or to make a firm decision about
    Synonyms: solve, decide
MALICE (<u>maal</u> ihs) *n.*
  animosity, spite, hatred
    Synonyms: malevolence, cruelty, enmity, rancor,
    hostility
IMBUE (ihm <u>byoo</u>) *v.* -ing,-ed.
  to infuse; to dye, wet
    Synonyms: charge, freight, permeate; moisten
COUNTENANCE (<u>kown</u> tuh nuhns) *n.*
  appearance, facial expression
    Synonyms: face, features, visage
PERVADE (puhr <u>vayd</u>) *v.* -ing,-ed.
  to become diffused throughout every part of
    Synonyms: permeate, spread, fill, transfuse
TOTTER (<u>tah</u> tuhr) *v.* -ing,-ed.
  to stand with much unsteadiness
    Synonyms: wobble, sway, reel, stagger
CONFOUND (kuhn <u>fownd</u>) *v.* -ing,-ed.
  to baffle, perplex; to mistake something for another
    Synonyms: overwhelm, disconcert, entangle,
    muddle; confuse, misidentify
MULTITUDE (<u>muhl</u> tuh tood) *n.*
  a great number, the state of being many, a crowd
    Synonyms: mass, myriad, slew
INCOHERENT (ihn koh <u>hihr</u> uhnt) *adj. (See page 234.)*
VIVACITY (vih <u>vahs</u> ih tee) *n. (See page 348.)*
DOGGED (<u>daw</u> gihd) *adj.*
  stubborn or persistent
    Synonyms: tenacious, obstinate, pertinacious
GAIT (gayt) *n. (See page 380.)*

economic **ingenuity** of Dr. Bransby had also fitted up as dormitories; although, being the merest closets, they were capable of accommodating but a single individual. One of these small apartments was occupied by Wilson.

One night, about the close of my fifth year at the school and immediately after the **altercation** just mentioned, finding every one wrapped in sleep, I arose from bed and, lamp in hand, stole through a wilderness of narrow passages from my own bedroom to that of my rival. I had long been plotting one of those ill-natured pieces of practical wit at his expense in which I had hitherto been so **uniformly** unsuccessful. It was my intention, now, to put my scheme in operation and I **resolved** to make him feel the whole extent of the **malice** with which I was **imbued**. Having reached his closet, I noiselessly entered, leaving the lamp, with a shade over it, on the outside. I advanced a step and listened to the sound of his tranquil breathing. Assured of his being asleep, I returned, took the light, and with it again approached the bed. Close curtains were around it, which, in the prosecution of my plan, I slowly and quietly withdrew, when the bright rays fell vividly upon the sleeper, and my eyes at the same moment, upon his **countenance**. I looked—and a numbness, an iciness of feeling instantly **pervaded** my frame. My breast heaved, my knees **tottered**, my whole spirit became possessed with an objectless yet intolerable horror. Gasping for breath, I lowered the lamp in still nearer proximity to the face. Were these—*these* the <u>lineaments</u> of William Wilson? I saw, indeed, that they were his, but I shook as if with a fit of the <u>ague</u>, in fancying they were not. What *was* there about them to **confound** me in this manner? I gazed—while my brain reeled with a **multitude** of **incoherent** thoughts. Not thus he appeared—assuredly not *thus*—in the **vivacity** of his waking hours. The same name! The same contour of person! The same day of arrival at the academy! And then his **dogged** and meaningless imitation of my **gait**, my voice, my habits, and my

CREDULITY (kreh juh luh tee) *n.*
gullibility, willingness to trust
Synonyms: naïveté, innocence
SKEPTICISM (<u>skehp</u> tih sih zuhm) *n.*
doubt, questioning
Synonyms: disbelief, incredulity, cynicism
LEVITY (<u>leh</u> vih tee) *n.*
humor, frivolity, gaiety
Synonyms: lightness, amusement, cheer
PROFLIGACY (<u>prah</u> flih guh see) *adj.*
corruption, degeneration, immorality
Synonyms: dissolution, impurity, baseness
ELUDE (ih <u>lood</u>) *v.* **-ing,-ed.**
escape, avoid
Synonyms: evade, dodge
VIGILANCE (<u>vih</u> juh lehnts) *n.*
attention, watchfulness
Synonyms: alertness, awareness, care
DISSIPATION (dihs uh <u>pay</u> shuhn) *n.*
the pursuance of pleasure to excess; a scattering
Synonyms: self-indulgence, squandering,
consumption; dispersal, diffusion
DEBAUCHERY (dih <u>bahch</u> uh ree) *n.*
an instance of excessive eating or drinking, overindul-
gence; corruption, seduction from virtue or duty
Synonyms: intemperance; riot, debasement
PROTRACT (proh <u>traakt</u>) *v.* **-ing,-ed.**
to prolong, draw out, extend
Synonyms: lengthen, elongate, stretch

manner! Was it, in truth, within the bounds of human possibility, that *what I now saw* was the result, merely, of the habitual practice of this sarcastic imitation? Awe-stricken, and with a creeping shudder, I extinguished the lamp, passed silently from the chamber, and left, at once, the halls of that old academy, never to enter them again.

After a lapse of some months, spent at home in mere idleness, I found myself a student at Eton. The brief interval had been sufficient to enfeeble my remembrance of the events at Dr. Bransby's, or at least to effect a material change in the nature of the feelings with which I remembered them. The truth—the tragedy—of the drama was no more. I could now find room to doubt the evidence of my senses; and seldom called up the subject at all but with wonder at the extent of human credulity, and a smile at the vivid force of the imagination which I hereditarily possessed. Neither was this species of skepticism likely to be diminished by the character of the life I led at Eton. The vortex of thoughtless folly into which I there so immediately and so recklessly plunged, washed away all but the froth of my past hours, ingulfed at once every solid or serious impression, and left to memory only the veriest levities of a former existence.

I do not wish, however, to trace the course of my miserable profligacy here—a profligacy which set at defiance the laws, while it eluded the vigilance of the institution. Three years of folly, passed without profit, had but given the rooted habits of vice, and added, in a somewhat unusual degree, to my bodily stature, when, after a week of soulless dissipation, I invited a small party of the most dissolute students to a secret carousal in my chambers. We met at a late hour of the night; for our debaucheries were to be faithfully protracted until morning. The wine flowed freely, and there were not wanting other and perhaps more dangerous seductions; so that the gray dawn had already faintly appeared in the east while our delirious extravagance was at its height. Madly flushed with

PROFANITY (proh <u>faan</u> ih tee) *n.*
   impurity, religious contradiction, sacrilege; foul language
      Synonyms: vulgarity, blasphemy; swearing

NOVEL (<u>nah</u> vuhl) *adj.*
   new, original
      Synonyms: fresh, newfangled, innovative, unusual, different
PETULANT (<u>peh</u> chuh luhnt) *adj.*
   rude, peevish
      Synonyms: irritable, querulous, testy, fretful
SOBER (<u>soh</u> buhr) *adj.*
   not intoxicated; self-controlled; serious
      Synonyms: dry, not drunk; subdued, sedate; grave
TREMULOUS (<u>treh</u> myoo luhs) *adj.*
   trembling, quivering; fearful, timid
      Synonyms: shaking, palsied; timorous, anxious
UNQUALIFIED (uhn <u>kwah</u> luh fied) *adj.*
   absolute and unconditional
      Synonyms: outright, clear, total, unfaltering
SOLEMN (<u>sah</u> luhm) *adj.*
   quiet, deeply serious; somberly impressive
      Synonyms: earnest, brooding; dignified, ceremonial
ADMONITION (aad muh <u>nih</u> shuhn) *n.*
   cautionary advice, an earnest warning
      Synonyms: reprimand, rebuke, counsel

EVANESCENT (eh vuh <u>nehs</u> uhnt) *adj.*
   momentary, tendency toward vanishing
      Synonyms: transient, ephemeral, fleeting, fugitive

cards and intoxication, I was in the act of insisting upon a toast of more than wonted **profanity**, when my attention was suddenly diverted by the violent, although partial, unclosing of the door of the apartment, and by the eager voice of a servant from without. He said that some person, apparently in great haste, demanded to speak with me in the hall.

Wildly excited with wine, the unexpected interruption rather delighted than surprised me. I staggered forward at once, and a few steps brought me to the vestibule of the building. In this low and small room there hung no lamp; and now no light at all was admitted, save that of the exceedingly feeble dawn which made its way through the semi-circular window. As I put my foot over the threshold, I became aware of the figure of a youth about my own height, and habited in a white kerseymere morning frock, cut in the **novel** fashion of the one I myself wore at the moment. This the faint light enabled me to perceive; but the features of his face I could not distinguish. Upon my entering, he strode hurriedly up to me, and, seizing me by the arm with a gesture of **petulant** impatience, whispered the words "William Wilson" in my ear.

I grew perfectly **sober** in an instant.

There was that in the manner of the stranger, and in the **tremulous** shake of his uplifted finger, as he held it between my eyes and the light, which filled me with **unqualified** amazement; but it was not this which had so violently moved me. It was the pregnancy of **solemn admonition** in the singular, low, hissing utterance; and, above all, it was the character, the tone, the *key*, of those few, simple, and familiar, yet whispered syllables, which came with a thousand <u>thronging</u> memories of by-gone days, and struck upon my soul with the shock of a <u>galvanic</u> battery. Ere I could recover the use of my senses he was gone.

Although this event failed not of a vivid effect upon my disordered imagination, yet was it **evanescent** as vivid.

MORBID (<u>mohr</u> bihd) *adj.*
    abnormally gloomy; relating to disease; gruesome
        Synonyms: dismal; pathological, unhealthy; grisly,
        macabre, unwholesome

SINGULAR (<u>sihn</u> gyuh luhr) *adj.* *(See page 384.)*

PERSEVERINGLY (pehr suh <u>veer</u> ihng lee) *adv.*
    with unwavering determination
        Synonyms: persistently, enduringly, ploddingly

INSINUATE (ihn <u>sihn</u> yoo ayt) *v.* **-ing,-ed.** *(See page 382.)*

ASCERTAIN (aa suhr <u>tayn</u>) *v.* **-ing,-ed.** *(See page 330.)*

INDULGE (ihn <u>duhlj</u>) *v.* **-ing,-ed.** *(See page 252.)*

LUXURY (<u>luhg</u> zhoor ee) *n.* *(See page 372.)*

VIE *v.* **vying,vied.**
    to compete, contend
        Synonyms: strive, rival, vie, emulate

PROFUSENESS (pruh <u>fyoos</u> nehs) *n.*
    plenty, abundance; lavish extravagance, richness
        Synonyms: prosperity; exuberance, profusion

HAUGHTY (<u>haw</u> tee) (<u>hah</u> tee) *adj.* *(See page 76.)*

CONSTITUTIONAL (kahn stih <u>too</u> shuh nuhl) *adj.*
(See page 366.)

TEMPERAMENT (<u>tehm</u> puhr uh mehnt) *n.* *(See page 366.)*

ARDOR (<u>ahr</u> duhr) *n.* *(See page 128.)*

SPURN (spuhrn) *v.* **-ing,-ed.**
    to reject or refuse contemptuously; to scorn
        Synonyms: ignore, cut, snub; disdain, ostracize

RESTRAINT (rih <u>straynt</u>) *n.*
    a rule or limitation; control, repression, restriction
        Synonyms: barrier, order, rein; confinement

REVEL (<u>reh</u> vuhl) *n.*
    boisterous festivity, joyful behavior
        Synonyms: merrymaking, cavorting, gaiety, jollity

MULTITUDE (<u>muhl</u> tuh tood) *n.* *(See page 386.)*

NOVEL (<u>nah</u> vuhl) *adj.* *(See page 390.)*

ADEPT (uh <u>dehpt</u>) *n.*
    an expert
        Synonyms: ace, superstar, whiz, genius

ENORMITY (ih <u>nohr</u> muh tee) *n.*
    state of being gigantic or terrible
        Synonyms: outrageousness, atrociousness

For some weeks, indeed, I busied myself in earnest enquiry, or was wrapped in a cloud of **morbid** speculation. I did not pretend to disguise from my perception the identity of the **singular** individual who thus **perseveringly** interfered with my affairs, and harassed me with his **insinuated** counsel. But who and what was this Wilson— and whence came he—and what were his purposes? Upon neither of these points could I be satisfied—merely **ascertaining**, in regard to him, that a sudden accident in his family had caused his removal from Dr. Bransby's academy on the afternoon of the day in which I myself had eloped. But in a brief period I ceased to think upon the subject, my attention being all absorbed in a contemplated departure for Oxford. Thither I soon went, the uncalculating vanity of my parents furnishing me with an outfit and annual establishment, which would enable me to **indulge** at will in the **luxury** already so dear to my heart—to **vie** in **profuseness** of expenditure with the **haughtiest** heirs of the wealthiest earldoms in Great Britain.

Excited by such appliances to vice, my **constitutional temperament** broke forth with redoubled **ardor**, and I **spurned** even the common **restraints** of decency in the mad infatuation of my **revels**. But it were absurd to pause in the detail of my extravagance. Let it suffice, that among spendthrifts I out-Heroded Herod,[77] and that, giving name to a **multitude** of **novel** follies, I added no brief appendix to the long catalogue of vices then usual in the most <u>dissolute</u> university of Europe.

It could hardly be credited, however, that I had, even here, so utterly fallen from the gentlemanly estate as to seek acquaintance with the vilest arts of the gambler by profession and, having become an **adept** in his despicable science, to practice it habitually as a means of increasing my already enormous income at the expense of the weak-minded among my fellow-collegians. Such, nevertheless, was the fact. And the very **enormity** of this offence

SENTIMENT (<u>sehn</u> tuh muhnt) *n.*
  an attitude, thought, or judgment prompted by
  feeling, a romantic or nostalgic feeling
    Synonyms: idea, emotion

LIBERAL (<u>lihb</u> uh ruhl) (<u>lihb</u> ruhl) *adj.*
  generous, lavish; tolerant, broad-minded
    Synonyms: bounteous, munificent; progressive,
    permissive

PARASITE (<u>paar</u> uh siet) *n.*
  person or animal that lives at another's expense
    Synonyms: leech, sycophant

INIMITABLE (ih <u>nihm</u> it uh buhl) *adj.*
  unable to be copied or imitated
    Synonyms: matchless, exceptional, unrivaled

WHIM (wihm) *n.*
  a playful or fanciful idea
    Synonyms: caprice, impulse, dream, vision, fantasy

CONTRIVE (kuhn <u>triev</u>) *v.* **-ing,-ed.**
  to devise, plan, or manage; to form in an artistic manner
    Synonyms: concoct, scheme; create, design

SOLICITOUSLY (suh <u>lih</u> sih tuhs lee) *adv.*
  in a concerned manner, with eager attentiveness
    Synonyms: thoughtfully, considerately, anxiously,
    meticulously

DUPE (doop) *n.*
  fool, pawn
    Synonyms: chump, sucker, victim

PROTRACT (proh <u>traakt</u>) *v.* **-ing,-ed.**
  to prolong, draw out, extend
    Synonyms: lengthen, elongate, stretch

ANTAGONIST (aan <u>taag</u> uh nihst) *n.*
  foe, opponent, adversary
    Synonyms: enemy, rival

against all manly and honorable sentiment proved, beyond doubt, the main if not the sole reason of the impunity with which it was committed. Who, indeed, among my most abandoned associates, would not rather have disputed the clearest evidence of his senses, than have suspected of such courses, the gay, the frank, the generous William Wilson—the noblest and most liberal commoner at Oxford—him whose follies (said his parasites) were but the follies of youth and unbridled fancy—whose errors but inimitable whim—whose darkest vice but a careless and dashing extravagance?

I had been now two years successfully busied in this way, when there came to the university a young *parvenu*[78] nobleman, Glendinning—rich said report, as Herodes Atticus—his riches, too, as easily acquired. I soon found him of weak intellect, and, of course, marked him as a fitting subject for my skill. I frequently engaged him in play, and contrived, with the gambler's usual art, to let him win considerable sums, the more effectually to entangle him in my snares. At length, my schemes being ripe, I met him (with the full intention that this meeting should be final and decisive) at the chambers of a fellow-commoner (Mr. Preston), equally intimate with both, but who, to do him justice, entertained not even a remote suspicion of my design. To give to this a better coloring, I had contrived to have assembled a party of some eight or ten, and was solicitously careful that the introduction of cards should appear accidental, and originate in the proposal of my contemplated dupe himself. To be brief upon a vile topic, none of the low finesse was omitted, so customary upon similar occasions, that it is a just matter for wonder how any are still found so besotted as to fall its victim.

We had protracted our sitting far into the night, and I had at length effected the maneuver of getting Glendinning as my sole antagonist. The game, too, was my favorite *écarté*. The rest of the company, interested in the extent of our play, had abandoned their own cards,

INDUCE (ih <u>doos</u>) (ihn <u>dyoos</u>) *v.* **-ing,-ed.**
  to persuade, to bring about
    Synonyms: prevail, convince, lead, effect, occasion
FEIGN (fayn) *v.* **-ing,-ed.**
  to pretend or give a false impression, to invent falsely
    Synonyms: assume, affect, simulate, fake
PIQUE (peek) *n.*
  a fleeting feeling of hurt pride
    Synonyms: vexation, resentment, indignation,
    dudgeon, umbrage
COMPLIANCE (kuhm <u>plie</u> uhnts) *n.*
  submission, yielding
    Synonyms: malleability, complacency, acquiescence
COMPLY (kuhm <u>plie</u>) *v.* **-ing,-ied.**
  to yield or agree, to go along with
    Synonyms: accord, submit, acquiesce, obey, respect
COUNTENANCE (<u>kown</u> tuh nuhns) *n.*
  appearance, facial expression
    Synonyms: face, features, visage
FLORID (<u>flohr</u> ihd) (<u>flahr</u> ihd) *adj.*
  ruddy, flushed; gaudy, extremely ornate
    Synonyms: reddish; flamboyant, ostentatious
TINGE (tihnj) *n.*
  a slight shade of color, stain, odor, or taste
    Synonyms: hint, hue, tincture, tone, wash
PEREMPTORILY (puhr <u>ehm</u> tohr uh lee) *adv.*
  absolutely, in a commanding manner; immediately
  putting an end to
    Synonyms: urgently, imperatively; decisively, finally
EJACULATION (ih <u>jaak</u> yuh lay shuhn) *n.*
  a sudden exclamation
    Synonyms: chatter, vociferation, expletive
EVINCE (ih <u>vihns</u>) *v.* **-ing,-ed.**
  to show clearly or display
    Synonyms: express, exhibit, demonstrate, manifest
DUPE (doop) *n.*
  fool, pawn
    Synonyms: chump, sucker, victim
PROFOUND (pruh <u>fownd</u>) *adj. (See page 320.)*

and were standing around us as spectators. The *parvenu*, [78] who had been **induced** by my artifices in the early part of the evening to drink deeply, now shuffled, dealt, or played with a wild nervousness of manner for which his intoxication, I thought, might partially but could not altogether account. In a very short period he had become my debtor to a large amount, when, having taken a long <u>draught</u> of port, he did precisely what I had been coolly anticipating—he proposed to double our already extravagant stakes. With a *well*-**feigned** show of reluctance, and not until after my repeated refusal had seduced him into some angry words which gave a color of **pique** to my **compliance**, did I finally **comply**. The result of course, did, but prove how entirely the prey was in my toils: in less than an hour he had quadrupled his debt. For some time his **countenance** had been losing the **florid tinge** lent it by the wine; but now, to my astonishment, I perceived that it had grown to a <u>pallor</u> truly fearful. Glendinning had been represented to my eager inquiries as immeasurably wealthy; and the sums which he had as yet lost, although in themselves vast, could not, I supposed, very seriously annoy much less so violently affect him. That he was overcome by the wine just swallowed was the idea which most readily presented itself; and, rather with a view to the preservation of my own character in the eyes of my associates than from any less interested motive, I was about to insist, **peremptorily**, upon a discontinuance of the play, when some expressions at my elbow from among the company and an **ejaculation evincing** utter despair on the part of Glendinning, gave me to understand that I had effected his total ruin under circumstances which, rendering him an object for the pity of all, should have protected him from the ill offices even of a fiend.

What now might have been my conduct it is difficult to say. The pitiable condition of my **dupe** had thrown an air of embarrassed gloom over all; and, for some moments, a **profound** silence was maintained, during which I could

REPROACH (rih <u>prohch</u>) *n.*
  expressed disappointment or displeasure; discredit
    Synonyms: rebuke, blame; disgrace

IMPETUOSITY (ihm peh choo <u>ah</u> sih tee) *n.*
  rapid force, violence; quickness to act without thinking
    Synonyms: ferocity, rage; impulsiveness, passion

EXPEDITIOUS (ehk spih <u>dihsh</u> uhs) *adj.*
  fast and efficient
    Synonyms: speedy, rapid, prompt

CAPACIOUS (kuh <u>pay</u> shuhs) *adj.*
  large, roomy, extensive
    Synonyms: ample, commodious

PROFOUND (pruh <u>fownd</u>) (proh <u>fownd</u>) *adj.*
  deep, infinite; intelligent; difficult to understand
    Synonyms: bottomless, unending; smart; thorough,
    weighty

REPROCURE (ree proh <u>kyoor</u>) *v.* **-ing,-ed.**
  to obtain again
    Synonyms: acquire, secure, get, gain

not help feeling my cheeks tingle with the many burning glances of scorn or **reproach** cast upon me by the less abandoned of the party. I will even own that an intolerable weight of anxiety was for a brief instant lifted from my bosom by the sudden and extraordinary interruption which ensued. The wide, heavy folding doors of the apartment were all at once thrown open, to their full extent, with a vigorous and rushing **impetuosity** that extinguished, as if by magic, every candle in the room. Their light, in dying, enabled us just to perceive that a stranger had entered, about my own height, and closely muffled in a cloak. The darkness, however, was not total; and we could only feel that he was standing in our midst. Before any one of us could recover from the extreme astonishment into which this rudeness had thrown all, we heard the voice of the intruder.

"Gentlemen," he said, in a low, distinct, and never to-be-forgotten *whisper* which thrilled to the very marrow of my bones, "gentlemen, I make an apology for this behavior, because in thus behaving, I am fulfilling a duty. You are, beyond doubt, uninformed of the true character of the person who has to-night won at *écarté* a large sum of money from Lord Glendinning. I will therefore put you upon an **expeditious** and decisive plan of obtaining this very necessary information. Please to examine, at your leisure, the inner linings of the cuff of his left sleeve, and the several little packages which may be found in the somewhat **capacious** pockets of his embroidered morning wrapper."

While he spoke, so **profound** was the stillness that one might have heard a pin drop upon the floor. In ceasing, he departed at once, and as abruptly as he had entered. Can I—shall I describe my sensations? Must I say that I felt all the horrors of the damned? Most assuredly I had little time for reflection. Many hands roughly seized me upon the spot, and lights were immediately **reprocured**. A search ensued. In the lining of my sleeve were found all

DISPOSITION (dihs puh <u>zih</u> shuhn) *n.*
  mood or temperament
    Synonyms: behavior, tendency, inclination, nature
DUPE (doop) *n.*
  fool, pawn
    Synonyms: chump, sucker, victim
ANTAGONIST (aan <u>taag</u> uh nihst) *n.*
  foe, opponent, adversary
    Synonyms: enemy, rival
INDIGNATION (ihn dihg <u>nay</u> shun) *n.*
  anger caused by something mean or unjust
    Synonyms: fury, ire, wrath
CONTEMPT (kuhn <u>tehmpt</u>) *n.*
  disrespect, scorn
    Synonyms: derision, disdain
LUXURIOUS (luhg <u>zhoor</u> ee uhs) *adj.*
  sensual, pleasurably indulgent
    Synonyms: elaborate, fancy, impressive, posh
PRESUME (prih <u>zoom</u>) *v.* **-ing,-ed.**
  to assume or believe something without proof; to dare
    Synonyms: take for granted; venture
ABASED (uh <u>bays</u>d) *adj.*
  shamed, disgraced
    Synonyms: humbled, humiliated, demeaned
GALLING (<u>gahl</u> ihng) *adj.*
  exasperating and irritating
    Synonyms: vexing, fretful, irksome
FASTIDIOUS (faa <u>stihd</u> ee uhs) (fuh <u>stihd</u> ee uhs) *adj.*
  careful with details
    Synonyms: meticulous, painstaking, scrupulous,
    punctilious, precise
FRIVOLOUS (<u>frihv</u> uh luhs) *adj.*
  petty, trivial, flippant, silly
    Synonyms: frothy, light, vapid
UNWITTINGLY (uhn <u>wih</u> ting lee) *adv.*
  unconsciously, unintentionally
    Synonyms: obliviously, inadvertently

the court cards essential in *écarté* and, in the pockets of my wrapper, a number of packs, <u>facsimiles</u> of those used at our sittings, with the single exception that mine were of the species called, technically, *arrondis*; the honors being slightly convex at the ends, the lower cards slightly convex at the sides. In this **disposition**, the **dupe** who cuts, as customary, at the length of the pack, will invariably find that he cuts his **antagonist** an honor; while the gambler, cutting at the breadth, will, as certainly, cut nothing for his victim which may count in the records of the game.

Any burst of **indignation** upon this discovery would have affected me less than the silent **contempt**, or the sarcastic composure with which it was received.

"Mr. Wilson," said our host, stooping to remove from beneath his feet an exceedingly **luxurious** cloak of rare furs, "Mr. Wilson, this is your property." (The weather was cold; and, upon quitting my own room, I had thrown a cloak over my dressing wrapper, putting it off upon reaching the scene of play.) "**I presume** it is <u>supererogatory</u> to seek here (eyeing the folds of the garment with a bitter smile) for any farther evidence of your skill. Indeed, we have had enough. You will see the necessity, I hope, of quitting Oxford—at all events, of quitting instantly my chambers."

Abased, humbled to the dust as I then was, it is probable that I should have resented this **galling** language by immediate personal violence, had not my whole attention been at the moment arrested by a fact of the most startling character. The cloak which I had worn was of a rare description of fur; how rare, how extravagantly costly, I shall not venture to say. Its fashion, too, was of my own fantastic invention; for I was **fastidious** to an absurd degree of <u>coxcombry</u>, in matters of this **frivolous** nature. When, therefore, Mr. Preston handed me that which he had picked up upon the floor, and near the folding-doors of the apartment, it was with an astonishment nearly bordering upon terror, that I perceived my own already hanging on my arm (where I had no doubt **unwittingly**

MINUTE (mie <u>noot</u>) (mih <u>noot</u>) *adj.* *(See page 328.)*
SINGULAR (<u>sihn</u> gyuh luhr) *adj.*
   uncommon, peculiar
     Synonyms: unusual, odd, rare, unique, individual
RETAIN (rih <u>tayn</u>) *v.* **-ing,-ed.** *(See page 360.)*
RESOLUTE (reh suh <u>loot</u>) *adj.*
   determined; with a clear purpose
     Synonyms: firm, unwavering; intent, resolved
EXALTATION (ihg zahl <u>tay</u> shuhn) *n.*
   an intense sense of power or exhilaration; praise
     Synonyms: joy, ecstasy, rapture; reverence, worship
DETESTABLE (dee <u>tehst</u> uh buhl) *adj.*
   deserving of intense and violent hated
     Synonyms: disgusting, despicable, loathsome
OFFICIOUSNESS (uh <u>fihsh</u> uhs nehs) *n.*
   intrusiveness, unwanted help or advice
     Synonyms: eagerness, curiosity, nosiness, prying
INSCRUTABLE (ihn <u>skroo</u> tuh buhl) *adj.*
   impossible to understand fully
     Synonyms: mysterious, impenetrable, cryptic, enigmatic
PESTILENCE (<u>peh</u> stihl ehnts) *n.*
   epidemic, plague, illness
     Synonyms: contagion, scourge, sickness, disease
SCRUTINIZE (<u>skroot</u> niez) *v.* **-ing,-ed.** *(See page 270.)*
SCRUTINY (<u>skroot</u> nee) *n.*
   careful observation
     Synonyms: examination, study, surveillance
IMPERTINENT (ihm <u>puhr</u> tuh nuhnt) *adj.*
   rude, audacious; improper
     Synonyms: forward, bold; impolite, discourteous
CONJECTURE (kuhn <u>jehk</u> shuhr) *n.*
   speculation, prediction
     Synonyms: postulation, hypothesis, supposition, guess
IMPERIOUSLY (ihm <u>pihr</u> ee uhs lee) *adv.*
   in a majestic or domineering manner; urgently
     Synonyms: arrogantly, overbearingly; imperatively

placed it), and that the one presented to me was but its exact counterpart in every, in even the **minutest** possible particular. The **singular** being who had so disastrously exposed me, had been muffled, I remembered, in a cloak; and none had been worn at all by any of the members of our party, with the exception of myself. **Retaining** some presence of mind, I took the one offered to me by Preston; placed it, unnoticed, over my own; left the apartment with a **resolute** scowl of defiance; and, next morning ere dawn of day, commenced a hurried journey from Oxford to the continent, in a perfect agony of horror and of shame.

I fled in vain. My evil destiny pursued me as if in **exaltation**, and proved, indeed, that the exercise of its mysterious dominion had as yet only begun. Scarcely had I set foot in Paris, ere I had fresh evidence of the **detestable** interest taken by this Wilson in my concerns. Years flew, while I experienced no relief. Villian! At Rome, with how untimely, yet with how spectral an **officiousness**, stepped he in between me and my ambition! At Vienna, too—at Berlin—and at Moscow! Where, in truth, had I not bitter cause to curse him within my heart? From his **inscrutable** tyranny did I at length flee, panic-stricken, as from a **pestilence**; and to the very ends of the earth *I fled in vain.*

And again, and again, in secret communion with my own spirit would I demand the questions "Who is he? Whence came he and what are his objects?" But no answer was there found. And now I **scrutinized**, with a **minute scrutiny**, the forms, and the methods, and the leading traits of his **impertinent** supervision. But even here there was very little upon which to base a **conjecture**. It was noticeable indeed that, in no one of the multiplied instances in which he had of late crossed my path, had he so crossed it except to frustrate those schemes or to disturb those actions, which, if fully carried out, might have resulted in bitter mischief. Poor justification this, in truth, for an authority so **imperiously** assumed! Poor indemnity

PERTINACIOUSLY (puhr tihn <u>ay</u> shuhs lee) *adv.*
  stubbornly, persistently
     Synonyms: obstinately, tenaciously, steadily, doggedly
SCRUPULOUSLY (<u>skroop</u> yuh luhs lee) *adv. (See page 380.)*
DEXTERITY (dehk <u>stayr</u> ih tee) *n.*
  physical or mental skill, ability
     Synonyms: aptitude, adroitness, proficiency
WHIM (wihm) *n. (See page 394.)*
CONTRIVE (kuhn <u>triev</u>) *v.* **-ing,-ed.** *(See page 394.)*
EXECUTION (ehk sih <u>kyoo</u> shuhn) *n. (See page 344.)*
AFFECTATION (aaf ehk <u>tay</u> shun) *n.*
  fakeness, phoniness, artificiality, false display
     Synonyms: insincerity, pose, pretension
ADMONISHER (aad <u>mahn</u> ihsh uhr) *n.*
  one who cautions or reprimands
     Synonyms: reprover, chider, rebuker
THWART (thwahrt) *v.* **-ing,-ed.**
   to block or prevent from happening; to frustrate
     Synonyms: oppose, defeat, foil, balk; hinder, baffle
AVARICE (<u>aa</u> vuhr ihs) *n.*
  greed
     Synonyms: cupidity, rapacity
ARCH *adj.*
  having the highest rank, most important;
  mischievous, roguish
     Synonyms: chief, top; impish, saucy, ironic
IMPERIOUS (ihm <u>pihr</u> ee uhs) *adj.*
  arrogantly self-assured, domineering, overbearing
     Synonyms: authoritarian, despotic
SENTIMENT (<u>sehn</u> tuh muhnt) *n. (See page 394.)*
IMPLICIT (ihm <u>plih</u> siht) *adj. (See page 374.)*
ARBITRARY (<u>ahr</u> bih trayr ee) *adj.*
  depending solely on individual will; inconsistent
     Synonyms: discretional; whimsical, impulsive
INDUCE (ih <u>doos</u>) (ihn <u>dyoos</u>) *v.* **-ing,-ed.** *(See page 396.)*
DIMINUTION (dih mih <u>noo</u> shuhn) *n.*
  the act of lessening or shrinking, reduction
     Synonyms: shortening, decrease

for natural rights of self-agency so **pertinaciously**, so insultingly denied!

I had also been forced to notice that my tormentor, for a very long period of time (while **scrupulously** and with miraculous **dexterity** maintaining his **whim** of an identity of apparel with myself) had so **contrived** it, in the **execution** of his varied interference with my will, that I saw not, at any moment, the features of his face. Be Wilson what he might, *this*, at least, was but the veriest of **affectation**, or of folly. Could he, for an instant, have supposed that, in my **admonisher** at Eton—in the destroyer of my honor at Oxford—in him who **thwarted** my ambition at Rome, my revenge at Paris, my passionate love at Naples, or what he falsely termed my **avarice** in Egypt— that in this, my **arch**-enemy and evil genius, I could fail to recognize the William Wilson of my school-boy days— the namesake, the companion, the rival—the hated and dreaded rival at Dr. Bransby's? Impossible! But let me hasten to the last eventful scene of the drama.

Thus far I had <u>succumbed</u> <u>supinely</u> to this **imperious** domination. The **sentiment** of deep awe with which I habitually regarded the elevated character, the majestic wisdom, the apparent omnipresence and <u>omnipotence</u> of Wilson, added to a feeling of even terror, with which certain other traits in his nature and assumptions inspired me, had operated, hitherto, to impress me with an idea of my own utter weakness and helplessness, and to suggest an **implicit**, although bitterly reluctant submission to his **arbitrary** will. But, of late days, I had given myself up entirely to wine; and its maddening influence upon my hereditary temper rendered me more and more impatient of control. I began to murmur—to hesitate—to resist. And was it only fancy which **induced** me to believe that, with the increase of my own firmness, that of my tormentor underwent a proportional **diminution**? Be this as it may, I now began to feel the inspiration of a burning hope, and at length nurtured in my

RESOLUTION (reh suh <u>loo</u> shuhn) *n.*
  a firm decision
    Synonyms: determination, will, explanation
MASQUERADE (maas kuh <u>rayd</u>) *n.*
  a costume ball; disguise, action that conceals the truth
    Synonyms: carnival, party; charade, façade
INDULGE (ihn <u>duhlj</u>) *v.* **-ing,-ed.**
  to give in, as to a craving or desire; to spoil
    Synonyms: humor, gratify, allow; pamper
DOTING (<u>doht</u> ihng) *adj.*
  lavishing attention, loving to excess
    Synonyms: adoring, cherishing, tendering
UNSCRUPULOUS (uhn <u>skroop</u> yuh luhs) *adj.*
  immoral, dishonest; hasty and imprecise
    Synonyms: unrestrained, deceitful; unconscientious

WRATH (raath) *n.*
  anger, rage
    Synonyms: fury, ire, resentment, indignation

SUSTAIN (suh <u>stayn</u>) *v.* **-ing,-ed.**
  to support, uphold; endure, undergo
    Synonyms: maintain, withstand, prop; confirm,
    encourage

DRAW *v.* **-ing, drew, drawn**
  to pull or pull out (in this instance, he is "drawing" a
  sword), drag; to lead, to bring about on purpose; to
  attract or be attracted to
    Synonyms: haul, tow, yank; provoke, elicit; lure, entice

secret thoughts a stern and desperate **resolution** that I would submit no longer to be enslaved.

It was at Rome, during the Carnival of 18—, that I attended a **masquerade** in the palazzo of the Neapolitan Duke Di Broglio. I had **indulged** more freely than usual in the excesses of the wine-table; and now the suffocating atmosphere of the crowded rooms irritated me beyond endurance. The difficulty, too, of forcing my way through the mazes of the company contributed not a little to the ruffling of my temper; for I was anxiously seeking (let me not say with what unworthy motive) the young, the gay, the beautiful wife of the aged and **doting** Di Broglio. With a too **unscrupulous** confidence she had previously communicated to me the secret of the costume in which she would be habited, and now, having caught a glimpse of her person, I was hurrying to make my way into her presence. At this moment I felt a light hand placed upon my shoulder, and that ever-remembered, low, damnable *whisper* within my ear.

In an absolute frenzy of **wrath**, I turned at once upon him who had thus interrupted me, and seized him violently by the collar. He was attired, as I had expected, in a costume altogether similar to my own; wearing a Spanish cloak of blue velvet, begirt about the waist with a crimson belt **sustaining** a rapier. A mask of black silk entirely covered his face.

"Scoundrel!" I said, in a voice husky with rage, while every syllable I uttered seemed as new fuel to my fury. "Scoundrel! Impostor! Accursed villain! You shall not— you *shall not* dog me unto death! Follow me, or I will stab you where you stand!" And I broke my way from the ballroom into a small antechamber adjoining, dragging him unresistingly with me as I went.

Upon entering, I thrust him furiously from me. He staggered against the wall, while I closed the door with an oath, and commanded him to **draw**. He hesitated but for an instant; then, with a slight sigh, **drew** in silence, and put himself upon his defence.

MULTITUDE (<u>muhl</u> tuh tood) *n.*
a great number, the state of being many, a crowd
Synonyms: mass, myriad, slew

ANTAGONIST (aan <u>taag</u> uh nihst) *n.*
foe, opponent, adversary
Synonyms: enemy, rival

AVERT (uh <u>vuhrt</u>) *v.* **-ing,-ed.**
to turn away; avoid
Synonyms: deflect, parry; deter, forestall, preclude

TOTTERING (<u>tah</u> tuhr ihng) *adj.*
barely standing
Synonyms: unsteady, wobbly, swaying, reeling,
staggering

GAIT (gayt) *n.*
the way one moves on foot, a manner of walking
Synonyms: tread, walk, march, pace

SINGULAR (<u>sihn</u> gyuh luhr) *adj.*
uncommon, peculiar
Synonyms: unusual, odd, rare, unique, individual

The contest was brief indeed. I was frantic with every species of wild excitement, and felt within my single arm the energy and power of a **multitude**. In a few seconds I forced him by sheer strength against the wainscotting, and thus, getting him at mercy, plunged my sword, with brute ferocity, repeatedly through and through his bosom.

At that instant some person tried the latch of the door. I hastened to prevent an intrusion, and then immediately returned to my dying **antagonist**. But what human language can adequately portray *that* astonishment, *that* horror which possessed me at the spectacle then presented to view? The brief moment in which I **averted** my eyes had been sufficient to produce, apparently, a material change in the arrangements at the upper or farther end of the room. A large mirror—so at first it seemed to me in my confusion—now stood where none had been perceptible before; and as I stepped up to it in extremity of terror, mine own image, but with features all pale and dabbled in blood, advanced to meet me with a feeble and **tottering gait**.

Thus it appeared, I say, but was not. It was my **antagonist**—it was Wilson, who then stood before me in the agonies of his <u>dissolution</u>. His mask and cloak lay, where he had thrown them, upon the floor. Not a thread in all his raiment—not a line in all the marked and **singular** <u>lineaments</u> of his face which was not, even in the most absolute identity, *mine own!*

It was Wilson; but he spoke no longer in a whisper, and I could have fancied that I myself was speaking while he said:

"You have conquered, and I yield. Yet henceforward art thou also dead—dead to the World, to Heaven, and to Hope! In me didst thou exist—and, in my death, see by this image, which is thine own, how utterly thou hast murdered thyself."

ENDNOTES

1. *rara avis in terris*: "a rare bird upon the earth"

2. In this instance, *baroques* means "a deceptive sentence." However, *baroque* usually refers to an elaborate type of European art or music from the 17th and 18th centuries.

3. *Bas-relief* is a type of sculpture in which the subject matter protrudes slightly from the background creating a somewhat three-dimensional effect.

4. *Ashtophet* is the Egyptian goddess of fertility.

5. *Hyacinthine* refers to one's hair curling like the petals of the hyacinth flower.

6. In alchemy, the precursor to modern chemistry, *Saturnus* was the name for lead.

7. *Azrael* is the angel of death.

8. *Druidical* pertains to the Druids, a group of ancient British priests who were believed by some to be sorcerers.

9. *Saracenic* describes a type of Arabic architecture used in mosques and temples in which arches and domes are part of the design.

10. *Elysium* is a place of total happiness, a paradise. According to Greek mythology, this is where happy souls go after death.

11. *Palladian*: Andrea Palladio (1518-1580) was an Italian architect with a classicist style.

12. In botany, the genus *Acanthus* contains a group of prickly herbs and shrubs. Pliny was a Roman scholar whom Poe believed to have once described an acanthus plant as having "soft and almost liquid" characteristics. According to recent historians, Poe was mistaken.

13. *bienséance*: appropriateness

14. *bedizen*: to adorn tastelessly

15. Giovanni Cimabue (1240-1302) was an influential Florentine painter. He is sometimes referred to as the father of modern European painting because he broke away from the ancient Byzantine style.

16. "The best artist has no concept which the marble itself does not contain."

17. A *bugbear* is an obsolete term for something imaginary that causes needless fright, such as a goblin or bogeyman.

18. *Moresque* is a type of ornate and detailed decoration in which a symmetrical pattern radiates out from a focal point, much like a flower and its petals.

19. "His heart is a pendant lute which resounds the moment touched." Pierre-Jean de Béranger was a well-known poet of the early 1800's.

20. John Henry Fuseli (1741-1825) was a famous Swiss-English painter of fantasies.

21. The Greek word *Porphyro* means *purple*, a color traditionally recognized in the Victorian era as a color reserved for royalty. *Porphyrogene* suggests a royal issue.

22. *Alarum* is the Old English word for *alarm*.

23. *Rue* is the French word for *road*.

24. In Greek mythology, the Syrens (or Sirens) were a group of island nymphs who used their beautiful singing voices to lure mariners to destruction on their island.

25. Achilles was a mythical Greek hero of Homer's *Iliad*. His mother, Thetis, did not want him to be sent to war. With the permission of the king of the island of Scyros, she hid Achilles among the maidens of the king's court. Achilles is also known for the one weak and vulnerable part of his body, his heel.

26. *Théâtre des Variétés* (The Variety Theater) was a place where comedy performances were staged.

27. *Crébillon's Tragedy* was a play about Xerxes, a powerful Persian king who was defeated by the Greeks.

28. *Pasquinaded*: ridiculed

29. *et id genus omne*: "and all of that sort"

30. *charlatânerie*: fraud or quackery

31. Epicurus was a Greek philosopher who studied atomism, the theory that everything in the universe is comprised of tiny indestructable particles.

32. Actors in tragedies often wore a type of boot called a *buskin*.

33. "The first letter has lost its ancient sound."

34. *gendarmes*: French policemen

35. *sacré* and *diable*: "holy" and "devil"

36. *mon Dieu*: "my God"

37. A *robe-de-chambre* is a dressing robe. "*Pour mieux entendre la musique*" means *in order to hear the music better*. Jean Baptiste Poquelin Moliere, an author, wrote about a character, M. Jourdain, who once asked for his chamber robe so that he could better hear the chamber music.

38. Francois Eugene Vidocq (1775-1857) was the French Minister of Police.

39. *loge de concierge*: "a doorkeeper's apartment"

40. *Je les ménageais*: "I handled them tactfully."

41. *a posteriori*: "after the fact"

42. *grotesquerie*: vileness

43. *Maison de Santé*: an insane asylum

44. "*of denying that which is, and of explaining that which is not.*"

45. "He who has only a moment longer to live has no longer anything to conceal." Phillippe Quinault (1635-1688) was a French dramatist who wrote the text to the opera *Atys*.

46. In ancient Greece, Pyrrho was the founder of a school for skeptics. *Pyrrhonism* means *skepticism*.

47. *ignes fatui*: something alluring, yet misleading

48. *Coir* is the fiber of a coconut husk, *jaggeree* is a coarse sugar made from a palm tree sap, and *ghee* is a butter-like product made from buffalo milk.

49. The *kraken* is a huge, legendary Norwegian sea monster.

50. *Hove in stays* is a nautical phrase which means "in the process of sailing against the wind."

51. *ratlin*: the rope material used to make a ladder which is fastened to the shrouds of a ship

52. *sibyl*: a woman fortune-teller

53. *Eld* is antiquity or ancient times.

54. Balbec, Tadmor, and Persepolis are ancient cities of the Middle East.

55. Democritus (460-360 B.C.) was a philosopher and considered to be one of the fathers of atomism. Poe's mention of the "well of Democritus" is actually an indirect reference to one of his sayings—*"Of a truth we know nothing, for truth is in an abyss* [the well]."

56. *Mare Tenebrarum*, "sea of darkness," refers to the Atlantic Ocean.

57. *Sexagesima Sunday* is the second Sunday before Lent.

58. In Greek mythology, the *Phlegethon* is the river of fire.

59. "Here an insatiable band of torturers long wickedly nourished their lusts for innocent blood. Saved, now, our homeland; destroyed, the funereal dungeon." In the French Revolution, the Jacobins were a group of radicals during the Reign of Terror. However, Poe's "The Pit and the Pendulum" is about the Spanish Inquisition, and he is drawing a comparison between the political

radicalism of the French Revolution and the more controversial practices enforced by the Spanish Inquisition.

60. The *inquisitorial voices* refer to the members of the Spanish Inquisition, who would cruelly punish non-Catholics.

61. *Hades,* in Greek mythology, is hell.

62. The *auto-da-fés* was the public announcement and the actual execution of the Inquisition's sentence.

63. A *scythe* is a long, curved metal blade used to cut grass.

64. The *Ultima Thule* is "the most extreme way or form."

65. A *scimitar* is an Asian sword with a curved, convex edge.

66. *cottage orné* is a small villa or cottage with rustic architecture.

67. Poe writes that *Crepuscularia* is the scientific family name of the strange creature the narrator sees. However, this name is now outdated.

68. *Lepidoptera* is the name of the scientific order which contains the families of butterflies and moths, under class Insecta (insects).

69. *Pharonnida* is a long romantic verse written by William Chamberlain.

70. *Elagabalus* is a name used to represent an emperor generally remembered for extremely evil practices and excessive debauchery.

71. Draco was a politician and law writer in ancient Athens in the early 600's. His *Draconian Laws* were very harsh and severe.

72. *peine forte et dure*: "long and hard pain"

73. *outré*: "strange"

74. Carthage was an ancient city in northern Africa that was repeatedly destroyed and rebuilt. *Carthaginian medals* or money survived the destruction and provide proof of the city's existence.

75. *"Oh, what a good time is this century of iron!"* This quote indirectly refers to the Industrial Age.

76. A *praenomen* is a person's first name. In this story, *William* is the praenomen.

77. Herod was the King of Jews who is famous for attempting to kill Jesus by ordering all children under the age of two in Bethlehem to be killed.

78. A *parvenu* is a person who has recently become rich.

GLOSSARY

The following words appear underlined throughout the text:

abbey (aa bee) *n.*
  a religious and secluded convent or monastery

abstruse (aab stroos) *adj.* difficult to understand

advent (aad vehnt) *n.*
  an arrival or approach of something

adventitious (aad vehn tih shuhs) *adj.*
  additional, inadvertent, unexpected

advert (aad vuhrt) *v.* **-ing,-ed.**
  to bring up, to turn attention to

ague (ay gyoo) *n.* a state of chills or shivering

albatross (aal buh trahs) *n.*
  the largest sea bird, capable of flying very long and far

aperture (aa puhr chuhr) *n.* a hole or narrow opening

apothegm (aap uh thehm) *n.* a witty saying or remark

arabesque (aa ruh behsk) *n.; adj.*
  Arabic decorative art

aquiline (aak wih lien) *adj.*
  curved and hooked, like the beak of an eagle

assignation (aas sihg nay shuhn) *n.*
  a romantic meeting, a tryst

ballast (baa lihst) *n.*
  a heavy material loaded on a ship that adds stability

benighted (bih nie tihd) *adj.*
  enveloped or overtaken in darkness

bestir (bih stuhr) *v.* **-ring,-red.**
  to motivate or become active, to rouse

betrothed (bih trohthd) *n.*
  a person to whom one is to be married

bruit (broot) *v.* **-ing,-ed.** to report or spread information

burr (buhr) *n.* a buzzing noise or sound

cadaverously (kuh daa vuhr uhs lee) *adv.;* **cadaverousness**, *n.*
  in a corpselike manner; a state of emaciation or death

GLOSSARY

cadence (<u>kayd</u> ihnts) *n.*
a musical chord sequence; the rhythm of sounds

cant (kaant) *n.*
a special type of ambiguous vocabulary or speech

career (kuh <u>reer</u>) *v.* **-ing,-ed.** to move with great speed

caryatides (kaa ree <u>ah</u> tih deez) *n. pl.*
architectural columns sculpted like robed women

casement (<u>kays</u> mehnt) *n.*
a window with hinged coverings that open outward

castellated (<u>kaast</u> uh lay tihd) *adj.* resembling a castle

cataleptical (kaa tuh <u>lehp</u> tik kuhl) *adj.*
characterized by having rigid muscles and the inability
to react or respond to stimuli

cataract (<u>kaat</u> uh raakt) *n.*
a tall waterfall or large downpour

censer (<u>sehn</u> suhr) *n.*
a container in which incense is burned

cerements (<u>sehr</u> eh muhnts) *n. pl.*
burial cloths used to wrap a corpse

charnel (<u>chahr</u> nuhl) *adj.*
ghastly, gruesome; able to receive or contain the dead

chiromancy (<u>kie</u> ruh maan see) *n.*
the practice of palm reading

chrysalis (<u>krih</u> suh lihs) *n.*
a protective cocoon containing a pupa or young insect

clangorous (<u>klaang</u> ohr uhs) *adj.*
having a loud, metallic, ringing sound

collocation (kah luh <u>kay</u> shuhn) *n.*
the act of grouping or arranging things, often words
in a sentence

commingle (koh <u>mihng</u> guhl) *v.* **-ing,-ed.**
to blend or mix, to fuse

consign (kuhn <u>sien</u>) *v.* **-ing,-ed.**
to hand over permanently, to surrender oneself

GLOSSARY

conspicuous (kuhn spihk yoo uhs) *adj.*
obvious, easily noticed

cosmogony (kahz mah guh nee) *n.*
the study of or theory of the evolution of the universe

coxcombry (kahk skohm ree) *n.*
the behavior of a showy, conceited man (a coxcomb)

crank (krangk) *adj. Nautical.* unstable, likely to capsize

cupola (kyoo puh luh) *n.*
a dome-like structure set upon a roof

dalliance (daal ee ehnts) *n.*
the act of wasting time, dawdling, playing

dank (dangk) *adj.* moist, damp, dewy

decanter (dih kaan tuhr) *n.*
a vessel used to hold wine or liquor before it is served

decrepitude (dih krehp ih tood) *n.*
weakness or deterioration due to old age or long use

deity (dee ih tee) (day ih tee) *n.*
a supreme being, god, goddess

denizen (dehn ih zehn) *n.*
a resident, one who is very familiar with a certain place

depend (dih pehnd) *v.* -ing,-ed.
to hang downward; to rely on or trust

depute (dih pyoot) *v.* -ing,-ed. to assign or appoint

descant (dih skaant) (dih skaant) *v.* -ing,-ed.
to make lengthy comments or criticisms

desultory (dehs uhl tohr ee) *adj.*
disconnected, lacking order or logical sequence

diametrically (die uh meh trihk lee) *adv.*
across the center or diameter of a circle

dint (dihnt) *n.* persistent effort, power

dissimulation (dih sihm yuh lay shuhn)
the act of hiding the truth, concealment

dissolute (dihs uh loot) *adj.*
unrestrained, reckless, wild, lewd

GLOSSARY

dissolution (dih suh <u>loo</u> shuhn) *n.*
    disintegration, decomposition

donjon (<u>dahn</u> jihn) *n.* the main tower of a castle

dotage (<u>doh</u> tihj) *n.*
    lack of mental strength, mental deterioration

doughty (<u>dow</u> tee) *adj.* courageous, valiant, fearless

draught (drawft) *n.* a drink or gulp of a liquid

éclat (<u>ay</u> klah) *n.* great success, exceptional brilliance

educe (ih <u>doos</u>) *v.* **-ing.-ed.** to draw out, evoke

effulgence (ih <u>fuhl</u> jehns) *n.*
    extreme radiance, brilliant luster

encrimson (ehn <u>krihm</u> zihn) *v.* **-ing.-ed.**
    to make reddish, to give a crimson hue

endue (ehn <u>doo</u>) *v.* **-ing,-ed.** to give a quality to; to endow

enfeeble (ehn <u>fee</u> buhl) *v.* **-ing,-ed.**
    to weaken, to drain of strength

ensue (ehn <u>soo</u>) *v.* **-ing,-ed.**
    to follow afterward, to happen subsequently

enthral (ehn <u>thrahl</u>) *v.* **-ing,-ed.** to hold captive

epoch (<u>eh</u> pihk) *n.* a memorable period of time

excavation (ehks kuh <u>vay</u> shuhn)
    a hole or cavity in the ground formed by digging

excoriate (ehk <u>skor</u> ee ayt) *v.* **-ing,-ed.; excoriation,** *n.*
    to tear or scratch the skin; a lesion or open skin cut

exequy (<u>ehk</u> sih kwee) *n.* a death wish, a funeral rite

exergue (<u>ehk</u> suhrg) *n.*
    the space on a coin listing the engraving date and place

facsimile (faak <u>sih</u> muh lee) *n.*
    a reproduction of a document

fain (fayn) *adv.; adj.* gladly, rather; glad, content, happy

feint (faynt) *n.*
    deception, the act of distracting for a purpose

fête (fayt) *n.* an elaborate celebration, a feast

GLOSSARY

filigreed (<u>fihl</u> ih greed) *adj.*
  decorated or embellished with delicate jewel work

firmament (<u>fuhr</u> muh mehnt) *n.* the sky or heavens

fissure (<u>fihsh</u> uhr) *n.* a deep, narrow crack or opening

fob (fahb) *n.*
  a small pants or vest pocket used to hold a watch

fortnight (<u>fohrt</u> niet) *n.* a two-week period of time

fretted (<u>freh</u> tihd) *adj.*
  adorned with a band of repeated geometrical shapes

fulvous (<u>fuhl</u> vuhs) *adj.*
  yellow, mixed with brown and gray

gallows (<u>gaa</u> lohs) *n.*
  a structure with a suspended noose used for hanging

galvanic (gaal <u>vaan</u> ik) *adj.*
  relating to chemically-produced electricity

garret (<u>gaa</u> reht) *n.* an attic

gauntleted (<u>gawnt</u> leh tihd) *adj.*
  covered by an armored glove

genera (<u>jeh</u> neh ruh) *n. pl.*
  kinds, categories, groups with similarities

girt (guhrt) *v.* **-ing,-ed.** to surround or encircle

grave (grayv) *v.* **-ing,-ed, graven.** to sculpt, engrave, stamp

habiliment (haa <u>bihl</u> ih mehnt) *n.*
  clothes associated with a specific occasion or purpose

habit (<u>haa</u> biht) *v.* **-ing,-ed.** to dress or clothe

hearken (<u>hahr</u> kihn) *v.* **-ing,-ed.** to listen

idolatry (ie <u>dahl</u> uh tree) *n.*
  extreme devotion or worship of something

imbibe (ihm <u>bieb</u>) *v.* **-ing,-ed.**
  to absorb, as if by soaking or drinking

immolation (ih moh <u>lay</u> shuhn) *n.*
  an act of sacrifice with the use of fire

GLOSSARY

impotent (<u>ihm</u> puh tehnt) *adj.*
  ineffective, powerless

impunity (ihm <u>pyoo</u> nih tee) *n.*
  exemption from being punished or harmed

inanition (ihn uh <u>nihsh</u> uhn) *n.*
  exhaustion or weakness due to lack of food or energy

incongruous (ihn <u>kahn</u> groo uhs) *adj.*
  incompatible, not in agreement, inappropriate

incubus (<u>ihn</u> kyuh buhs) *n.*
  a terrifying or oppressive burden, a terrible dream

indemnity (ihn <u>dehm</u> nih tee) *n.*
  compensation for loss or damage

ineffable (ihn <u>eh</u> fuh buhl) *adj.*
  indescribable, unspeakable

inordinate (ihn <u>ohr</u> dih niht) *adj.*; **inordinately**, *adv.*
  excessive or immoderate; excessively

insoluble (ihn <u>sahl</u> yuh buhl) *adj.*
  impossible to explain or solve

interjectional (ihn tuhr <u>jehk</u> shuhn uhl) *adj.*
  short, sudden, and abrupt

interleaf (<u>ihn</u> tuhr leef) *n.* a blank page inserted in a book

interminableness (ihn <u>tuhr</u> mihn uh buhl nehs) *n.*
  endlessness, infinity

intonation (ihn tuh <u>nay</u> shuhn) *n.*
  the pitch of one's voice

involute (<u>ihn</u> vuh loot) *adj.* complex

lambent (<u>laam</u> bihnt) *adj.*
  gently glowing or flickering

lattice (<u>laat</u> ihs) *n.*
  a window with a criss-crossed pattern of wood or metal

lee *n.* the side of a boat which is sheltered from the wind

lineaments (<u>lihn</u> ee uh mihnts) *n. pl.*
  outlines or contours

locution (loh <u>kyoo</u> shuhn) *n.*
a manner of speaking, a way of expressing oneself

maelström (<u>mayl</u> struhm) *n.*
an enormous whirlpool

mandible (<u>maan</u> dih buhl) *n.*
a mouth part of an insect; also commonly used to refer to the jawbone of mammals and other vertebrates

manifold (<u>maan</u> ih fohld) *adj.*
multiple, having many forms

meekly (<u>meek</u> lee) *adv.* submissively

menial (<u>mee</u> nee uhl) (<u>meen</u> yuhl) *n.* a servant

metaphysical (meh tuh <u>fihz</u> ih kuhl) *adj.*
relating to the study of the nature of reality

moiety (<u>moy</u> ih tee) *n.* a portion of something, a half

mouldering (<u>mohl</u> duhr ihng) *adj.* decaying, rotten

ocular (<u>ah</u> kyuh luhr) *adj.* visual

omnipotence (ahm <u>nih</u> puh tehnts) *n.* limitless power

orb (ohrb) *n.*
1. a spherical object, sometimes used to describe eyes
2. a celestial body (moon or sun)

orthodox (<u>ohr</u> thuh dahks) *adj.*
traditional, conventional

overawe (oh vuhr <u>aw</u>) *v.* -ing,-ed.
to control by causing a feeling of awe, to scare into submission

pall (pahl) *v.* -ing,-ed. to close over, cover

pallor (<u>paa</u> luhr) *n.* unnatural paleness

parley (<u>pahr</u> lee) *n.* a discussion, often to settle a dispute

paroxysm (puh <u>rahk</u> sihz uhm) *n.*
an outburst of passion or emotion; a convulsion

patronymic (paa truh <u>nihm</u> ihk) *n.*
a name derived from one's father

peevish (<u>pee</u> vihsh) *adj.;* **peevishness**, *n.*
discontented, cranky; discontent

GLOSSARY

phantasmagoric (faan taaz muh <u>gohr</u> ihk) *adj.*
surreal, imaginary

phosphoric (fahs <u>fohr</u> ihk) *adj.*
relating to light emitted due to oxidation of phosphorus

phrenologist (frih <u>nahl</u> uh jihst) *n.*
one who studies the shape of the skull to determine
character traits and mental capacity

pinion (<u>pihn</u> yuhn) *n.* the wing or feather of a bird

pomp (pahmp) *n.* a display of magnificence, splendor

prismatic (prihz <u>maa</u> tihk) *adj.* iridescent

proboscis (pruh <u>bahs</u> kihs) *n.*
a long, tubular feeding organ of many insects

prolixity (pruh <u>lihk</u> sih tee) *n.*
wordiness, great length

promontory (<u>prah</u> muhn tohr ee) *n.*
a high, mountainous point that juts out into the sea

propinquity (pruh <u>pihng</u> kwih tee) *n.* nearness, proximity

protuberance (proh <u>too</u> buhr ehnts) *n.*
a bulge, something that projects outward

quondam (<u>kwahn</u> duhm) *adj.* former, once

rampart (<u>raam</u> pahrt) *n.*
a fort or embankment used for defense

rank (rangk) *adj.*
growing excessively; offensively odorous

recherché (reh shehr <u>shay</u>) *adj.* uncommon, rare

recusant (<u>reh</u> kyuh zehnt) *n.*
a nonconformist, especially one who denounced the
King's supremacy in the church of England

redolent (<u>rehd</u> lihnt) *adj.* diffusing an aroma or odor

remand (rih <u>maand</u>) *v.* **-ing,-ed.**
to order or send back into custody

rencontre (rehn <u>kawn</u> tuhr) *n.* an unexpected meeting

revivification (ree vih vih fih <u>kay</u> shuhn) *n.*
the renewal of life or vitality

GLOSSARY

rheum (room) *n.* a watery discharge from the eyes

sable (<u>say</u> buhl) *adj.* gloomy and dark; black in color

sally (<u>saa</u> lee) *v.* **-ing,-ied.** to set out, to leave for a trip

sarcophagus (sahr <u>kahf</u> uh gihs) *n.*; **sarcophagi,** *n. pl.*
a sculpted coffin made of stone

sate (sayt) *v. Archaic.* the past tense of the verb *sit*

scantling (<u>skaant</u> lihng) *n.*
small boards used for building

scud (skuhd) *v.* **-ding,-ded.** *Nautical.*
to move swiftly before the wind with no sail spread

sedge (sehj) *n.* a grassy plant that grows in wet places

self-gratulation (sehlf graach uh <u>lay</u> shuhn) *n. Archaic.*
congratulation of oneself, pride in oneself

simoon (sih <u>moon</u>) *n.*
a very hot and sandy wind typical of Africa and Arabia

smack (smaak) *n.* a small fishing boat

sooth *n. Archaic.* reality or truth

specious (<u>spee</u> shuhs) *adj.* seemingly truthful, but false

statuary (<u>staa</u> choo ayr ee) *n.* a sculptor

stereotomy (stayr ee <u>ah</u> tuh mee) *n.*
the art of cutting stone

sublunary (suhb <u>loo</u> nuh ree) *adj.* earthly

succumb (suh <u>cuhm</u>) *v.* **-ing,-ed.**
to give up, to collapse under a stronger force; to die

sulphurous (<u>suhl</u> fuhr uhs) (suhl <u>fyoor</u> uhs) *adj.*
bitter, caustic, harsh

sunder (<u>suhn</u> duhr) *v.* **-ing,-ed.** to break, to separate

supererogation (soo puhr ehr ih <u>gay</u> shuhn) *n.*
an effort beyond what is required or expected

supererogatory (soo puhr eh <u>rahg</u> uh tohr ee) *adj.*
unnecessary, not required

supervene (soo puhr <u>veen</u>) *v.* **-ing,-ed.** to follow after

supinely (soo <u>pien</u> lee) *adv.* passively, carelessly

GLOSSARY

supposition (suh puh <u>zih</u> shuhn) *n.*
an assumption, a hypothesis based on little evidence

tarn (tahrn) *n.* a lake in the mountains

tarry (<u>taa</u> ree) *v.* **-ing,-ied.** to wait

tenure (<u>tehn</u> yuhr) *n.* the act of holding

throng (thrahng) *n.*; *v.* **-ing,-ed.**
a crowd or large group; to gather together

tincture (<u>tihngk</u> shuhr) *v.* **-ing,-ed.** to tint, to instill

trammel (<u>traam</u> uhl) *n.* a shackle or net used to capture

transcendentalism (traan sehn <u>dehn</u> tuhl ih zuhm) *n.*
a philosophy that focuses on spiritual reality versus
scientific fact

treble (<u>treh</u> buhl) *v.* **-ing,-ed.**; *n.*
to triple; a high singing voice

unction (<u>uhnk</u> shuhn) *n.* earnest devotion

unprepossessing (uhn pre puh <u>zehs</u> ihng) *adj.*
unimpressive, not showy

unwonted (uhn <u>wahn</u> tihd) *adj.* uncommon, unusual

uprear (uhp <u>reer</u>) *v.* **-ing,-ed.** to lift, to raise up

vagary (<u>vay</u> guh ree) *n.* a fanciful thought, a whim

veritable (<u>vehr</u> iht uh buhl) *adj.*; **veritably,** *adv.*
genuine, authentic, real; genuinely, truely

viand (<u>vie</u> uhnd) *n.* a food item

vignette (vihn <u>yeht</u>) *adj.*; *v.* **-ing, -ed.**
having softened edges that fade, as in a portrait; to
fade the edges of a portrait

volute (vuh <u>loot</u>) *n.* an ornament of spiral formation

vortex (<u>vohr</u> teks) *n.*; **vortices** (<u>vohr</u> tih seez) *n. pl.*
a whirling or circular mass that draws in
everything near it

welter (<u>wehl</u> tuhr) *v.* **-ing,-ed.** to wallow, roll around

witticism (<u>wih</u> tih sih zuhm) *n.* a joke, a funny phrase